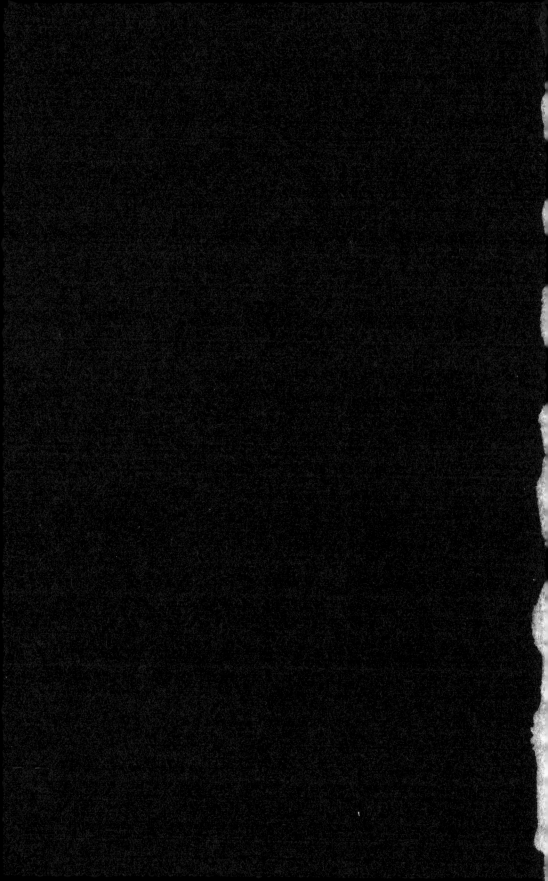

a special AGENT

AIDS IS
KILLING ARTISTS
NOW HOMOPHOBIA
IS KILLING ART

a special AGENT

Gay and Inside the FBI

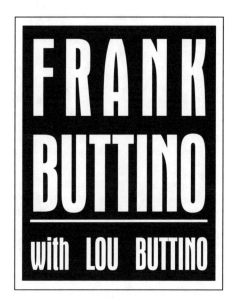

FRANK BUTTINO

with LOU BUTTINO

William Morrow and Company, Inc. • New York

In writing this book, I have tried to protect the privacy of people I have mentioned. In a few instances, names and depictions of personal friends have been changed, and facts altered to achieve this result.

HV
7911
B87
A3
1993

Copyright © 1993 by Frank Buttino and Lou Buttino

It is the policy of William Morrow and Company, Inc., and its imprints and affiliates, recognizing the importance of preserving what has been written, to print the books we publish on acid-free paper, and we exert our best efforts to that end.

Library of Congress Cataloging-in-Publication Data

Buttino, Frank.
    A special agent : gay and inside the FBI / by Frank Buttino with
Lou Buttino.
        p.   cm.
    ISBN 0–688–11958–1
    1. Buttino, Frank.   2. United States. Federal Bureau of
Investigation—Officials and employees—Biography.   3. Gay men–
United States—Biography.   I. Buttino, Lou.   II. Title.
HV7911.B87A3   1993
363.2'092–dc20
    [B]   92–46238
                                                            CIP

Printed in the United States of America

First Edition

1   2   3   4   5   6   7   8   9   10

BOOK DESIGN BY LINEY LI

To our parents

Kathryn and Tony Buttino

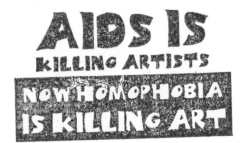

acknowledgments

Numerous people provided us with assistance in a variety of ways.

For me, Frank Buttino, I would like to acknowledge my appreciation to attorneys Richard Gayer, Michael Fitzgerald, and Gary Hall for their wise counsel during the writing of this book. I am appreciative of the enormous support, encouragement, and inspiration I have received from the gay and lesbian community. Heartfelt thanks to my close friends Raymond Lee, Richard Tanner, Steve Cantine, and Larry Durkay for their friendship, encouragement, and assistance over the years. And special thanks to Everett Waldo for long hours spent going over the text with me and for always being there during some very difficult times. My appreciation to my brother Lou, without whom this book would never have been written.

For me, Lou Buttino, reliance on Missy Francisco, Michael Di-Giorgio, Laurie Ward, and Sonia Basko for research and the handling of numerous other details was essential. My assistant, Renee Locke, stuck with me through the many starts and alterations of the manuscript, and to say that I am extremely grateful is an understatement. Lin Mocejunas was always there when backup was needed, and I am grateful to her. I acknowledge Dr. Robert George, whose grammatical and critical sugges-tions were astute and kindly given. Judy VanBuskirk, Diane Lucas, Nancy Martin, and Puck Winqvist, reference librarians at St. John Fisher Col-lege, answered my numerous queries promptly, professionally, and with good cheer. Special thanks to Dr. William L. Pickett, president of the college, and Dr. Thomas McFadden, now president of Marymount College, Rancho Palos Verdes, California, for their unflinching support. My wife, Kathleen, read and reread the text through it several drafts, saying the tough things a writer often does not want to hear. She provided me with perspective and encouragement and kept our family intact through the long days when I was away in mood and mind.

We both wish to acknowledge the wise counsel of John Harney, who assisted us in obtaining a top-notch agent who in turn helped us obtain a top-notch publisher. John is friend, confidant, and seasoned veteran of publishing ins and outs. We acknowledge our literary agent, Julian Bach, whom writer Pat Conroy described as one of the finest men he'd ever met. We can only add to this his considerable talent as an agent. Finally, we wish to thank Will Schwalbe, director of special publishing projects at William Morrow and our editor. Quite simply, we think we got the best in the business.

contents

introduction

I was born on February 18, 1945. I joined the FBI as a special agent on July 28, 1969. For more than twenty years I worked organized crime, narcotics, and foreign counterintelligence investigations. Some of these assignments were undercover; others involved highly publicized cases. On January 31, 1990, my Top Secret security clearance was revoked. I was fired on June 20, 1990. I am gay. This is my story.

Frank Buttino

part one
passageways

1.

I have always liked being an FBI agent.

When I was a new agent, I liked the cops-and-robbers part of the job—kicking in doors at daybreak, the high-speed car chases, arresting criminals at gunpoint. But as I grew older, all that seemed to change.

I remember an old-timer in the bureau saying once that "some people liked playing checkers and others liked chess." I was a thirty-nine-year-old special agent who had been with the bureau for fifteen years—and I wanted to be one of its better chess players.

■ ■ ■

It was Monday, August 6, 1984. I was at my desk in the organized crime (OC) unit of the FBI when I heard my name being called. Jack Blair, my squad supervisor, stood in the doorway to his office. I could tell from the look on his face that something was wrong. I grabbed a pen and notebook. Jack's office was small, with full-length glass walls. He closed the door behind me, and I noticed other agents watching, no doubt wondering what the meeting was about.

Jack was a well-liked and respected supervisor. He cared about his people and set high standards for our work. We were, as a result, loyal to him and had a reputation as being one of the best organized crime squads in the bureau.

He was normally easygoing and friendly, but he seemed tense as he moved behind his desk. He didn't sit or ask me to. I wondered if there was a problem with one of my cases or if it had to do with me personally.

"I just got a call from headquarters," he began. "They've got a special going in Miami they want you to help with."

"What's it about?"

Jack shrugged. "They didn't say much. Something about drugs. That—a bureau informant and an FBI undercover operation."

He thought the assignment might take a couple of weeks, but my hunch was that it would be longer. Drug cases were complex and time-consuming.

"Do you think you can go, Frank?"

I asked when headquarters wanted me in Miami.

There was a trace of embarrassment when he answered. "They said Thursday."

There were out-of-town guests at my house for the week. I also wanted to make long-range plans in case the "special" lasted longer than expected. "How about if I fly out on Sunday and be there Monday morning?"

Jack seemed relieved. "That'll be fine. I'll let headquarters know."

I started to leave when he added, "HQ wants this kept secret."

I nodded.

He put his hand on my shoulder as we reached the door. "Thanks, Frank," he said.

I walked to an interview room down the hallway from his office, thinking about what cases ought to be reassigned in my absence. The room was empty, and I pulled the door shut. The phone wasn't "secure," so I would have to make the conversation brief. An outside intelligence source could be monitoring the call.

Brian answered on the second ring, and I told him I had to go out of town. I asked him if he would mind taking care of my house while I was away.

He wanted to know how long I'd be gone.

"I'm not sure. They think a couple of weeks."

He was disappointed. "Frank, I'm sure my ship is going overseas again this fall. I thought this was the summer we were going to spend a lot of time together."

"This sounds exciting, and maybe it won't take long," I told him.

Other questions tumbled from him. "Why do you always get chosen for these things? . . . It always takes longer than they tell you. . . . Is it going to be dangerous?"

I was anxious about being on the phone too long. "Brian, I really can't talk now. We'll go for a walk in the canyon later."

Brian's family was at my house. They were from the East Coast and didn't know about our relationship. We had to be careful around them. Brian slept on board ship at night rather than with me.

■　■　■

It was midmorning, Sunday, August 12, and I had just finished packing when Brian came into the bedroom. His family was in the backyard, but he closed the door anyway. I could feel his eyes on me as I shut the suitcase. I looked up.

"I'm going to miss you," I said.

He walked over to me in that slow, lumbering way he had and put his arms around me. Brian was the type of person who usually kept what he was feeling inside. I could feel his body tremble slightly.

"I love you, Frank," he told me, and I said that I loved him, too. We kissed and kept hold of each other, swaying a little, as if trying to lock on the rhythm of our life together.

Despite the sadness of the moment, it was—overall—a high point for me. I was in a loving gay relationship. And the bureau, in assigning me to the "special," was acknowledging my emergence as one of its better chess players.

But the journey to that moment had been difficult. And I have never shared all its passageways with anyone, including Brian, until now.

2.

How does a person account for who or what he or she becomes? Is it biology? Environment? Culture? Had I grown up at a different time in a different place, would I be somebody different now?

■ ■ ■

I once told Brian that growing up in Canastota, New York, during the late 1950s was a lot like growing up as a character on the TV program *Happy Days*. Canastota is a village of about five thousand, and my fondest memories were the school dances, the hours we whiled away at the Chatterbox, and the Saturday afternoon football games.

There was work, too. Plenty of it. My brothers, Tony and Lou, and I spent our summers on ''Black Beach,'' which was better known to out-of-towners as the mucklands. Canastota farmers, including my father and his father before him, raised onions in its rich black soil. I was the third-generation son of Italian immigrants who had settled in the area to work the soil or to work on the railroad. My father did both.

Canastota's main claim to fame is native son Carmen Basilio. He was an onion farmer who went on to be one of the most admired boxers of all time. He was the world welterweight and world middleweight champion and beat legendary fighters, including Sugar Ray Robinson. Carmen was a friend of our family. His parents and my grandparents came from the same small town of Campochiaro in Italy.

But even in adolescence a shadow began to stalk me. In junior high school I was horsing around with another boy out on the playground when I experienced an intense pleasure from innocent physical contact with him. I felt awkward around the boy after that but didn't know why. I also felt an inordinate amount of interest in watching certain male actors on television, such as Ricky Nelson. I didn't know the words to express these things. And even when I did, years later, I still wasn't able to say them out loud.

I had a steady girlfriend in high school. She, too, was a good student, involved in school activities, and popular. I think our parents believed we would get married someday and settle down in Canastota, as they had done.

Friends sometimes talked about their physical attraction to certain girls or their sexual experiences with some of them. I knew, at some level, I wasn't feeling what they were feeling. My girlfriend and I spent a lot of time together, yet I had no overwhelming desire to do anything more than kiss her good-night. I loved her as a friend and kissed her because it was expected of me. I tried to convince myself that when the right girl came along, all I was feeling would change.

The word "queer" was used to describe homosexuals. It was a profoundly degrading epithet. Yet by my senior year I wondered if I was one of them. My strong attraction to certain males in my class persisted.

What prevented me from believing it was true was that I didn't fit the prevailing stereotype. I was the starting defensive halfback on my high school football team and a hard-nosed wrestler. I was voted class president all four years and in my senior year also picked as the "Most Likely to Succeed."

I couldn't be queer! I felt like a younger version of my father. I was convinced that shadow stalking me would disappear in time, that the confusion I felt would resolve itself with age.

There were no girls at Colgate University when I enrolled as a freshmen in 1963. It was an intellectually demanding school, and I quickly immersed myself in my studies. Dating on a steady basis wasn't expected, so I didn't feel some of the pressures I had felt in high school. At one point in my freshman year my high school girlfriend sent me an eight-by-ten photograph of herself. I thanked her and kept the picture out for a while but didn't feel any deep connection to her. We saw each other a few times that year and drifted apart.

I had my first sexual experience with a woman during college and was physically intimate with a few others after that. But I carry no deep or lasting impressions of these intimacies. Instead, unexpected and troubling feelings toward certain male classmates returned.

One night three other students and I were making our way back from a road trip to an all women's school. I was in the back seat with one of the guys; the other two were in the front seat. I had always been attracted to the student who now slept next to me, and it felt strangely satisfying just to press my hand against his leg. He didn't awaken until we arrived back at school and I'm sure was unaware of my closeness to him. I knew I had crossed the line of appropriateness and promised myself not to do it again.

Yet it happened one other time. There was a party at our fraternity, and I drank too much. I had gone back to my room to sleep it off when I noticed a student from another fraternity sleeping on the bunk above me. I touched his leg, and he immediately woke up and began to mumble something. I pretended to be asleep. I worried for a long time afterward that he would remember and say something about it, but he never did.

In hindsight, these two instances seem so pitiable. It was as if I had been restricted to solitary emotional confinement. Part of me felt naturally inclined to give and receive affection from certain males, yet I knew this was forbidden. The slightest hint of it could cast me into exile. I'd be an outcast of the worst order and couldn't even imagine the repercussions in terms of family, friends, and hometown.

I didn't venture geographically much beyond Colgate and Canastota until my senior year, when my older brother, Lou, and I drove through the South. I had my first experience with racial discrimination. We saw drinking fountains and motels that had signs that read: WHITES ONLY or NEGROES ONLY. One time we went in the wrong door of a restaurant. A white waitress immediately escorted us to the whites-only section of the restaurant. The difference in appearance between the two was extraordinary.

Though the civil rights movement was to have a profound effect upon me, I never saw my own plight in a similar vein. African-Americans were perceived by bigots to be less than human in intelligence and social standing because of the color of their skin; gays were considered less than human because of a "moral sickness." While I would stand up for African-Americans, I would not stand up for me. I did not see that all prejudice is rooted in the need to judge but not to be judged.

After graduating from Colgate in 1967 with a B.A. in history, I went back to Canastota to teach high school history and coach football and basketball. I enjoyed my life there but soon got restless. America was undergoing great changes, and I wanted to be a part of it, not just teach about it.

I was dating a woman fairly steadily during that time. She was fun and intellectually stimulating, and we were sexually intimate. For some reason, I didn't feel any strong attraction toward other males during this time. I thought the feelings had vanished, just as I had hoped they would. Yet the intensity of the relationship with the woman I was dating was not as powerful as I expected it should be. I thought—once more—that I hadn't found the right person. I also wondered if I would ever be able to find the right woman or if I would ever at least feel what I thought I should feel during sexual intimacy.

■　■　■

Because of the rioting and other violence in America in the late 1960s, Congress authorized the Federal Bureau of Investigation to hire a thousand new agents. I saw this as my chance to do something different. The FBI had an excellent reputation, the work sounded exciting, and the pay was good. Being an FBI agent would afford me the opportunity to see the country and do something for my country.

The application process consisted of an examination, interview, and background investigation. Word spread fast throughout our small town as friends and neighbors were being interviewed by FBI agents. My excitement and hopes mounted while I waited to hear their decision. Then, on July 28, 1969, I was given a gold-plated badge and sworn in as a special agent of the FBI.

The new FBI Academy at Quantico wasn't built yet, so we trained at various quarters in Washington, D.C. My instructors were all white; there was one African-American, no Latinos, and no women in our training class of fifty. I became the stereotypical FBI agent: white, in my mid-twenties, and wearing the uniform of dark suit, white shirt, and tie. Photographs of J. Edgar Hoover seemed to be everywhere in the training facilities. Instructors referred to him deferentially as the director or Mr. Hoover.

I got my first glimpse of Hoover in the basement of the Department of Justice. He was waiting for an elevator with longtime companion, and the FBI associate director, Clyde Tolson, who glared at everyone around him, apparently not wanting anyone to bother Hoover or join them on the elevator. I walked quickly by. Stories circulated about FBI careers ending because Hoover or Tolson didn't like an agent's looks.

Pride and loyalty were stressed in new agent training. We were repeatedly told that the current President, Richard M. Nixon, had been rejected by the FBI because he wasn't aggressive enough. We new agents became heirs to past bureau glories; the pursuit of ''Baby Face'' Nelson, the shoot-out with John Dillinger, the emergence of FBI agents as G-men (government men).

My father didn't hunt or own a gun, so firing a revolver for the first time was a new experience for me. We were given the standard bureau issue revolver—a .38 caliber Smith & Wesson—upon graduation. As we strapped them to our sides, our instructor cautioned us that now we had "half the power of God."

The four months of training had passed quickly, and in early November 1969 I packed my 1966 Chevrolet Impala convertible and headed for Tampa, Florida, my first-office assignment. I felt I had left my youth truly behind in the small towns of central New York and was entering a more worldly arena where the chance to grow was exceeded only by my willingness to do so.

I was assigned fairly routine cases as a first-office agent but soon made my first arrest. Two more experienced agents accompanied me. Though we didn't have any problems, I saw the importance of preparation and staying observant, rational, and cool.

I also saw, in my first-office assignment, how Hoover used fear to maintain control over his employees. I was warned not to say anything negative about him in the office or in public. Agents lived by the phrase: "Don't embarrass the bureau." Saying or doing anything to tarnish Hoover's reputation or his carefully crafted image of an FBI beyond reproach could incur the wrath of the director or his associate director, Clyde Tolson, who was Hoover's hatchet man for employee discipline.

At that time FBI field offices were required to send local newspaper articles and all other publicity, favorable or unfavorable, about the bureau to FBI headquarters. Negative publicity about or emanating from an agent could result in disciplinary action or firing.

We lived in fear that somebody would write a personal letter to the director criticizing our personal or professional conduct. Whether the criticism was justified or not made little difference. If it "embarrassed the bureau," an agent might receive a "disciplinary transfer" to a remote field office. An agent I knew was abruptly transferred when one of his neighbors complained to FBIHQ about the noisy motorcycle his son drove.

Places such as Butte, Montana, were the destination for agents transferred for disciplinary reasons. It was like being sent to Siberia. But what HQ didn't know was that with the high cost of living and increasingly high crime rates found in most American cities, being transferred to places such as Butte became viewed as something to celebrate.

FBI agents were seldom given an opportunity to explain or defend themselves against allegations made by the public or HQ. Outside of legal action *after* termination, there was no review process inside the FBI. Hoover had established an agency that was not subject to outside scrutiny or susceptible to the social changes sweeping the country. Agents served at his whim and did not racially, ethnically, or in terms of gender represent the America we were pledged to serve. Homosexuals were totally excluded from even being considered for FBI employment.

■ ■ ■

The FBI moves new agents around in the beginning. The agency wants to expose them to different experiences. The policy also provides the bureau with an opportunity to observe agents in different settings and situations.

I was assigned to the Detroit field office of the FBI in late 1970. Riots had ravaged parts of the city in 1967. From 1967 to the date of my arrival, handgun sales had doubled, reaching a record-high half million. The city's homicides had also doubled during this same time. In 1972 Detroit had the highest homicide rate of any city in America.

I worked on a case in Detroit that resulted in the arrest of Ku Klux Klan members who were responsible for the bombing of school buses in nearby Pontiac, Michigan. I also worked cases involving the radical left. The FBI was under mounting criticism because of the attempt by Hoover and others to link the antiwar movement to international communism. I didn't think this was appropriate or necessary, and I was uncomfortable for the first time about my supportive role in this line of thinking. There were, however, elements of the New Left, such as the Weathermen, which were convinced America could be changed only through violence. I felt this was the problem.

While in Detroit, I began to date women and after a while became the fairly steady companion of one woman in particular. A few times, when we were making love, the thought of having sex with a man flashed across my mind. Since these images seemed so minuscule, in view of all that was happening in my life, I thought their occurrence might be just something fleeting. I had not worried or thought much about those feelings since college.

I wanted to meet Hoover, despite all the warnings that it wasn't a good idea. I learned that I would have to make a written request well in advance and could either have my picture taken with him or talk to him—

but not both. I had to return to FBI headquarters for a training session in 1972 and decided to meet him at that time.

Another agent waited with me outside Hoover's office. I went in first and walked over to where Hoover was standing. He greeted me, extending his hand. I thought about my first job as a small-town high school teacher. It was hard to believe I was standing face-to-face with someone many believed to be more powerful than presidents.

There was also something unusual about the encounter, something I thought about much later. Hoover held on to my hand longer than seemed appropriate. He also kept staring into my eyes in a way that made me uncomfortable. It was, I later learned, a way gays made contact with one another.

I waited for the other agent to come out of the building, and I could see he was upset. "I didn't get a chance to say anything," he said. "Hoover launched into a tirade about Jack Anderson, Angela Davis, and the Chappaquiddick Kid [Ted Kennedy], and that was it."

In May 1972, three months after my meeting with Hoover, he died in his sleep. He was seventy-seven years old and had been FBI director for nearly forty-eight years. With his death we knew great changes would come to the bureau. What we didn't know was how much and how swiftly they would come. Hoover's old guard, men with the same mind-set as Hoover, was still in place at FBIHQ. They were expected to challenge the initiatives of the newly appointed acting director, L. Patrick Gray III.

As I watched and experienced these and other changes at the FBI, I felt less like a newcomer and more like a veteran. I was glad for the changes. A truly "new" FBI was emerging. I also knew I had developed a lifelong commitment to the bureau and began to think about the shaping of my own career.

In 1972 President Nixon became the first American President to visit Communist China. The normalization of relations between America and China was in the offing, and I thought the ability to speak Chinese might make me more valuable to the bureau and offer some interesting work. The government would need information about Communist China's economy, politics, military, and social structure. The FBI would be interviewing American visitors to China and monitoring the activities of Chinese officials and emigrees.

My request to study the Cantonese dialect of Chinese at the Defense Language Institute in Monterey, California, was approved, and in June 1972 I left Detroit for California. I said good-bye to the woman I had been dating, but there was nothing traumatic about the farewell. We had never talked about or alluded to a long-term commitment. I was sad, knowing I would miss her. But I know now that the loss I felt had more to do with friendship than with love. I had never been to the West Coast, and California had always been this magical place in my mind.

Language training was academically the most demanding year of my life. I spent six hours a day in class and an equal amount of time at my apartment studying. Because of the demands of the course, a normal social life was out of the question. Occasionally, however, I'd drive the hundred miles or so to San Francisco for sight-seeing. From reading the newspaper I also knew that San Francisco had a sizable gay population.

I drove along Polk and Castro streets when I went to San Francisco. I saw the gay bookstores and movie theaters advertising all-male movies. Sometimes I'd park and get out. I noticed that other men would glance at me, and it felt both strange and exhilarating. I didn't go into any of the stores, theaters, or restaurants. I was afraid somebody in the FBI might see me and I'd be questioned about what I was doing there.

After finishing language school, I requested a transfer to San Diego. There was an opening on the security squad, and I liked the city's weather and the fact that it was a little less fast-paced than other major California cities.

I did a little of everything on the security squad investigating the Communist Party USA (CPUSA) and working cases that involved sabotage, subversive activity, radicals and radical groups, spies, espionage, and counterespionage. My specialty, however, was cases involving Chinese people and activities.

Hoover had committed enormous manpower and resources to infiltrating and monitoring the activities of the rather moribund Communist party of the United States. FBI agents joked privately that if it weren't for our informants within the party, the CPUSA would probably fold. Hoover also ordered investigations of individuals and groups within the country he considered subversive and threats to national security. I never learned that these investigations involved homosexual individuals and groups until the nation itself learned of them in the late 1980s.

I found security work interesting and quickly adjusted to the relatively small-town feel of San Diego. I bought a house and, as I settled in, began dating again.

The FBI had changed even in the one year I had been away. An FBI assistant director once told us that ''the greatest threat facing the FBI in the future was the possibility of having female agents,'' yet I now worked alongside female agents. I grew a mustache before going to work in San Diego, and nobody seemed to notice or comment; mustaches and beards had been strictly forbidden in Hoover's FBI.

One day, while looking at magazines in a bookstore, I came across a copy of the *Advocate*. This is a national gay publication and at the time contained pictures of attractive gay men. I was intrigued. I bought a copy to take home with me. In hindsight, this was the point from which I was no longer able to deny my feelings. Despite the inherent risks, I thought about answering one of the personal ads.

After putting much thought into how to make initial contact with the gay community, I rented a post office box. A face-to-face meeting in San Diego would be too risky, so I would use the mails and travel out of town. I wished I had somebody to talk with about all this. I didn't know if I was going about it in the right way or if I was making a mistake. All I knew was that I had a compelling desire to know somebody who was gay.

Because of the easygoing nature of his letters, I became interested in a guy named Ted from Los Angeles. He eventually gave me his phone number, and I called to talk to him from a pay phone. Ted had been out of the closet for a while, was easy to talk with, and seemed comfortable with his homosexuality. I told him my fears and feelings, and I experienced enormous relief in finally talking about this side of me that had never been revealed to anyone before. It also scared me to think I was actually doing this.

In late September Ted and I decided to meet, and I drove to Laguna Beach, a beautiful city bordering the ocean in Orange County. I could feel my excitement and trepidation mount.

I found Ted attractive and as easygoing as he had been in his letters and on the phone. We walked along the beach for a long time. He talked about growing up in the Los Angeles area and his sexual experiences with a couple of Hollywood stars, including Rock Hudson. The more we talked, the more enticed I became about the possibility of having sex with him.

"Would you like to find a place where we can be together?'' Ted asked. His voice was confident and relaxed.

I nodded slowly.

We found a motel in South Laguna Beach. I was nervous and awkward, but Ted was patient. Though I had enjoyed having sex with women, this was clearly different. For the first time I felt both a mental and physical connection with another person. The lovemaking with Ted was a completely satisfying experience.

But I felt guilty, afterward, driving home. I had betrayed all the values taught me and all the expectations of me. I was also afraid I might slip up in some way, among family and friends and even at work. Would others be able to tell I had slept with a man?

I started to add bricks to a wall I had been building since my youth. Yet there was one question that continued to reverberate for me: How could something so bad feel so good?

For a long time I thought I might be bisexual. I continued to see Ted and to date women. Sex with women even seemed more pleasurable than before. Maybe I didn't have so many expectations. Maybe I knew Ted was there, too.

I never gave Ted my telephone number even though he asked. I diverted his questions about what kind of work I did. He must have grown weary of my evasions because suddenly I couldn't reach him anymore. But though saddened and hurt, I realized that I wanted and needed some kind of relationship with a man.

I began to go to Los Angeles to meet other gay men and on one trip went into a gay bar for the first time. I was nervous about being seen by someone from the bureau and also wasn't sure how to act. But it was fun to meet other men like me and dance to songs I had never thought were for me. It was like seeing and hearing the world for the first time.

During one of these trips I met Roger and Phil, two longtime gay lovers. They both worked in business, and both were ex-military people. We became friends, and they were a great help to me in understanding what was going on inside me and what it meant. They gave me one piece of advice that had a major impact on me: They said failure to accept my homosexuality could eventually lead to self-destructive behavior.

3.

The FBI continued to change. Hoover had emphasized statistical crimes that made the bureau look good, like recovering stolen cars. Now the FBI began major initiatives in the more difficult crime areas, such as La Cosa Nostra (LCN).

An organized crime (OC) squad was being formed in San Diego in 1976, and the assistant special agent in charge (ASAC) asked if I wanted to be a part of it. I told him I wanted to stay in security because of my language training, but I was "drafted" into OC anyway. My initial assignment involved conducting surveillances, but I volunteered to go undercover. I liked the challenge and wanted to keep growing in my bureau experiences.

Hoover had been opposed to undercover work. He had been afraid we'd be corrupted. Undercover operations had nevertheless been conducted in the bureau—without his knowledge or approval. These old undercover operations really didn't amount to much, as evidenced by the remark a veteran agent made to me, after seeing my long hair and beard. He said undercover work used to mean taking off your tie!

When my assignment began, I stopped going into the office or associating with colleagues. Such contact carried the risk I might be spotted. I did, however, meet with my contact agent from time to time. The contact agent's responsibility is to look after the undercover agent's needs and report on the progress of the case.

I was relatively free of bureau contact and consequently felt more safe in pursuing a gay relationship in San Diego. I casually met a guy I was immediately attracted to. He had clean-cut all-American looks and a warm smile. Bill was attracted to me, too, even though I looked somewhat scruffy with my long hair and beard. We saw each other steadily for a while. It was my first experience of close contact with another gay man on a steady basis, and I liked the feeling.

I was undercover for two years. The hours were long, and I maintained two residences, driving back and forth in an old car. My family was aware I was undercover, but I never shared the details with them. My father remarked once that it must be difficult living two lives. In fact, I was living three.

It took a long while before I told Bill I was an FBI agent; he didn't take the news well. It precipitated more and more arguments until he finally told me one day that he had been raped by a policeman in his hometown.

I was outraged that anyone had done this to him, even more so because it involved someone in law enforcement. But no matter what I said or how I tried to comfort him, I think he believed everyone in my line of work was, beneath the surface, brutish and mean. I had never experienced brutality against gays or any other minority in my career, nor did I ever hear local or state police or FBI agents brag about such experiences. If such a thing had occurred in front of me, I would have intervened.

Bill wasn't the first gay to talk to me about police brutality. I also read about this in the *Advocate* and other gay publications. At the time little about this was being reported in the mainstream media, and there were no special training sessions conducted in the bureau to sensitize agents and administrators to prejudice against minorities.

I was pretty much on the sidelines in regard to the struggle for gay rights. Yet even there I couldn't express my encouragement. Worse still, whenever I got close enough to another gay man to tell him I was with the FBI, more often than not I was treated like the enemy.

Midway through the second year of our relationship Bill told me he had met somebody else. It didn't surprise me, and I hadn't had much hope of the relationship's surviving. I was a constant reminder of his rape.

■　■　■

By the late 1970s our organized crime squad became involved in a series of high-profile cases involving the Teamsters and La Cosa Nostra. High-profile cases are highly publicized, in contrast with much of our work, which the public knows little about. In 1978 Jimmy "The Weasel" Fratianno broke the LCN oath of *omertà* (silence) and agreed to talk. A hundred-thousand-dollar contract was put out on his life. Fratianno was one of the highest-ranking LCN members ever to cooperate with law enforcement officers.

He was being held under tight security in the Metropolitan Correctional Center in San Diego, and FBI agents from all around the country were anxious to interview him. One morning the assistant special agent in charge of our office surprised me by asking if the bureau could use my house to debrief Fratianno. The bureau believed he would be more cooperative in a comfortable setting. The agent asked me because I didn't have a family and lived alone in a house on a quiet street in a quiet neighborhood. The bureau believed all these factors afforded Fratianno the maximum in terms of security.

Fratianno was transported from the correctional center to my house in a windowless van. Armed agents preceded and followed the van; agents with shotguns also waited inside my house. The drapes were closed, and no one exited the van until the garage door was closed.

The next two days with Fratianno were reminiscent of the scene in *The Godfather* when the Corleone family goes into hiding. We ate Italian food, drank a lot of coffee, and listened as Fratianno talked about his past and the workings of the LCN. Fratianno was a slender man of about sixty who talked in a gruff, show-off kind of way. He talked without emotion about his involvement in mob contract murders, using the word "clipping" as a euphemism for murder. He had the habit of biting off the end of the Cuban cigars he smoked and spitting it on the floor. About a half dozen times he did this, and I told an agent standing next to me that if he did it one more time, *I* was going to "clip" him!

Fratianno was questioned about a recent mob hit where a car bomb was used, and he suddenly became angry. He said the "old days" were much better. Then you just brought out some guns and blasted away. He told how he had killed people by being more clever than they were. Ovid Demaris later wrote a book about Fratianno's exploits entitled *The Last Mafioso*. With us, though, Fratianno looked like a scared old man trying to save his skin.

Movies like *The Godfather* tend to glamorize organized crime figures, but in real life there is little admirable about them. They're usually grotesquely self-centered with a total disregard for the feelings, opinions, or very lives of others. For two days a murderer sat at my dining-room table, and when it was over, I was sorry he had come.

Fratianno went into the witness protection program and spent several more years testifying against his former associates. Many high-ranking LCN members were sent to prison as a result of his testimony, and Fratianno did provide a rare look inside the LCN. The last I heard, he had changed his appearance and was still in hiding.

■ ■ ■

After breaking up with Bill and after my undercover assignment ended, I went back to dating women. I guess I was still trying to take the easy way out, still hoping, in the face of all evidence to the contrary, that I wasn't gay.

I took these dates to FBI parties and other social events and was intimate with some of them. But I missed the special quality a gay relationship had for me. I started to meet gay men in San Diego—through the personals, while I was running or working out at the gym, or through mutual gay friends. Sometimes a gay man would tell me he was married. I never pursued these relationships because they made me uncomfortable.

I always tried to be discreet meeting and being with others. I never disclosed my name or occupation until I knew a person well. Since most of the people I met were also closeted, they were as discreet and guarded as I was. I knew these contacts and my ever-widening circle of gay friends were putting me at risk of being found out by the FBI. But I also knew I couldn't deny my heart.

When I first began to date men, I wasn't sure what type of man I was interested in. Now I was more certain. I liked good-looking, athletic men in their twenties or thirties. Sometimes, as with heterosexuals, meeting someone might lead to a sexual relationship. There was also the same frustration of meeting someone you were interested in but who wasn't interested in you. As is true in any relationship at whatever age, endings were usually painful.

For a while it seemed I had the best of both worlds. I dated women *and* men. Dating women was socially far easier. I could go nearly anywhere and show public affection. Despite this, I was gradually coming to accept that sexual intimacy with men was more gratifying and meaningful to me. I would spend the evening with a woman but would want to be with a man for the weekend.

I also began to want a long-term gay relationship. I had a lot of friends in both the straight and the gay worlds, but there was hardly anyone who knew all of me.

■ ■ ■

In 1980 I became the case agent for a major bureau investigation. The case agent is in charge of an investigation, and this was a significant milestone in my career.

This particular investigation involved a large-scale gambling operation allegedly being run by San Diego resident Chris Petti, an associate of LCN members. On the basis of information we developed through informants, surveillance, and other investigative tools, court-authorized wiretaps were obtained for telephones used by Petti and others in San Diego, Los Angeles, and Las Vegas. In addition to supervising our own investigation, I coordinated FBI efforts in these other cities.

We obtained an arrest warrant for Petti a year after the case began. It was midmorning on August 7, 1981, as, accompanied by several other agents, I approached the front door of Petti's house. I saw him standing in the kitchen talking with an elderly woman. Petti spotted me at the same time and immediately came to the door. We did not draw our weapons. I told him that we had a warrant for his arrest for violating federal gambling statutes. He explained that his mother was visiting and asked that we not upset her.

His mother remained in the kitchen, and we accompanied Petti to the bedroom, where he changed clothes. I handcuffed him and led him away. He became his usual wise guy self after we left—the same person I had heard month after month on our wiretaps. He didn't know me, but I felt I knew him well.

We brought Petti to the FBI office using a back elevator. Most of the other agents knew about the arrest and noticed as we took him to be photographed and fingerprinted. Grand jury indictments of Petti and others were unsealed that morning, and the media were waiting as we exited bureau space to take Petti to prison.

When we stepped into the hallway that morning, with Petti beside me, I turned away as soon as I saw the cameras. Most FBI agents are concerned about becoming publicly known. It can impair an investigation—especially undercover and surveillance work. It is also personally dangerous to an agent. I had the additional concern of protecting my identity from gay people who didn't know I was an agent. When pictures of the incident were later published and broadcast, all you could see was the back of my head.

Several others, along with Petti, were convicted in a multimillion-dollar bookmaking ring. FBI headquarters was pleased with my work, and I received another letter of commendation and my first cash incentive award. The letter from Director William Webster was read before the entire office, and afterward I expressed my thanks to those who had assisted me.

■ ■ ■

By the early 1980s drug trafficking had become a serious crime problem for the country. The FBI received authorization from Congress in 1982 to assist the Drug Enforcement Administration (DEA) in its efforts. This was another major change for the bureau. Hoover hadn't wanted the bureau involved in drug investigations because they were too risky and too complex and might corrupt his agents.

In early spring 1982 I volunteered for the first drug-training session of FBI agents conducted by the DEA. The two-week class held at DEA headquarters in Glencoe, Georgia, made me realize that the nation's drug problem was far worse than I had thought. The amount of illegal drugs being imported into the United States was staggering, as was the number of drug users.

Such usage not only destroyed individual lives and ravaged communities but also increased this country's crime rate. In 1979 drug offenders accounted for only 6 percent of state prison populations, but in little more than a decade that figure climbed to 22 percent. Long-term studies at the time also showed that the rate of recidivism (the tendency to repeat criminal behavior) was extremely high for those in prison. The more people we put in prison, the more the crime rate increased. And the United States already had proportionately more prisoners than most other countries.

The DEA and other law enforcement agencies had already experienced corruption in their ranks as the result of drug investigations, and I believed FBI agents were not going to remain immune from such corruption for long. Drug trafficking was an extremely lucrative enterprise.

Involvement in drug investigations increased the danger level for those in law enforcement. Most of our DEA instructors had been in drug-related shoot-outs, and some had been wounded. I personally had never yet had to fire a weapon, nor had many agents I knew.

Beginning then, we were issued bulletproof vests, which we were required to wear when making arrests. Since drug raids often involved several law enforcement groups, agents were also issued windbreakers and baseball caps with the letters *FBI* clearly visible. Other law enforcement personnel were issued similar identifying clothing. I found myself mentally preparing for the increased possibility of violence.

From my training and conversations it seemed that the DEA was like a poor stepchild. In comparison with the manpower and resources of the FBI, the DEA was understaffed and underfunded. Yet there was no mistaking the perseverance, dedication, and bravery of its agents.

Soon after returning to San Diego, I was assigned as co-case agent for a major drug investigation. An FBI informant had identified an individual in San Diego who was, he said, dealing cocaine "like he had a license to do it." The information proved accurate, and we began identifying others who were involved. We learned who was in charge, and an undercover agent made contact. The operation was known as "the corporation," and in fact, it was run as if it were a legitimate business enterprise.

Months of investigation led to court-authorized wiretaps. These were run twenty-four hours a day for several months more, and agents from around the country were brought in to assist. I was often on the job working long hours seven days a week. Our wiretaps finally enabled us to identify both operatives of "the corporation" in New York City and the Colombian source of the cocaine. During the first week in December 1982 we obtained search warrants and arrest warrants for several of the organization's participants.

We had to assemble a small army of local, state, and federal law enforcement personnel to assist us in executing our warrants simultaneously throughout the country. The seizures produced cocaine, money, weapons, and drug records. Until then it was the biggest drug investigation in San Diego FBI office history, and our work received substantial local and national media coverage.

I didn't socialize much during this period. But then, through a mutual friend, I met a very attractive woman. We enjoyed each other's company and saw each other whenever we could. One night, as we lay on the couch together, she said suddenly, "We've been dating for a while, yet you've shown so little affection toward me."

She knew I was an FBI agent, so I couldn't tell her about my attraction to men even if I had wanted to.

"Don't you find me attractive?" she asked, sitting up at this point. It was as if she had just become aware of her feelings.

I started a story about how I had just broken up with somebody, but she got up and, without saying a word, left my house.

While I had been enjoying the best of both worlds, I hadn't given due consideration to the feelings of women whose long-term interests often tended toward a permanent commitment. It was wrong for me to continue to date women.

I had maintained the notion, however self-deceptive, that I could still find the right woman able to give me the satisfaction I found in relationships with men. I was also torn between what I was raised to believe and what I knew was right for me. I had sabotaged relationships with both men and women because of my inability or unwillingness to face the truth about myself.

Not long afterward I was invited by an FBI employee to a house party. While dancing with a female agent, I spotted a guy standing with several others. He was looking at me, too. Later in the evening I spoke with him briefly.

He was slender, had brown hair, and looked as though he might be in the Navy. He was shorter than I was, and younger, and appeared mild-mannered and shy. I felt very comfortable being with him, but he left the party before I got a chance to talk to him again. I suspected he was gay. His name was Brian.

The following week the same female agent and I went out dancing. One of the bars I suggested was predominantly gay. I told her this, but she said it didn't matter; she had a number of gay friends. While dancing, I saw Brian again. He was dancing with another guy, and later, while my date was in the ladies' room, I went over to talk with him. He was alone at the bar. Before the other agent returned, I slipped Brian my telephone number and told him to give me a call sometime. Giving him my phone number was risky, but I wanted to see him again.

Brian called the following week, and I invited him to dinner at a downtown San Diego restaurant. I hoped my initial positive feelings about him would prove correct.

As I had thought, Brian was in the Navy. He said he was living on board his ship, which was stationed in San Diego. He had finished two years of college but had run out of money. At that point he had joined the service in the hopes of putting some money away to complete his education and to see the world. Brian said he had been in San Diego only two days before meeting me.

"I'm glad you called," I said as we neared the end of dinner.

He smiled. "When I saw you at the party and later at the bar with that same woman, I just assumed you were straight. I was really surprised when you gave me your number."

My other two homosexual relationships failed in part because I wasn't forthcoming, and I wasn't about to let it happen again—especially when I had a hunch that this could work out. "I would like to get to know you better," I said, "but there is something I want to share with you first. I hope you will keep it confidential."

Brian nodded though he looked a little apprehensive. No one was seated near us.

"I can appreciate your concern about the military finding out you're gay. I hope this doesn't bother you, but I'm an FBI agent."

Brian didn't respond immediately but then smiled. "That doesn't bother me. For a minute I thought you were going to tell me you were married!"

I took Brian back to his ship, and we made plans to see each other the following weekend. I thought about him a lot the rest of the week, and on Friday I picked him up near my office, and we drove to my home. We continued talking as I prepared dinner. He was intelligent, well mannered, and charming—all in a low-key sort of way—and I was liking him more and more.

After dinner we went into the den, and I built a fire. As we sat on the couch together, talking and watching the fire, I sensed he was as physically attracted to me as I was to him. The fire started to die down, and I asked him if he wanted to go into the bedroom.

We stayed in bed for a long time the following morning, drinking coffee and talking. We spent the entire weekend together, and early Monday morning I took him back to his ship. I told him that it had been one of the best weekends in my life and that I looked forward to seeing him again. He said he would call me that evening. Meanwhile, when I went to work that morning, others asked about my weekend. I wished I could say that I'd met somebody nice.

In many ways Brian was my opposite. He was laid-back while I tended to be impatient and intense, especially when at work on an investigation. Even when I was home, I thought about an investigation, but Brian was a big help in this regard. I was more relaxed when I was around him.

We started spending every weekend together. We would be outside during the day—either at the beach or throwing a football or Frisbee around. At night we would go back to my house, fix dinner together, and rent a movie.

"The corporation" drug case wasn't completely over when I met Brian, but we began to see each other almost on a daily basis. He didn't own a car and would take a bus to my house late in the afternoon. He would spend the night, and I would take him back to the base on my way to work in the morning.

Like me, Brian felt the stress of living two lives. He hadn't acted on his homosexual feelings until very recently and was still in the process of sorting through many of the conflicts I had already come to terms with. I tried to help him as much as I could in these matters.

Brian was keeping his homosexuality hidden from his family and the Navy. He wasn't sure how his family would react, but he knew he'd be discharged if the military found out. Brian told me about the "fag" jokes and other derogatory comments his shipmates made from time to time, and I could tell how much this hurt him. I also was afraid that Brian might be physically assaulted if his shipmates ever found out he was gay. Fortunately they bought his story about having a girlfriend in San Diego. They seldom bothered him about socializing while off duty.

My neighbors must have noticed that Brian and I were together a lot and perhaps even saw us leave some mornings. When we were outside the house, we were very circumspect in our conversations and actions. Occasionally we bumped into an FBI employee or someone from Brian's ship. We treated the situation casually.

Being new to San Diego and in the military, Brian had very few gay friends. I introduced him to mine. Several were successful in their professions and good role models for Brian. My friends, in turn, liked Brian's sincerity and easy manner.

Brian and I promised to be honest with each other no matter how much it might hurt. Neither of us was interested in seeing others but agreed that if this should change, we would talk about it.

Occasionally someone at the office wanted to play matchmaker and offered to introduce me to a single woman. I usually declined by saying I was already dating someone. Sometimes this created a problem: I was invited to bring whomever I was dating. Normally I'd make up an excuse about having a previous engagement. I'm sure some wondered why I was so antisocial outside the office.

My parents often asked if I was dating anyone, and if I answered yes, they would want to know all about "her" and when they were going to have a chance to meet "her." My mother usually punctuated such conversations in a half-kidding way by saying she wanted more grandchildren. My relationship with Brian was the most important nonwork thing in my life, yet I couldn't share it with them. I stopped saying I was dating anybody, however, though their questions persisted.

The price I was paying for remaining closeted was that my family and co-workers never saw me as a whole person. They never saw me in a loving relationship and perhaps wondered if I was self-centered or incapable of loving another human being. Keeping my life hidden from my friends at the FBI did not bother me as much as keeping it hidden from family. Aside from Brian, they were the people who loved me most.

■ ■ ■

Brian called me at work one morning from a pay phone. I had been expecting the call. "Our ship just got orders to head overseas," he said.

His ship was going to the Far East, and he expected to be gone for at least seven months. Most of that time he would actually be at sea, and we had no idea when we would be able to talk with each other again. We had less than a month together and spent as much of that time as possible with each other.

On the night he was scheduled to leave, I prepared a special candle-light dinner for him. We drank champagne, and I told him that the past year with him had been the most wonderful in my life. As usual he said very little in response. I could tell by his eyes, though, that he felt the same way.

It was nearing the time when we had to leave for the ship. I cleared the table, and Brian left the room to finish packing. He was taking longer than expected, and I went into the bedroom to see how he was doing. The room was dark, and I turned the dimmer switch up a little. Brian was lying on his back with his hand over his eyes. He was crying. I lay down beside him and started to cry, too. I put my arm around him and told him that I loved him.

For several weeks after he left, I felt lost. Though I shared this with a few close gay friends, I'm sure neither my family nor the people at work detected anything different about me. I spent a lot of my spare time at work, and it took awhile before I could get use to the fact that he was really gone.

■ ■ ■

We had arrested several people involved in "the corporation," and we now had the enormous task of helping the prosecution prepare its case. This took several months, but in the end we successfully obtained guilty verdicts for everyone we had arrested. Early in 1984, after nearly two years, the drug investigation was finally over. Several of us received letters of commendation and cash incentive awards from Director Webster. The timing couldn't have been better. Brian's ship was heading back to San Diego.

■ ■ ■

I felt a little out of place standing alone on the dock at the Thirty-second Street Naval Base, south of downtown San Diego. Mostly women with small children were gathered, waiting for that first glimpse of the ship. Someone suddenly spotted it, and people began to clap and cheer.

The ship slowly made its way toward us, and we began to see the sailors on deck in their white uniforms. I strained to find Brian among the hundreds of sailors waving to us as tugboats carefully guided the ship into position at the dock. I finally saw him, and he was smiling and waving back at me. It seemed to take forever to secure the ship. Most of the others hugged and kissed and cried, but Brian and I only shook hands.

He told me how excited they had been when they saw the California coastline. They cheered, and the ship's sound system played Neil Diamond's "America."

It was good to have him home.

■ ■ ■

A few weeks later, in March 1984, while Brian and I were having supper at my house, I asked, "What do you think about taking a trip cross-country together?"

It had been more than a year since either of us had seen our families. After working the drug case for two years, I was anxious for a vacation. Being on board ship for most of seven months had been equally difficult for Brian.

"We could take my pickup truck, camp along the way, and visit our families."

"I'd love to," Brian answered, but then paused.

"What's the matter?"

"I don't think I can afford it, Frank. In fact, I know I can't."

I told him I'd like to pay for it. "People along the way have been generous to me, and whenever I asked to pay them back, they simply said to pass it on to someone else someday. This is one of those days."

Because of the differences in our incomes, I was careful about wanting to do things that would pose a financial hardship on him or make him indebted to me. I usually paid for our expenses when we were together, and Brian reciprocated by helping me with the house, yard, and dog.

"They say if you go on a long trip with someone and are still friends afterward, you'll be friends for life," I joked.

"It will be a great trip if you relax and forget you're an FBI agent!" he replied.

FBI agents have to be available twenty-four hours a day. Sometimes when Brian and I were together, I'd get a call from the office or have to stop what we were doing and go into work. If we were away from home for a while, I'd call to tell the office my whereabouts and also check my answering machine for bureau messages. Brian would get after me from time to time when he caught me thinking about work.

Because we had to hide our relationship from others, we felt as if we were in a fishbowl in San Diego. We couldn't go dancing together or have a drink together at a gay piano bar. Leaving San Diego would allow us to leave these concerns behind.

In April we packed our bikes and sleeping bags and headed east. We took our time, slowly meandering through the Southwest and the South, stopping in major cities along the way. Brian and I went into gay bars together. And we danced with each other. It was an extraordinary feeling to be with the person you loved and not have to hide your affection. We met other gay people along the way, and they gave us tips about what to see and do, and some even invited us into their homes.

I met Brian's family for the first time and stayed with them a few days before traveling alone to Canastota. Brian told his parents we were good friends, and they treated me warmly. Yet I also sensed they suspected us of having a homosexual relationship. I was closer in age to them than to Brian, and though we were very careful around them, I felt they could pick up on how close we were.

Later Brian flew to Canastota, and we spent a few days together at my parents' home. I had talked to my family about Brian, and they looked forward to meeting him. Everyone seemed to like him. It had been ten years since I had last brought someone home with me. Although I was not prepared to tell anyone I was gay, introducing Brian to my family and friends was a major step in sharing my personal life with them. If people suspected that we had a homosexual relationship, they kept it to themselves.

A few weeks later, after passing through twenty-six states and driving more than ninety-six hundred miles together, we returned to San Diego. There had been a few minor disagreements along the way, but overall, the experience had brought us even closer together. We agreed it was the trip of a lifetime, and we were looking forward to a long summer at the beach together.

The special in Miami now had changed all that. But I thought our relationship could endure whatever lay ahead.

part two

worlds colliding

4.

I was a little anxious that Monday morning, August 13, 1984, meeting the seven other agents assigned to the "special." We all were from different parts of the country but were all experienced investigators. Most of us were in our late thirties. John Morris, a supervisor from Boston, was assigned as the special supervisor. I had a feeling we would be spending a lot of time together. Little did I know the case would become one of the most important in FBI history.

Our meeting took place at the Holiday Inn in downtown Miami. An executive suite had already been converted into a mini-FBI office. Our whereabouts and purpose were known to only a few top supervisors at HQ and in Miami.

The investigation involved one of the FBI's first undercover drug operations. The code name for it was Operation Airlift, and it had originated in Miami. But the operation had been shut down by FBI headquarters for its lack of success. The bureau also said it had been mismanaged by the Miami office, and several agents involved in the case had been censured. The FBI's undercover agent Dan Mitrione, Jr., had quit the bureau soon after the operation was terminated.

Hilmer Sandini, our informant, was suspected of selling cocaine in the Pittsburgh area, and we were assigned to determine if this was true— and whether the cocaine came from our own drug operation. Cocaine had been allowed to "walk" at a key point in Operation Airlift, meaning that it had been permitted to enter into commerce. The purpose had been to trace the flow of cocaine sales so that all those involved could be caught. Allowing drugs to walk was not done often.

Sandini was the ultimate con man and had a lengthy criminal record. He had volunteered his services to help the FBI in Miami to keep from going to prison for fifteen years on a previous drug-smuggling conviction.

I could see we had our work cut out for us. The daily reports, surveillance records, tape recordings, background investigations, and other activities usually associated with major undercover operations were virtually nonexistent for Operation Airlift. We had to piece the story together ourselves, and the trail was cold.

We brought the co-case agents working on the Sandini drug-trafficking investigation in Pittsburgh to Miami. I normally don't make snap judgments about people but found I couldn't stand the DEA agent who came. He was overbearing, pompous, and a chain smoker. The FBI agent working with him seemed barely able to tolerate his counterpart.

The ten of us spent a full week in a smoke-filled room working out a chronology of key events and people involved in Operation Airlift. On occasion, we heard the DEA agent suggest that the undercover agent Dan Mitrione, Jr., was "dirty." As the week drew to a close, I confronted him on this.

"I talked to some people who saw him accept money during the operation," he said smugly.

"He was an undercover agent in an undercover drug operation," I shot back. "You can't assume because he took money he's dirty."

Our investigation the following week expanded to include secret interviews with FBI agents from headquarters and Miami who were involved in the operation. The friction between HQ and the Miami office was soon apparent. HQ thought Miami had botched the operation; Miami blamed HQ for poor planning and leadership. We had requested government, law enforcement, and business records, and they began to arrive.

The eight of us working on the "special" spent most of our off-duty time together and were becoming friends. A month had passed, and some of the agents, most of whom were married, talked about missing their families and home. I missed Brian but, of course, said nothing. John Morris arranged for us to have a long weekend off.

Brian prepared a special dinner for me on my first night home, complete with wine and candles. "This house is not the same without you, Frank," he said as we walked from room to room together later.

That night, when we were in bed, Brian told me his ship was leaving again for another long cruise. With that he started to cry. I held him, telling him I would try to get home one more time before he left. I wondered if it had been a mistake to accept the assignment.

■   ■   ■

The DEA agent's hunch was proving correct. The more we learned about Sandini's criminal behavior, the more questions we had about Mitrione's conduct. John Morris and several agents interviewed Mitrione in Miami, and he denied any criminal involvement. But he still couldn't adequately answer some of the most important questions we had about his actions. At this point the investigation became even more intense for us all. Mitrione was one of our own.

We began questioning others who had been involved in Operation Airlift. Our hope was that by widening our net and keeping the pressure on, we would force a break—or someone out into the open.

Special Agent Jim Brown and I were assigned to interview a drug smuggler at Leavenworth Federal Prison in Kansas. Though convicted felons, like informants, could not be relied upon to tell the truth, sometimes they offered that one single detail that could prove crucial to solving the case.

Leavenworth is known as the hothouse because of the effect of the intense summer heat on the massive brick structure. Built in the early 1900s, the walls of the prison begin thirty-five feet underground and rise another thirty-five feet in the air. An FBI agent from the Kansas City field office accompanied us, and once the big front doors had slammed shut, we were told to surrender our weapons. There were more than a thousand inmates inside, but none of the guards carried weapons. It was prison policy: If the guards did not have weapons, they could not be used against them by prisoners.

The Kansas agent unfastened his gun and joked, "Now remember, they all have weapons and we don't!"

Jim and I didn't smile back.

Prisoners watched from behind bars as we walked through the main corridor to the security supervisor's office. We were, of course, dressed in suits and ties, and I assumed they knew exactly who we were. The supervisor apologized for the mess inside his office. "We're putting steel reinforcements in the walls," he said. "We caught inmates trying to break in last week, looking for the names of prison snitches."

The body alarm he was wearing then went off, and he jumped up. He yelled back over his shoulder, "Lock the door!"

The Kansas City agent was quick to lock it. I turned to Jim. "Good timing on our part. First time here, and they have a riot."

"How long do you think we'll last, Frank?" he answered.

About a half hour later the supervisor returned, saying it had been only a "minor" disturbance. He led us to a vacant infirmary across the prison compound where the interview was to take place. The warden feared for the prisoner's safety should others find out about it.

Jim and I took turns questioning the convict, but did not uncover much new information. Unlike most of what is portrayed on television and in the movies, FBI investigations are often routine and tedious. I occasionally told people my job was often unexciting—interrupted by moments of sheer terror!

Jim and I had some spare time that afternoon and visited Harry Truman's home in Independence, Missouri. A passage in Merle Miller's biography about Truman (*Plain Speaking*) always stuck out in my mind— especially since the book was published in the same year (1974) I had my first homosexual experience.

Responding to a question about J. Edgar Hoover, Truman said, "One time they brought me a lot of stuff about his personal life, and I told them I didn't give a damn about that. That wasn't my business. It was what he did *while* at work that was my business."

■   ■   ■

Human beings are incredibly complex, and Dan Mitrione, Jr., was no different. After interviewing him, his bureau supervisors, co-workers, associates, friends, and members of his family, we were still not sure if he was capable of criminal activity.

Mitrione was a graduate of the University of Maryland and had served in Vietnam. After military service he joined the FBI and worked at the New York City field office. A couple of agents on the "special" knew Mitrione personally and spoke highly of him. A former Miami supervisor told us, "If Mitrione took a dime, you can have my house." But there were others, both in the bureau and out, who thought Mitrione was moody, even arrogant. They claimed it was difficult to get to know him.

During Operation Airlift Mitrione had driven a flashy car, rented a posh apartment, and lived lavishly. Witnesses claimed he snorted cocaine; others, that he hired prostitutes for drug dealers. Mitrione was playing a role, but the question was whether he had gone too far. Mitrione's immediate supervisor had been sick during most of Operation Airlift, yet none of the relief supervisors picked up the slack. Mitrione had no contact agent to whom he could talk or who could observe him.

At one point during the undercover operation Mitrione met with the Miami special agent in charge (SAC) and a supervisor. When Mitrione left the meeting, the SAC said, "He's [Mitrione] no longer acting or talking like an FBI agent. Whose side is he on?" The SAC told the supervisor to keep an eye on Mitrione, but nothing was done about it. Mitrione went back to the streets to work alongside our informant, Hilmer Sandini.

Sandini called Mitrione "son," telling others Mitrione was the son he had never had. Mitrione referred to Sandini as "the old man." Mitrione's own father, a former chief of police in Indiana, had gone to work as a police instructor in Uruguay for the Agency for International Development (AID). He was later kidnapped by leftist Tupamaros who believed he was working for the CIA. They killed him, and the incident was the basis for Costa-Gavras's film *State of Siege*. Two years after his father's murder Mitrione went to work for the FBI. Some believed it was a way to avenge his father's death. Whatever the reason, we were shocked when we came across a picture of Mitrione's father one day. He bore a remarkable resemblance to Sandini.

Word of our investigation had now gotten around HQ and the Miami field office. Some thought of us as a goon squad out to get a good agent.

■ ■ ■

Sometimes an agent in our group would ask me why I wasn't dating. I'd answer that I was seeing somebody back in San Diego and we had agreed not to see others. I even produced a photograph of a woman I had once dated, hoping that would satisfy the curiosity. I didn't like doing this. It bothered me to deny my relationship with Brian—and even his existence.

Once in a while the desire to relax around other gay people got to be too much, and I would go out to a gay bar. I thought the odds of running into someone from work were fairly remote. But I couldn't tell gays I met who I really was or what I was doing in Miami. I couldn't form any friendships, so I decided, instead, to focus almost exclusively on my work. I knew the time would come when I could go home.

■ ■ ■

John Morris was required to keep headquarters informed about the investigation and sometimes a few of us went back with him. On one such trip I made a presentation and, after returning to Miami, got a call from a bureau supervisor. He said that headquarters was impressed with me and wanted to know if I was interested in an administrative post in Washington. I was flattered, but said, "No thanks." I added, half-kiddingly,

"If I go back there, who's going to solve cases in the field and make all of you look good?"

Administrative advancement in the bureau never appealed to me. I didn't want to sit behind a desk all day reviewing other agents' investigations; I wanted to be in charge of solving them. Ironically, the complex cases I was now assigned put me behind a desk more often than I wanted.

■ ■ ■

I called my father on October 3, 1984, to wish him a happy birthday. He was seventy years old—or "seventy big ones," as he said. He got me laughing with the line "If I knew I was going to live this long, Francis, I would have taken better care of myself!"

After hanging up, Jim Brown called. "Have you heard the news?" he said.

It sounded as if somebody had died. "I'm afraid to ask."

"An FBI agent in Los Angeles has been arrested for espionage. A guy named Miller. The networks are carrying the story."

I turned on the TV. NBC's Tom Brokaw was saying that for the first time in history an FBI agent was being charged with espionage. Richard W. Miller, a twenty-one-year veteran in Los Angeles, had allegedly given classified information to Soviet agents.

Our investigative team gathered for dinner that night at our usual Italian restaurant, but there was none of our usual lighthearted banter. Toward the end of dinner John Morris said, in a voice reflecting concern, "Let's hope we don't have another scandal on our hands. But if we do, let's conduct the investigation thoroughly and not make the bureau look any worse."

I talked to Brian later, and he said his ship was scheduled to leave by week's end. I told him I was sorry I wouldn't be home to say good-bye.

I couldn't sleep that night. I wondered why I put my career ahead of my relationship with Brian. I also wondered what motivated Miller to betray our country. I knew agents with financial and drinking problems and others who engaged in extramarital affairs. Perhaps something along these lines had caused Miller's downfall.

Being gay made me careful about my conduct and appreciative of my work. I knew somebody might try to use the fact that I was gay against me one day, but I also knew that nothing on earth could cause me to betray my country.

I couldn't let the fear of being fired dominate my life. If I did, I would no longer be effective as an agent. I would second-guess every remark and decision; I would be looking every which way instead of at what was in front of me.

That night I recommitted myself to being the best agent possible. After all, somebody might one day say that an agent who helped solve this case was gay.

■ ■ ■

In November Sandini's attorney, Joel Rosenthal, contacted us and said Sandini wanted to talk to us about Mitrione. John Morris told Rosenthal we'd listen, but there wouldn't be any deals.

Jim Brown and I were in Indianapolis when John Morris called. I could hear only Jim's part of the conversation but could tell the news wasn't good.

"Morris finished questioning Sandini," Jim said. "Sandini claims Mitrione helped him steal cocaine from our drug operation. He also says he paid Mitrione hundreds of thousands of dollars from its sale."

One loose end from the investigation now loomed larger. Sandini had previously claimed someone tried to kill him by placing a bomb beneath his car. At the time Sandini was about to testify before a federal grand jury on drug-trafficking charges. If Mitrione thought Sandini was going to "roll over" and cooperate with authorities, Mitrione would have a motive to see him dead.

Jim and I returned to Miami along with other agents, and we got another call, this time from Mitrione's attorney, Dan Forman. He wanted to set up a meeting with John Morris.

We had determined Sandini's guilt in the sale of cocaine and we were fairly certain it had come from our operation. Because the investigation had been so broad, word had evidently reached Sandini about this. He then must have stepped forward to save his own skin. This, in turn, could have drawn Mitrione out. He knew Sandini was capable of just about anything to avoid serving time. Now we would have to determine which one—if either—would tell us the truth.

Dan Forman met briefly with John Morris at a poolside table at the hotel. When Forman left, John called us together. His voice was somber. "Forman said Mitrione took the money. He's coming in tomorrow to confess. We'll meet again at seven to discuss strategy."

I noticed tears form in the eyes of some of the agents who knew Mitrione. No one said a word as we left the room, almost in single file.

A second FBI agent had gone bad. Miller was the first for espionage; Mitrione could be the first for drug trafficking.

I changed clothes quickly but didn't stretch much before beginning my six-mile run north along the familiar Miami shoreline. I pushed hard at the six-mile mark and kept running. My shock at what Mitrione had done turned to anger, and I knew I had to get rid of it. Mitrione was a former agent and would be able to tell a great deal about our investigation by our questions. We had to be at our best.

At our meeting that night, agents volunteered to ask questions based upon their specialized knowledge of the case. John Morris, after talking with a psychiatrist on retainer by the bureau, also advised us that sometimes people who confess become violent or commit suicide. We took precautions with our sixth-floor suite. Some of us would also be armed.

The bureau seldom tape-records confessions. Recording can inhibit or otherwise intimidate a person. And if the machine malfunctions, it can cause problems in court. Moreover, defense attorneys make an issue out of how and why certain questions are asked.

We usually take notes of interviews or confessions in longhand. The agent who does so is responsible for making sure that all key areas are covered and that the information recorded is accurate and complete. This agent is also responsible for preparing the all-important FD-302 afterward. The 302 is a narrative of the interview and is subsequently used as evidence in court. Others, including the judge, defense attorneys, other law enforcement agencies, and sometimes the public see the 302, and it reflects the quality of our work.

John asked for a volunteer to take notes, but no one responded right away. All of us knew it would be a difficult job, considering the amount and complexity of information available to us. The commitment I had made the night before to doing the best job possible urged my hand up. "I'll do it, John," I said, and he nodded his thanks.

The meeting ended, and I immediately went to work. I reviewed our files and other reports, making an outline of key areas to be covered. I got to bed late that night and was up early the following morning. We reconvened at 10:00 A.M., and I distributed copies of my twelve-page outline. We went over it together, making changes and additions.

We finished our work about 10:45 and waited mostly in silence. Mitrione was scheduled to arrive at 11:00. I was by a window that looked out over the Miami River. There was a knock at the door, and John Morris moved to answer it. Dan Mitrione, Jr., stood in the doorway looking every bit the FBI agent he once had been. Tall and slender, with a sport jacket and tie, Mitrione showed little emotion as John introduced him to us. Mitrione didn't offer his hand, not even to the agents who knew him. To me, his face seemed puffy and a little reddish.

He was led to the conference table, and I followed directly behind. I couldn't determine whether or not he was armed. Because I have some hearing loss, I sat next to Mitrione, on his left. I put my outline, notes, notepad, and pens on the table and placed my briefcase on the floor near my leg. I purposely left it unlocked. Inside was a gun that I could have gotten to in a matter of seconds.

John Morris advised Mitrione of his Miranda rights and then gave him a waiver of rights form to sign. As I was witnessing the form with my signature, I heard John say, "Dan, why don't you just give us an overview of what happened and we can go over it in detail later?"

There was an awkward moment of silence as we waited for Mitrione to begin. He seemed nervous, unsure of himself. But then, in a voice barely audible, he told a story of such tragic proportions that it nearly froze us in place. Nobody seemed to cough, sigh, or shift in his chair. The only sound, other than Mitrione's voice, was my pen racing line after line down the page.

5.

Mitrione told us that he and Sandini initially set up a legitimate under-cover drug operation at Fort Lauderdale Executive Airport. But the longer he worked with Sandini, the more he realized that Sandini was making illegal drug deals on his own. At times Mitrione witnessed the deals but didn't report them to the bureau. Eventually he realized he could no longer control Sandini.

Later Sandini gave Mitrione a nine-thousand-dollar Rolex watch and some money as gifts. Mitrione knew he should have refused the gifts and reported them to his supervisor, but he didn't. He also didn't give us a reason why.

None of us was prepared for what Mitrione told us next. He allowed Sandini to skim forty-two kilos of cocaine from a huge shipment that Operation Airlift arranged to be brought into the country. Although it was Sandini's idea, Mitrione had gone along with it, and Sandini personally transported cocaine from Memphis to Miami. Mitrione arranged for the rest of the shipment to be recovered by law enforcement officers in Florida.

I stopped writing for a moment. The street value of forty-two kilos of cocaine was in the neighborhood of ten million dollars! I glanced over at Mitrione, and though his eyes were misty, I didn't notice any tears. The side of his face was beginning to twitch slightly. We waited until he was ready to continue.

Mitrione advised us that Sandini began selling the cocaine a little at a time and gave Mitrione cash payments for several months afterward. The payments ranged from about $10,000 to as high as $85,000, and Mitrione was paid in public places, his car, and his home. Early on Mitrione was still an FBI agent, but the payments continued after he left the bureau. Mitrione estimated that his overall cut from the sale of the cocaine was about $850,000.

Mitrione must have anticipated one of our main concerns and said that there were no other FBI employees involved. He said he acted alone with Sandini and used the money to make investments and loans to friends, to take trips, and to buy cars and household items. He also paid his attorney Forman and had some money left, which he would turn over to us.

We sat riveted. I glanced at my watch. Mitrione had completed his confession in less than a half hour. John Morris rose.

"I'll be right back," he said, and left the room. Another agent continued the questioning. We knew John went to call headquarters, which was anxious to find out what Mitrione had said.

The questioning continued nonstop until we broke for dinner. I went for a long walk by myself and ate alone. I was tired from taking notes and needed to clear my head.

Mitrione was questioned late into the night, and when he left, we all seemed to be in a daze. Then one of the agents who knew Mitrione said, "I never thought he'd do it." We all mentioned something after that about our shock, anger, and disappointment.

We then began to focus on areas that still needed to be covered and the new leads his confession generated. When we finished, John Morris said he was proud of us—and so was headquarters. "It's going to be a major setback for the bureau, but we've got to find out the truth. Let's continue to take our time and be as thorough as possible, no matter how long it takes."

Three more days of intensive questioning followed, and then I went to work preparing the FD-302 report. I needed to get it done quickly. It would provide the basis for a statement Mitrione had to sign, and we didn't want him to change his mind. Headquarters, too, would be anxious to see it. I thought the report might take a week to finish, but it took more than two weeks of work every day. It came to eighty-seven pages. A much shorter statement was written from the 302, and Mitrione was called in to sign it.

Mitrione and Forman both read through each sentence of the statement carefully, occasionally making a minor change or correction. Mitrione signed the statement when he finished, and John Morris and another agent witnessed his signature.

After Mitrione and Forman left, John congratulated us on a job well done. In particular, he thanked me for my work, and the other agents joined in. I was pleased, but exhausted. John gave us a few weeks off. It was Christmas. Though Brian, still on board his ship, wouldn't be waiting for me, all his letters would be there.

■ ■ ■

I wrote Brian often while he was away, and he wrote me in San Diego. I was afraid one of his letters might go astray. In writing him, I used only my first initial and had a post office box as a return address. I composed my letters in such a way that anybody reading them wouldn't be able to decipher that they were written by a gay person. Despite these precautions, I continued to worry that somebody on board ship might find out and something would happen to Brian.

I spent Christmas Day with close friends but was alone on New Year's Eve. It was the first time Brian and I had been apart that night since we met. On New Year's Day I received a surprise phone call from him in the Philippines. It was good to hear his voice.

I returned to Miami in early January 1985. At that time we worked on strategy relative to the new leads developed by Mitrione. We also briefed Department of Justice attorneys who were preparing the case against Mitrione and others. The bulk of our assignment over, John Morris asked headquarters for replacement agents. My partner, Jim Brown, liked Florida and had asked to be permanently transferred there from Chicago. I figured I'd be going home in a short while.

Then John Morris called me into his office one afternoon. He asked if I would stay on with Jim at least until Mitrione pleaded guilty. "You know the case as well as anyone, Frank," he said. "We also need you to work with Jim to make certain that the new agents fully understand what we've been doing here. And if you decide to stay, I want you and Jim to be co-case agents for the remainder of the investigation."

The eight of us originally on the "special" went out to dinner one last time. We toasted each other and the bureau. When it came to me, I stood and looked over at John Morris. Raising my glass, I said, "To one of the best supervisors I've ever worked for."

The other agents chimed in with "Here! Here!" and John got up. He looked at each of us and then said, "To the best bunch of guys with whom I've ever worked. We can be proud of what we have accomplished here."

Except for John and Jim Brown, I never saw any of the other agents again. Only John and Jim from that group contacted me after I was fired.

■ ■ ■

With John's permission, I rented a small apartment in Coconut Grove, an area south of downtown Miami. I never like eating all my meals in a restaurant or the fact that I have no privacy. Coconut Grove was less than a ten-minute drive to work. I also knew it had a sizable gay population.

Jim Brown and I interviewed Mitrione a few more times in early 1985, and one thing he said haunted me. After the attempted bombing of Sandini's car Mitrione had gone into the Everglades, intending to kill himself. Telling us that was one of the few times he ever showed emotion.

Though the investigation was in its eighth month, the media were still unaware of our presence or Mitrione's confession. We were fortunate in this regard. Media attention could cause leads to dry up or suspects to disappear. It also would have increased pressure from headquarters.

After a series of high-level meetings with attorneys from the Department of Justice, it was decided that Mitrione would be polygraphed regarding the information he had provided. The date of the polygraph was set for March 13, 1985, the day before Mitrione was to appear in court.

■ ■ ■

I was finishing dinner at my apartment on March 13 when the phone rang. It was the Miami ASAC. "We need you at the United States attorney's office right away," he said. "I'll explain once you get here."

A number of conversations were taking place simultaneously when I arrived. I overheard the U.S. attorney for Miami, Stanley Marcus, trying to reach a top Department of Justice official in Washington. The FBI polygraph examiner was talking with an assistant United States attorney. I saw John Morris and Jim Brown and walked over to them.

"Mitrione failed the polygraph," Jim said. "He failed when he was asked if he had anything to do with the attempted bombing of Sandini's car."

I felt as though I had been blindsided. Stanley Marcus's voice boomed out over the crowd. "What do you guys think about all this?" he said, looking at us. The room instantly quieted.

John nodded for me to go ahead.

"We interviewed Mitrione several times. We compared what he told us with what we knew to be true, and at no time did we ever find him to be lying."

Marcus wasn't satisfied. "Well, what do you make of the results of the polygraph then?"

"We haven't developed any information tying him to the bombing."

Several others jumped in at that point, but Marcus's voice dominated. He said that he was going ahead with Mitrione's guilty plea but that he wanted the bombing issue resolved. He would ask the judge to postpone Mitrione's sentencing until then.

The meeting abruptly ended, but John, Jim, and I stayed behind. Their faces reflected the same shock and disappointment I was feeling. Had we been taken in by Mitrione? Had our eight months of work been for nothing?

"John," I said, "I want to take on the bombing investigation. I'd like to devote full time to it. That is, if it's all right with you and Jim."

John nodded, saying he would assist in whatever way he could.

■ ■ ■

We knew it was possible Mitrione might try to flee. A Miami surveillance team had been dispatched to watch him, but Jim and I drove out to his house anyway. It was dark and didn't look as if anybody were home. We had a rented car and so couldn't contact the surveillance team by radio.

Jim dropped me off at my car. "I wonder if he went into the Everglades again, Frank," he said.

I shrugged, thinking the same thing.

I went to the office early the following morning. John Morris arrived shortly afterward, and there was an unmistakable look of relief on his face. "Mitrione is at Forman's office. We're to meet him there in a half hour."

Mitrione and his wife were sitting in the reception area when we arrived. They were holding hands, and the strain was evident on their faces. Then their attorney, Dan Forman, came out of his office, and the three of them left in his car. We followed behind. As we made our way to the courthouse, Miami surveillance units moved in. It felt like a funeral procession.

John, Jim, and I took a seat in the front row. A short time later the judge, a gray-haired man, called our case. Stanley Marcus advised him that Mitrione was about to plead guilty to bribery and narcotics charges.

Before advising Mitrione of his legal rights, the judge commented how he never thought he would hear such charges brought against an FBI agent in his courtroom.

He asked Mitrione, "Is this a voluntary plea on your part?"

In a voice barely audible, Mitrione answered that it was.

"How do you plead to all of these charges?"

"Guilty," Mitrione said.

Federal marshals walked toward Mitrione to take him away. He turned to his wife and hugged her. He faced a possible forty-five years in prison and more than $2.6 million in fines.

Mitrione's guilty plea exploded into headlines across the country. Most accounts I saw were fairly accurate and well written, considering the complexity of the case. In nearly every story the point was made that this was the first time in history that a special agent of the FBI had been found guilty on drug corruption charges. A government official went so far as to say that the Mitrione case was "the biggest black eye in bureau history."

Time magazine titled its account of our investigation "The FBI Gets Its Man." But *Newsweek,* the *Wall Street Journal, Newsday,* and others, including television news coverage, focused on the growing number of law enforcement people nationwide corrupted by drug money while working undercover. One psychiatrist observed that Mitrione had lost his identity "out in the cold." Attorney Forman referred to him as a "fallen angel."

In addition to the Colombians, Mitrione and Sandini had met with drug traffickers in Panama City. This revelation led to closer scrutiny of Panama's drug ties to the United States. We went to war against Panama on December 20, 1989, and drug trafficking was cited as one of the reasons.

■ ■ ■

I started the investigation of the attempted bombing the same day Mitrione pleaded guilty. The basic facts of the case were fairly simple. Sandini was making his usual short drive from the Pompano Park Harness Track to his favorite night spot late on the night of April 2, 1984, when his car hit a rut in the road. His wife, Carol, driving behind, noticed wires dangling from the rear bumper of her husband's car. The police were called in and found that the wires were part of a highly sophisticated, powerful bomb. After all his swindling and drug deals, a number of people, including Mitrione, would have a motive to see Sandini dead.

I studied files, examined phone records, retraced events of that April night, and interviewed others, including Mitrione's family. Meeting

Mitrione's mother was particularly troubling. She reminded me of my mother. I often wondered if those who commit crimes ever consider the awful effect their actions have on those who love them.

I interviewed Sandini's attorney, Joel Rosenthal, because of his contact with Mitrione during this period, and some of what he said seemed to implicate Mitrione. We requested an interview with Sandini about the attempted bombing. When Rosenthal recontacted us, he said Sandini had a witness who could pinpoint Mitrione at the scene of the crime that evening.

"Sounds just like Sandini," Jim said. "I wonder what he's got up his sleeve."

"Whatever it is," I answered, "it should be a very interesting interview. After all these months we'll finally get a chance to meet him face-to-face."

■ ■ ■

Jim and I arrived in Memphis, Tennessee, late in the afternoon. We visited the Lorraine Motel, where Dr. Martin Luther King had been assassinated, and I experienced the feeling of sadness and loss I had had in Dallas, seeing where President Kennedy had been shot.

We arrived at the prison shortly before nine the following morning. Rosenthal joined us at the window of the interview room as an old man moved slowly across the prison yard, a guard following closely behind.

"That's Sandini," Rosenthal said.

Sandini had long white hair and a beard. We had heard he was in poor health, and he appeared to be walking with great difficulty. Jim looked at me, no doubt wondering the same thing. Was Sandini as frail as he appeared to be, or was this another con?

The door opened a few minutes later, and in walked Sandini. I knew he was over six feet tall, but he seemed bigger and more imposing than I anticipated. He looked down at us, then said hello to his attorney. We introduced ourselves and showed him our credentials. He scrutinized both closely.

Sandini shook hands with Jim and then turned to me. His hand was much larger than mine, and his handshake felt very strong. We looked at each other for a moment, and I wondered what he was thinking. I thought of the lives he had ruined. It felt as though I were shaking hands with the devil.

Sandini sat down opposite us at the conference table. Rosenthal restated the purpose of the interview, and while he spoke, Sandini sat with his hands clasped watching us.

Rosenthal finished, and I began the questioning. Sandini chose his words carefully. His voice was clear and strong, and his mind obviously sharp.

"Mr. Sandini," I asked at one point, "do you know who might be responsible for trying to kill you?"

Sandini hesitated and then began to talk with animation. He said Mitrione was the one who had tried to kill him. He said this repeatedly. He said he had a witness—a waitress who could put Mitrione at the scene of the crime.

Afterward Jim and I stood by the car without speaking. Then Jim commented, "The way he walked through the prison yard you would have thought he was on his deathbed. He was pretty sharp, though, wasn't he?"

"After being around him for a while you could see why he's so good at manipulating people. He's got presence, acting ability, and he's very clever."

We both were thinking of Mitrione.

"He'd be deadly if you were with him all the time," Jim said.

We returned to Miami and located the waitress. She said she'd seen a car that "looked" like Mitrione's, but it had pulled away before she got a chance to see the driver.

We were at a dead end as far as the investigation was concerned. The only thing left was perhaps to interview Mitrione again. I didn't need to stay in Miami waiting for the arrangements. Jim could contact me back in San Diego.

■　■　■

Brian had been discharged from the Navy and was making his way to Miami in my pickup truck, which I needed to take some things back with me. During this time I arranged a luncheon so that my partner, Jim Brown, could meet two agents I knew from San Diego. Dean Hughes and Jerry Dove had recently transferred to the Miami office.

Dean was a bachelor and had grown up on a farm in the West. Jerry and I had run and also socialized together. Jerry was a good-looking, good-natured guy, and I had kidded him that he looked a lot like Tom Cruise. During my career I had found some male FBI employees like Jerry to be attractive but of course had always kept it to myself.

FBI agents like to swap "war stories" when they get together, and that luncheon was no different. I told about the time Hughes, several other agents, and I had searched a Hell's Angels hangout for drugs. The place was filthy, and I sat at the kitchen table most of the day, making an inventory of what was being seized.

"Dean started searching in the kitchen and said, 'Hey, there's a snake under the sink!' I quickly got out of there and went to the living room. It became obvious no one else was crazy about snakes. Finally a female agent took control of the six-foot-long boa constrictor. So much for not allowing females to be FBI agents!"

Dean, who had worked in New York City for several years, retold the legendary story about the agent who took the subway to work daily. One morning, as the agent boarded the train, he bumped into another man. The agent felt for his credentials and discovered that they were missing. Agents are almost paranoid about losing their credentials. Their loss can result in a letter of censure or worse, so the agent reached for the man. But the subway doors slammed shut, and the train pulled away.

On the way into work, the agent tried to figure out how to explain the loss of his credentials to his supervisor. When he arrived, the phone was ringing at his desk. It was his wife. She told him he had left his credentials at home. With that the agent opened up his briefcase and threw into the wastebasket the sleeve he had torn from the man's coat.

■ ■ ■

I left work a little early the evening Brian was scheduled to arrive. He and I waited, as usual, until we got inside before holding each other and kissing. Brian was tan, all smiles, and relaxed, and it felt incredibly good to see him. We talked for a while and then went into the bedroom. We had not been intimate in nine months.

Later Brian said he was too tired from driving to want to go out for dinner.

"How about some linguine and clam sauce?" I asked.

We talked nonstop throughout dinner. I had missed him but until then hadn't known how much. Brian excused himself afterward, and I cleared the dishes. When he returned, he was holding a small package.

"I wasn't home for your birthday, so I got this for you in Hong Kong," he said, smiling broadly.

I took the wrapping off the box, opening it slowly. Inside was a beautiful gold Seiko watch. It was expensive, and I knew Brian didn't earn much as an enlisted man.

"Look on the back," he urged.

I turned the watch over and read the engraving: "For the good times we shared. Happy 40th."

I couldn't say anything right away.

"It's beautiful and one of the nicest gifts anybody has ever given me," I finally told him. I put my arm around him. "I'll wear it only on special occasions, and it will always remind me of you."

We kissed, and I told him again how much I had missed him. I looked at the inscription again. Brian had purposely left off his name, knowing it might cause suspicion if others saw it.

■ ■ ■

My co-workers in San Diego knew when I was returning, and as I entered the office that mid-August morning, I was greeted by a huge Welcome Home sign. The sign had an arrow directing me to still another sign, and there were several more of these, with people greeting me along the way. My last stop was the organized crime squad area, and I was led to a table that contained a number of cards and gag gifts.

Jack Blair came out of his office, and we shook hands.

"So much for a two-week assignment, Jack," I kidded.

"Yeah, but look how happy everyone is to have you back."

I finished opening the last gag gift. "If I knew you were going to go through all this trouble and expense," I said, "I would not have come back!"

Jack asked if I had been in the men's room yet.

"I'm afraid to look."

Several male agents crowded around as I went in. Above the urinals was a large banner welcoming me back. A number of agents had signed it, leaving little witticisms. Not to be outdone, I took out my pen and wrote, "This is Frank . . . and I'm *under*whelmed!"

■ ■ ■

A few days later I got a call to return to Miami to discuss the government's case against Sandini and others who were about to stand trial. Mitrione was to testify on behalf of the government yet still hadn't made up his mind on whether to talk to us about the bombing. A cloud of suspicion still hung over him. Not having the issue resolved might cause problems later-on with his testimony.

One night in late September, as Brian and I watched television, Jim Brown called. "Mitrione is ready to talk to us about the bombing. He's about to testify against Sandini, and we need to talk to him as soon as possible."

Jim met me at the Pittsburgh airport on September 24. We stood apart from the others, waiting for my suitcases. "The interview is scheduled for ten A.M. tomorrow," Jim said. "I've made arrangements to pick up Bruce Teitlebaum in the morning, and the three of us can drive out to the prison together." Teitlebaum was an assistant United States attorney from Pittsburgh assigned to the case.

When we arrived the following morning, a guard escorted us to a building housing inmates kept segregated from the others. We waited inside the conference room, and moments later Mitrione entered. He was much thinner than when we last saw him, and his skin looked pale. He didn't look at me, and I sensed something was wrong. The guard took off Mitrione's handcuffs and left the room. Mitrione turned to Bruce and said he didn't want to talk to us.

We waited out in the hallway while he talked to Bruce. "Maybe he's afraid of what we're going to find out," I said, but Jim only shrugged.

The guard occasionally looked through the small glass window of the door to the conference room. After about an hour Bruce came out. He looked at me, saying, "Mitrione says he's very upset about how you treated his family during your interviews with them."

Jim and I looked at each other in disbelief.

"He heard you were rude and disrespectful and doesn't want to talk with Frank in the room."

I felt myself start to get angry but tried to keep it in check. A temper can be detrimental, even dangerous, in law enforcement.

"Someone has obviously given him false information," Bruce continued. "We need to convince him that it isn't true."

We considered our options, and Bruce went back into the room. He was to go in and out three more times that day. "Good thing we had a big breakfast," I told Jim at one point.

We asked to see Mitrione's cell, and the guard led us to a room with a Plexiglas window. From there guards watched Mitrione twenty-four hours a day. The cell was small and had a bed, toilet, and sink. We saw a few books and magazines, but there was no television set or radio. The cell entrance had bars; the other two walls were concrete from top to bottom.

Mitrione had no contact with other prisoners and took all his meals in the cell. He was allowed to take a shower a few times a week. He was also allowed into the prison yard a few hours a week when none of the other prisoners was present.

"This is *hard* time," Jim observed.

It was after one o'clock when Bruce came out the third time. "He'll talk to Jim but still won't talk to you, Frank," he said wearily.

Jim shook his head. "Frank knows this investigation better than anybody else. Mitrione talks to both of us, or we don't do the interview."

"I'll tell him how you guys feel," he said, and walked back into the room.

He came out about 2:30 P.M., shaking his head. "We're at an impasse. Why don't you guys come in?"

Jim, in his usual sincere way, tried his hand at convincing Mitrione we had always conducted ourselves professionally. I affirmed this, adding, "I'm offended that you believe I was disrespectful. I treated your mother and the rest of your family the way I would want mine treated under similar circumstances. Someone is giving you erroneous information, and I would be concerned about that person and his motivation."

Mitrione did not take his eyes off me while I spoke, and I felt as though we were the only two people in the room.

"Jim and I want to resolve this issue, and we need your help," I continued. "If you want to talk to us, fine. We're prepared to stay as long as it takes. If you don't want to talk to us, that's fine, too. It's your choice."

Mitrione finally agreed to the interview, but it was so late at that point we decided to wait until the next day to begin. Jim and I were back at the prison at nine the following morning. Because of an important prior commitment, Bruce didn't return.

"What do you think he's going to say, Jim?" I asked as we got out of the car.

"I don't know. I think you believe he did it more than I do. But then again you know the bombing investigation better."

"We've got a lot of unanswered questions. A lot depends on what he has to say."

When Mitrione came into the room, he seemed more relaxed than on the previous day. I waited until he was settled and then asked, "Were you responsible for the attempted bombing of Sandini's car?''

Mitrione emphatically answered no.

"Do you have any knowledge who tried to kill Sandini on the night of April second, 1984?''

Again Mitrione answered no.

"All right, Dan," I said, "let's go back to the beginning.''

The interview took several hours, and at one point Mitrione raised the possibility that Sandini had staged the bombing himself. I told him we had considered this, but our investigation did not bear it out.

Mitrione sat passively as we put away our things. He told us, the bitterness in his voice plain, "I'm anxious to leave this place. I have no privacy, and I'm watched constantly, even when I'm sleeping. It's a strange feeling to have a guy with a high school education telling you everything you can and cannot do.''

Outside the prison I took a deep breath of the cool autumn air. The grass was dark green, the leaves on the trees a dazzling orange and gold, and the sky cloudless. I couldn't imagine doing anything that would cause me to lose my freedom.

"What do you think?'' Jim asked.

"Jump ball,'' I told him.

■ ■ ■

Autumn is beautiful in upstate New York, and my father and I went to a high school football game together. It felt good to put the Mitrione interview behind me, at least for a little while. Things were so much simpler in Canastota. It was so different from Miami and the world of con men and drugs and prisons.

If I weren't gay, I might still be living in Canastota—teaching high school, coaching sports, watching my own children grow. But because I was gay, I knew I could never go back there to live. It would be a lonely, frustrating life. I suddenly missed Brian.

My father and I talked about the football game as I drove the familiar route home.

"I don't go to the games very much anymore now that you boys are gone,'' he said, looking out his window. "Why don't you quit your job and move back here? Your mother and I worry about you. We're afraid something's going to happen.''

"It's not that dangerous,'' I said with a laugh. "I worry more about writer's cramp and being crushed under FBI files.''

"We miss you" was my father's reply.

My mother was standing at the kitchen stove, frying Italian sausage and peppers when we arrived home. I had seen her standing in that same spot for more than twenty-five years. I walked over and hugged her as I had so many times before.

"It's so good to have you home again, Francis," she said.

"It's always good to be home, Mamma," I told her.

She said she had something to tell me and took my arm as we walked into the living room. We sat down on the couch next to each other. She put her hand over mine. "I've got some bad news for you. Brian called while you were at the game. He said he had to put your dog, Buddy, to sleep. The vet said it was for the best."

Buddy was my Samoyed whose health had been deteriorating. I asked how Brian was doing.

"He sounded pretty sad. The vet gave Brian some time to be alone with Buddy. Brian said it sounded as though Buddy was crying when he left the office."

I told my mother I was going for a walk, and she asked if I was all right.

"He was such a good dog, Mom," I said. "I've spent so little time with him this past year, and it seemed to age him. I was in my twenties when I first got him. So much in my life has changed since then."

■ ■ ■

On November 14, 1985, I waited in the office for Jim's call. I had never noticed before how much you could tell about a person by listening to his voice. Jim's was sad.

"The judge sentenced Mitrione to ten years in prison. He also criticized the bureau for its supervision of the undercover operation and its failure to provide psychological testing and training for undercover agents."

"There's enough blame to go around," I said.

"The judge also commented that the lady of justice who holds the scales may be blindfolded, but she's got a tear on her cheek today. He said that if there was ever a time you could say, 'Damn this drug society,' it was today."

After a pause I asked how Mitrione and his family had taken the news.

"Mitrione didn't show much reaction, but his family is very upset with the bureau."

The following day there was a front-page *New York Times* story about the sentencing. In it, FBI Director William H. Webster was quoted as saying: "The corrupting power of drug money is one of the obvious reasons why this number one crime problem must be conquered in our country. It must be exposed and rooted out wherever it may be found. This sad case illustrates our relentless determination to police our own ranks."

In that same month, November, Hilmer Sandini's daughter, wife, and five other people were convicted for their role in an international drug conspiracy that had brought twenty-five million dollars' worth of cocaine into western Pennsylvania between 1981 and 1984.

I was to return to Miami two more times. In December 1985 I talked with FBI and DEA agents, and federal prosecutors, about the convictions, other prosecutions, and unresolved issues such as the attempted bombing. In January 1986 John Morris and I joined Jim Brown in discussing the overall investigation with bureau supervisors.

But as the months rolled by, I was troubled about the fact that Operation Airlift, and all that had happened to Mitrione, received scant attention *inside* the bureau. Rather than apply the lessons we had learned, it seemed the bureau wanted to forget any of it ever happened.

6.

I was lying in bed the morning of April 11, 1986, fighting off the flu, when the phone rang. I recognized the voice of our squad secretary. She asked how I was feeling, but I sensed there was more to the phone call than that. She said she was sorry to bring me the terrible news that two FBI agents had been murdered in Miami.

I put my hand over the receiver, trying to catch my breath. My former partner, Jim Brown, was still in Miami. So was Jerry Dove, Dean Hughes, and other agents I knew.

"One of the agents killed was Jerry Dove. I'm sorry, Frank."

Tears started up inside.

I asked how people at the office were doing.

"Everyone's in a state of shock. Several of the women who knew Jerry are crying."

I flicked on CNN. It was broadcasting live from Miami. The reporter commented that it was one of the bloodiest shoot-outs in FBI history. Then the camera panned the bodies and smashed cars. The crime scene investigation was still under way, and the telecast showed Jerry's face as his body lay in a pool of blood on the pavement.

Jerry and the other agent had been conducting a surveillance in an area south of Miami. Two men, suspected of more than a dozen armored car holdups and bank robberies, sped by in a stolen Monte Carlo. The agents gave chase and forced the stolen car into a tree. A gunfight ensued, and other agents arrived on the scene. CNN said it was only the second time in FBI history two agents had been killed in the same incident. The first occurred in El Centro, California, in 1979. I had known those agents, too.

I thought about my parents. I thought about the times I told Brian not to worry. I turned off the TV and lay back down on the bed. I said a prayer for Jerry, the other agent, and their families. I started to cry. I wished I had been at work that day. Only people in the FBI knew what this felt like.

I called the FBI switchboard and asked for an agent who had worked in Miami. He said the office just received word that another FBI agent had been shot in Cleveland in the performance of his duties.

"What the hell is going on?" I said. "Is this open season on FBI agents?"

The other agent was more subdued. "It's so much more dangerous now than when we came in, Frank. There's so much more violence. What's happening to this country?"

I hung up the phone. Those of us in law enforcement knew what was happening to this country—how it had become the murder capital of the world. Guns and drugs changed us. America's murder rate had more than doubled since 1960 and was now seven times higher than that of Britain or Japan.

The phone rang again. "Francis?" said the frightened voice. "Oh, thank God you're safe."

It was my father. He and my mother had seen the news and tried to reach me at work.

"They said you weren't there—" my mother began, but started to cry.

Dad finished her thought. "We thought maybe you were back in Miami."

I told them I knew one of the agents who had been killed.

"Leave that damn job and come back home and live with us!" my father said with uncharacteristic insistence.

I tried to calm them. "I love my job. Unfortunately danger is sometimes part of it."

This time when we said good-bye, the words "I love you" seemed difficult to get out.

I couldn't reach Brian at work. At five-fifteen his car pulled into the driveway. Once inside, he put his arms around me. Neither of us spoke. When he let go, he seemed more anxious. "Frank, listen to me," he said. "I don't want to upset you any more than you already are, but I worry about you all the time—"

"Please, Brian," I said, interrupting. "It's really not that dangerous."

Brian stopped *me* now. "You always try to minimize what you do by saying that! Or by saying that you spend all your time in the office doing paper work. But I know that they put you in charge of arrests. And I know that it's more dangerous for you now."

I was surprised by his intensity. "Okay, okay. It *is* dangerous at times. But mostly it isn't." I shook my head. "I'll never give it up, Brian. I'm sorry, but I just can't do that."

Brian spent the night, but we didn't talk much. I fell asleep on the couch with the TV on.

■ ■ ■

On May 16, 1986, the San Diego SAC called us together for an "all-employees conference." Such events usually marked a particular milestone in a career or called attention to major accomplishments. Nearly two hundred agents and support staff employees listened as the SAC began to read from a letter:

> DEAR MR. BUTTINO,
>
> *Your professional handling of the investigation of a former Agent on drug-related charges is indeed commendable. . . . Investigations of this nature are some of the most difficult to pursue. But you rose above the difficulties and dedicated yourself to discovering the full truth. . . . Your investigative talents were in full view throughout this case, and, without these important skills, it is doubtful whether the success which was attained could have been realized at all. I commend you on a job well-done.*
>
> *Sincerely yours,*
> WILLIAM H. WEBSTER, *Director*

While others applauded, I was called to the podium to receive my letter and a cash incentive award. Without disclosing the exact amount, the SAC said it was the largest cash award he had ever seen or heard about in the FBI.

"This case was a personal tragedy for Dan Mitrione, who had been a good agent," I told the gathering. "And it was a tragedy for his family and the bureau. It was sad that one of our own employees would betray his oath to uphold the law.

"Mitrione could have come forward after being compromised initially. Perhaps he would have lost his job, but he would not be serving a ten-year sentence. None of us is immune to the temptations that come with this job, especially now with drug investigations. If you get in a jam, come forward and tell someone. The end result of your silence could be far worse than you ever imagined.''

I called Brian later that morning from an interview room and told him about Webster's letter and the cash award. I invited him out to dinner. ''The restaurant of your choice,'' I said.

''How much did you get, Frank?''

''Fifteen hundred dollars!''

■   ■   ■

After returning from Miami, I resumed other activities and commitments that had been put on hold. For example, I had been involved in the Big Brother/Big Sister program since the early 1970s. This program matches adults with children who don't have either a father or a mother living in the home. I had been matched with several boys over the years and maintained friendships with them even after they reached adulthood. I didn't disclose my homosexuality to program leaders or to the young people with whom I was matched. I didn't want it to matter; I also didn't want the word to get back to the bureau.

At the time nearly a half million cases involving the sexual abuse of children were being reported annually. Studies showed that the perpetrators—sometimes as high as 99 percent of them—were heterosexuals. But the predominant stereotype remained that homosexuals were the ones largely responsible.

During the summer of 1986 I was best man for Cliff Callahan, one of my former ''little brothers.'' Cliff originally was from San Diego, but now, in his mid-twenties, he lived and worked in Washington, D.C. A few months later I was best man in my brother Lou's wedding.

My brother's wedding date was significant, for it fell on November 22—the date in 1963 that President Kennedy was killed. My parents always remembered where they had been on December 7, 1941, when the Japanese attacked Pearl Harbor. Our generation remembered November 22.

I was a freshman at Colgate University at the time and had just come out of English class. A student told us about the shooting, and we rushed back to the dormitory lounge, where others were watching a live television broadcast. Walter Cronkite was reporting, and it surprised me to see him not wearing a jacket. He glanced at a clock on the wall and announced that the President was dead. Several of my classmates began to cry. I thought of the closing lines in William Golding's *The Lord of the Flies,* where Ralph "wept for the end of innocence, the darkness of man's heart. . . ."

I had seen Kennedy's inauguration on a small black-and-white TV brought into the classroom by our tenth-grade history teacher. And as the new President spoke, I remember looking around the room to see if others were as stirred as I was. It was as if we no longer had to dig into history for our heroes; he was alive and breathing. And when Kennedy said, on that cold January day, that the torch had been passed to a new generation of Americans, he inspired me to a new level of idealism.

In hindsight I think I joined the FBI because I was answering Kennedy's call to do something for America. The FBI also afforded me the opportunity to do something about the darkness which inhabits the world and was manifested in his murder.

■ ■ ■

I flew to Syracuse, the closest airport to my parents' home, several days before my brother Lou's wedding. Quite a few times before we left for Rochester, where the wedding was to take place, my parents commented that since Lou was getting married, I would probably be next. My father said he joked with relatives about how I was waiting for my older brother to get married first. The morning we were leaving for Rochester, my parents brought the subject up again. This time, however, I said it wasn't necessary to explain to others why I wasn't married.

"What should we say at the wedding if someone asks?" my father persisted. "You know how people are."

I was getting tired of having to justify my life to others. "If they ask, just tell them it's none of their goddamn business!"

I seldom swore, especially in front of my parents, and they were shocked by my reaction. They did not respond, nor did they ever bring up the subject again.

Weddings are particularly painful to closeted gays. The focus and celebration are on heterosexual unity and the beginning of a new family with possible children. Such occasions remind us that we live beyond the bounds of society's sanctioned rituals and traditions. Memories and photographs of these occasions often do not include others whom we also love.

■ ■ ■

I "roasted" Lou at the rehearsal dinner the night before the wedding. Lou actually lived the role of the absentminded professor, and I assured his fiancée, Kathleen, that he would neither forget to show up nor get cold feet. I took a pair of handcuffs out and held them up.

I also said how plans for the reception had at first reminded me of the wedding scene in *The Deer Hunter*. But then, after reviewing the guest list and seeing the large number of Italian-sounding names, I said it more closely resembled the wedding scene in *The Godfather*. I informed them that FBI agents from the Rochester office also planned to attend. They would be taking photographs and writing down license plate numbers!

The men in the wedding party assembled at Lou's house the morning of the ceremony. We toasted Lou, and one another other, with shots of schnapps. At one point Lou took his teenage stepson into the kitchen. I overheard him telling Matt that there would be a few gay people at the wedding and to be sensitive to that. I suspected Lou knew I was gay, but it obviously hadn't mattered to him.

■　■　■

Carmen Basilio and his wife, Josie, were also at the wedding, and they invited my parents and me to their home in Rochester the following day. Carmen took us into his den, which was filled with memorabilia. I swung the bat Mickey Mantle had given him; I looked at photos of Carmen with Rocky Marciano, Ted Williams, and other sports legends. Carmen recounted stories from his boxing career, and it was the most time I had ever spent with him. I wish I had told him that day how good it was to know that my boyhood hero was still somebody I could look up to.

Three weeks later, back in San Diego, I was listening to messages on my answering machine when I heard my father's voice. It was unusual for my parents to call me. "We had to take your mother to the hospital," my father said. "Please call home as soon as you can."

I dialed their home number, but no one answered. I tried calling my brother Tony, who lived in a small town near my parents with his wife and daughter, but no one was at home. I tried my brother Lou in Rochester but couldn't reach him either. I finally called Oneida City Hospital to see if my mother had been admitted.

"Fran?" It was my sister-in-law, Barbara, a nurse at the hospital. "I was just passing by. Mom had a stroke. She's alive, but the stroke was massive. The doctors aren't sure of the extent of the damage to her brain or rest of her body.''

"Thank God she's alive," I said. "How's my father?''

"He's holding up pretty well." She said my brothers were with him, and they all were in my mother's room.

"Should I come home?''

"There is not much any of us can do at the moment. I'd wait until we know her condition better. The next few days are critical.''

I called Brian, and he came over. "I'm sorry," he said. "But maybe she'll be all right.''

I sat down on a kitchen chair. "They said it was massive. I wished I had danced with her more, Brian. She looked radiant, like she was going to live forever.''

"Frank, take it easy," Brian urged. "Barbara also said nobody knows for sure how bad it is.''

I got up and went to a drawer to get a tape. On it was the song my brother and mother had danced to at the wedding—"Through the Years" by Kenny Rogers.

I put the tape on and closed my eyes. Lyrics such as "You've never let me down" brought back memories that caught in my throat like a fishbone. When the song was over, I got up and went into the bedroom. A short while later Brian came in and lay beside me.

My father called later that evening. He said Mom was in a coma and unable to move. The doctors were not certain if she would improve. I asked if he was all right.

"I'm hanging in there," he responded, the way he always did, but this time his voice was different. "It seems strange to be in this house without your mother," he began, and then stopped. I could hear him crying and waited until he came back on the line. "We've been together forty-six years.''

We talked some more, but I knew I had to get off the phone. "I'll call you tomorrow, Dad. Tell Mom I love her.''

Lou told me a few days later that he had been alone with my mother that first night in the hospital. He said he didn't want her to fight to stay alive if it meant she would spend the rest of her life in a coma. Lou believed people in a coma can still hear you and told her it was all right for her to go if that was what she wanted. He said these were the hardest words he'd ever had to say. I tried to assure him he had done the right thing, knowing full well I might not have been able to do it.

I was prepared for danger, even death on my job, but with my mother it was different. I didn't know if I would be able to accept the death of the person who had given me life. "There's nothing like losing a mother," I remember my father saying once, even though both his parents had died.

After two weeks my mother opened her eyes. She then began to speak. The doctors started physical therapy at once, and the nurses marveled at her courage and tenacity. She hated being in the hospital and especially hated hospital food. "They're trying to poison me," she would tell my father. She was back home in just seven weeks.

My father and brothers tried to prepare me for the change in her, but I never let it fully sink in. She had been a woman of great energy and always looked younger than her years. "Momma," I said, walking into the living room that March afternoon. It shocked me to see how much she had aged.

She didn't know I was coming home. I wanted it to be a surprise for her. She looked at me and started to cry. I put my arms around her.

"Louis," she stammered.

I wiped away my own tears and gave her a big smile. "I'm Francis, Mom."

She shook her head. "I'm sorry. I knew it was you, but when I talk, I sometimes don't say what I mean."

I assured her she would get better in time but realized, as the week passed, that both my parents had become old without my really noticing.

7.

The nation was being rocked by a series of spy cases in the mid-1980s, and I wanted to be part of the FBI efforts in this regard. I knew that espionage or foreign counterintelligence cases were among the most complex and sensitive in the bureau. I also knew that if my homosexuality became known, the bureau's first concern would be that I was a spy.

No gay American citizen ever engaged in espionage in response to gay-related coercion or blackmail, but that didn't seem to matter as far as the prevailing myth was concerned. Ironically, while I was putting in for a transfer to a foreign counterintelligence (FCI) squad, still another spy story broke. Marine guards at the U.S. Embassy in Moscow, enticed by sex with women, were alleged to have allowed KGB agents access to national security concerns. There was no hue and cry about the dangers of heterosexuals in the military or in matters of national security.

The majority in this or any society seldom sees itself fully or accurately. This is true for the myth that gays cannot be trusted in uniform or in the FBI. And because gays like me stayed in the closet, the myth largely remained self-justifying. Little did I know when I switched to FCI work that I would be the first to challenge this myth as far as the bureau was concerned and that I would have to come out of the closet to do it.

■   ■   ■

There was an opening on Squad Six, which handled espionage cases, and its supervisor said he would welcome my transfer. I also talked with my OC supervisor. Though he was reluctant to see me go, he thought Squad Six needed some experienced agents.

The transfer of agents between squads is common. Supervisors try to obtain the best agents for their squads. Conversely, they try to get rid of agents who are liabilities. The process is akin to player trading in professional sports.

After my transfer I began to read as much as I could about FCI investigations. I also worked with the more experienced agents on the squad and attended a two-week basic FCI training course at the FBI Academy. In class we were told that the great scientific and technological advances of recent years had dramatically expanded the ability of hostile intelligence services (HIS) to obtain information. HIS, such as the Soviet Union's KGB, were also becoming more aggressive and successful in acquiring military and nonmilitary secrets from U.S. citizens both here and abroad.

Several FBI agents involved in successful bureau espionage investigations spoke at length about the damage U.S. security had suffered. Many of those who betrayed the country had been doing so for years without detection. The agents said espionage was being engaged in while they spoke. The motivation to be a spy, they said, varied from financial gain to ideological beliefs. No one mentioned homosexuality as a cause, and I was heartened. In some ways I felt like a new agent again. I was also certain I had made the right decision.

■   ■   ■

In late spring 1987 the Squad Six supervisor asked if I wanted to participate in a seminar being held at the Central Intelligence Agency headquarters in Langley, Virginia. He said FBI and CIA people from around the country would be attending to receive specialized training. Few FBI agents ever have an opportunity to train at the CIA, and I welcomed the opportunity.

The CIA required a background check on all non-CIA participants, and I was concerned that they might find out about my homosexuality. Yet I figured an extensive investigation wouldn't be conducted because of my record and length of service, and it wasn't.

Though I cared for Brian a great deal, something began to change in our relationship for me. I started to feel uncomfortable when he was affectionate toward me. Sometimes I would pull away from him, and physical intimacy between us became less and less frequent. I still felt close to Brian but found myself attracted to others. I knew I had to talk to him about this. I weighed how best to say what I was feeling.

One night we were walking on the pier in Ocean Beach. We passed several fishermen and looked out at the bright lights that lined the San Diego coastline for miles. I began talking about our relationship and how it had evolved since we first met. ''I think the best part of our relationship is that we've always been honest with each other," I said.

He didn't respond, but I think he knew where I was heading with the conversation.

"You know how much I enjoy being with you, but I also want to be honest with you. I'd like to start seeing other guys."

We walked for a while, and Brian still hadn't responded. This was not unusual. He had difficulty talking about personal matters. I tried to reassure him that I cared very much about him and would still like to see him but that I just didn't feel I could remain monogamous anymore.

In truth, little changed in our relationship after that. I continued to see him once or twice a week, though we tried to talk more frequently than that. We were occasionally intimate with each other, but I didn't detect any change in his attitude toward me.

For my part, it seemed strange at first to be with someone else. Brian had been so much a part of my life. Sometimes he'd call and I would have already made plans. He was never angry, only disappointed. It saddened me to have to hurt him. Still, I couldn't lie and pretend our life together hadn't changed.

The night before I left for CIA headquarters, Brian came over to my house as planned. He usually didn't talk or drink very much, but he did both that night. Sometimes when he drank, he became more emotional than usual and would talk about things he normally kept to himself.

I drove to a small Italian restaurant in Pacific Beach. I suspected that something was on his mind. We ordered a large pizza and a small carafe of wine.

"Are you sure you're not Italian?" I asked as Brian reached for his third slice of pizza. "If I ate as much as you, I would weigh three hundred pounds."

He smiled, finished the slice, and reached for still another.

"You're a light eater," I joked. "When it gets light out, you start eating!"

He had heard these lines several times before and shook his head. I repeated another of my favorites: "You eat like a bird, Brian—a vulture!"

Brian kept smiling, but his mind was on something else. He talked about school and several professions he was considering as a career. I sat back listening.

I poured the last of the wine into his glass. He started talking about meeting me for the first time. "I thought you were straight or married to that woman. You surprised me when you gave me your phone number.''

I smiled.

''We've had a lot of good times together, and I've learned a lot from being with you. You've helped me focus on my goals, and I feel good about what I'm doing with my life.''

''You've come a long way from your Navy days, and I'm proud of what you're accomplishing in school,'' I said. ''You're a lot smarter than I thought you were!''

He started to smile, but then his demeanor seemed to change. ''We don't see each other very much anymore,'' he said. ''You always seem to be so busy, and you're always taking off somewhere for the bureau.'' He looked down. ''I really miss you when you're gone.''

I wasn't sure what he was trying to say. ''I miss you, too,'' I told him.

''Everything seems so much more difficult now,'' he continued. ''I wish our relationship could be like it was before.''

As on the night on the pier when I was doing most of the talking, there was a long, awkward silence between us. I didn't know what to say and didn't respond. I loved him more than anyone else in my life, but something—some chemistry—seemed to be leaving.

Brian looked around. When he spoke again, he had tears in his eyes. ''I admire you more than anyone I've ever known. You're everything I've ever wanted in a man.''

I think he was waiting for me to say something in return, but I didn't. There was another period of silence, and he continued looking at me. Usually I would try to say something funny, but he had a sad look in his eyes. I reached over and picked up the bill, and we slowly got up from the table to leave.

I thought about that conversation for a long time afterward. I think Brian, like me on the pier, was trying to say good-bye to the romantic side of our relationship. He had summed up, also like me, where we had been, but there was only a hint of where he was heading. Perhaps he wanted me to step in, to have a change of heart, and be monogamous with him again. Perhaps he didn't know what was going to happen next either.

■ ■ ■

The CIA arranged for FBI agents who attended the seminar to stay at a nearby motel together. Each morning a van would pick us up and at the end of the day take us back. We were escorted to our classroom and back.

I got to know a CIA intelligence officer in the class, and he took me on a tour of the main building. As we walked, I noticed how different sections of CIA work were housed in separate office spaces. Throughout, I saw signs indicating that access to some areas was carefully controlled. Overall, security seemed far greater at the CIA than at FBI headquarters. But much of our work involves traditional law enforcement investigations as opposed to intelligence gathering.

The tour over, the intelligence officer and I ate in the building's large cafeteria. We talked about our respective backgrounds and generally about some of our professional experiences. We also discussed personnel policies at both agencies. At one point he said that the CIA routinely polygraphed its employees, mentioning that some of the questions had to do with homosexuality.

When I returned to San Diego, I received an undercover assignment in a nationwide FCI operation. It was "light cover" which meant I worked at it only part-time. I had kept my identification from previous undercover assignments, so preparations were minimal. I met with FBI agents from around the country in Atlantic City that fall to learn details of the operation and my role in it.

Afterward I went to Canastota for a few days to visit my family. My mother's health steadily improved, and we all were able to gather together as a family on my father's seventy-third birthday.

■ ■ ■

Throughout the winter and spring of 1988 I continued in the part-time undercover assignment while working other cases. In June I decided to return to Canastota to attend the twenty-fifth reunion of my high school graduating class.

Because of the original background investigation, most of my classmates, and many people in town, knew I was an FBI agent. Whenever I went home, people usually asked about my job and wanted to hear stories about it. Most agents come to expect this.

I also expected to be asked if I was married. My response was that I hadn't met the right person yet. I think most people assumed that because I was an FBI agent, it was difficult to have a wife and family. If anyone even suspected I was gay, I'm sure he'd dismiss it quickly, believing that the FBI would not hire gay people to be agents.

I knew many of my classmates would have partners with them and bring pictures of their children. As friendly as I felt around these people, meeting them had become increasingly uncomfortable for me over the years. I felt awkward showing up alone at the reunion, and it was dissatisfying not to be able to share these experiences with anyone.

I spent about ten days in Canastota and visited friends and relatives. Most of my time, however, was spent with my parents. It felt good to be able to carry on long conversations with my mother again.

As is probably true for most couples who had been together for a long time, my mother and father sometimes took each other for granted or argued over trivial matters. Before her stroke my mother was independent and strong-willed. My father was the same way, but he was more subtle about it.

There was a certain tenderness about my mother now. She laughed more and seemed more at ease about life's obstacles. The stroke had changed them and their life together. My father did most of the things my mother had done, including the cooking, cleaning, and laundry. He drove her around and acted like a doting nurse. Their love for each other was never more apparent to me.

Whenever I came home, they'd mention how they worried about me. They said they wanted me to quit or at the very least move closer to home. I told them it was difficult to transfer, even though this was untrue. With my seniority I could easily have come back to New York State.

Like many closeted gays, I had established a geographical wall between my parents and me. Gays often leave hometowns for the relative freedom and anonymity of cities. Concealment also separates us mentally and emotionally from families. The result is that parents wonder what happened to the relationship they once had with their children. They wonder why they no longer are a part of their child's life. Pain, heartache, and missed moments occur on both sides of the wall.

To come out of the closet can be a very painful and sometimes devastating experience. One friend I had who had grown up on a small farm in the Midwest told his parents he was gay when he was a teenager. His father was furious, and the boy fled the house. He called his mother, who told him his father had gone to get a shotgun. My friend's only return home, years later, was to attend his father's funeral.

My parents and I occasionally discussed the subject of homosexuality on my visits home. Once, after a *Donahue* show, we talked at some length, and I could see that their knowledge and understanding were limited. I also realized they had come to accept much of what the television evangelists were telling them.

I felt that Jesus loved *more,* not less, those whom society had chosen to reject. I also felt Jesus' warning about not judging others was the most important—and most ignored—lesson from the Bible. I knew that trying to convince my parents I wasn't some mistake God had made was going to be an uphill climb.

My parents would wonder if somehow they were "responsible," that they had said or done something that caused me to be gay. They would be concerned about AIDS. They would be concerned about what my aunts, uncles, cousins, and neighbors would say once they found out. I feared the ripple effect of telling them or others close to me. Somebody might slip or tell another as a secret, and the word would quickly spread. It could also get back to the FBI.

Despite all this, I still wanted to tell them. The wall didn't seem right. I felt this even more so after my mother's brush with death. Did I want my parents to die without ever really knowing me? Did I want to carry my secret to the grave with me?

As my stay in Canastota drew to a close, I began to prepare myself mentally and emotionally for my return to San Diego. I loved my parents, but I also missed the life I had carved out for myself on the other side of America. Brian was staying at my house, and I called him to check on things there. My parents talked to him and didn't seem to make much of it. They knew we spent a lot of time together. I often mentioned that he stayed at my house when I was away.

I thought that my parents might suspect Brian was gay and that I was, too. One time my mother and I were on the breezeway, and she was pressing me on whether or not I was dating. She suddenly asked if Brian was "homosexual." Her question caught me by surprise, and I wondered if she was really asking me if *I* was gay or not. I told her no.

■　■　■

A hard rain was falling the Friday afternoon before I was to leave. Despite it, we took our customary drive to Johnny's Diner on the shores of Oneida Lake for a fish fry. After returning home, we sat in the living room for a while talking.

My father got up and walked into the kitchen, but I thought nothing of it. He came back holding a legal-size envelope, his hands shaking slightly. I didn't know if he was nervous or if I just hadn't noticed this about him before. He glanced at my mother before handing the envelope to me. She turned her eyes downward.

"I got this in the mail a couple of weeks ago," he said. There was an unusual look on his face, and a terrible feeling began to come over me.

The postmark indicated that the envelope had been sent from San Diego a few weeks before. There was no return name or address on it. Everything was accurate in terms of my parents' address except the street was spelled phonetically. That was not at all uncommon. The address was handwritten.

I reached inside and took out a legal-size sheet of paper. I immediately recognized my handwriting. It was my response to a gay personal ad. My first thought was that I had sent the letter to my parents by mistake. But attached to the letter was a handwritten note that said:

DEAR MR. AND MRS. BUTTINO—
Thought you might like to see this letter I recently received from your son Frank. It might answer some questions you have about him. Just thought you would like to know.

W. J.

I looked the letter, note, and envelope over again. Out of the corner of my eye I could tell my mother was looking at me, as she rocked slightly in her chair. My father was on the other side of a table and lamp, and I couldn't see his face. The ticking of the grandfather clock in a corner of the room seemed loud.

"Do you know who wrote this?" my father asked. He didn't sound angry, only anxious.

I put the materials back into the envelope. "No."

"But that one letter looks like your handwriting."

The room was quiet again.

"It's probably someone I put in jail, trying to give me a hard time."

My mother looked down at the floor.

"How did he get our address?" my father asked. I leaned forward so I could see him. I remembered his being big, strong, and without fear. But he was elderly now—and vulnerable. His voice seemed to reflect his concern about something he didn't understand. Maybe he was just disappointed he could no longer protect my mother and me from some unknown danger.

"I wouldn't worry about it," I said, trying to calm them. "Your name, address, and telephone number are in the phone book. It would be easy for someone to find that information out."

"But who is this guy and why would he send this to us?"

"It's okay. Really. When I get back to San Diego, I'll do some checking and see if I can find out who he is. But in the meantime, I wouldn't worry about it. I'll let you know when I get back. He's out to cause trouble, not to hurt you."

I looked out the picture window, and the rain seemed to be coming down even harder than before. "I'm getting cabin fever," I said, starting to get up. "I think I'll get my umbrella and go for a walk."

They both looked outside and then back at me. "You better wait until it lets up, Francis," my father said.

I was already leaving the room. "It could stay this way for hours."

I walked to the spare bedroom and closed the door behind me. Early in the year I had written a letter to a person who had placed an ad in the personals section of a San Diego gay publication. I remembered his last name—and his first initials were W. J. I thought of the look on my parents' faces.

That son of a bitch, I thought. *Why did he do this to my parents?*

I wondered who he was and if he knew I was an FBI agent. I sensed deep down that my life would never be the same after that one afternoon.

8.

The flight back to San Diego had a stopover in Chicago. I called Brian and told him about the letter to my parents.

He groaned. "Do you know who it is?"

I told him no.

"How did your parents handle it?"

"Pretty well. But they're worried that somebody knows where they live." I looked at my watch. Was Brian scared? Did W. J. know about him, too?

"Did you tell them you were gay, Frank?"

It was at that moment that I realized they had never raised the question. Neither had they been angry. Knowing how they handled conflict, I was sure they had agonized a long time how best to tell me about the letter.

For the remainder of the flight I tried to think like an investigator. I tried to figure out who W. J. was, his motivation and ultimate purpose, but my emotions kept getting in the way. Had somebody set me up? Somebody who knew I used the personals and then got me to disclose my homosexuality in my own handwriting? Was it some right-wing zealot? Somebody who was angry with me? Jealous?

I'd want to discuss the matter with Brian, but in doing so, I would be revealing a part of my life I had kept hidden from him, too. I needed more in a relationship than Brian could provide. I knew that now. I also knew that if I had been content with him, probably none of this would have happened.

Brian waited near the security area at San Diego's Lindbergh Field. His face gave no hint of what he was thinking or feeling. Closeted gays and FBI agents both were adept at disguising their emotions. I wondered if Brian thought maybe W. J. had written to his parents, too.

In the car Brian said, "This doesn't make sense. You don't go to gay bars because you're an FBI agent. And you write to people using a post office box to be discreet so this kind of thing *won't* happen." He felt I had to know W. J.; that was how he got the names and address of my parents.

Brian pulled into the driveway of my house. I wanted to be inside before talking about it all. He got settled in a chair across from me in the living room.

I began by telling Brian I had written to a guy in Del Mar (located in San Diego County) in late January or early February 1988, after seeing his ad in a gay magazine. I said his name was W. J. ———— , and it was several weeks before I heard back from him.

"He apologized for the delay, saying he had been away. He invited me to his house Friday night of that week, but I wanted to talk to him before going, to get a sense what he was like. He didn't give me a phone number, and none was listed. I wrote back to him, saying I wanted to talk, but Friday arrived, and I hadn't heard from him. I decided to go anyway."

I thought for a moment, trying to piece together what happened next. Brian, all the while, sat motionless in the chair.

"I drove to the address, following the directions he had given me, but something was wrong. The house was on the wrong side of the street. I parked my truck up the street a little and sat watching for a while. Then I got out and walked to the front door. A large glass window was adjacent to it, and I was about to knock but noticed children's shoes on the entry-way carpet. I left immediately."

"Are you sure you had the right house?" Brian asked.

"I brought the directions with me."

"What happened next?"

I said I sat in my truck awhile but had an uneasy feeling. I wasn't about to enter a house if children were present.

"Then a light went on in what looked like a front bedroom, and I saw a man enter with a small child. Later the light went off. It was getting dark. There were a few other cars parked on the street, and a man came out and looked around. He lit a cigarette and appeared to be middle-aged and fairly big. He took a few more puffs from his cigarette before butting it out. He then climbed into a station wagon and drove off."

Brian got up from the couch. He was fidgety.

"What's wrong?" I asked.

"It's just strange."

"I'm sorry to have to tell you this."

"Oh, I know. I'm just trying to understand why the directions would be wrong at the very end." He turned toward me. "I'm glad you didn't go in."

I nodded. "And it gets even more strange."

Brian sat on the arm of the couch, his arms folded, and I continued. "The second letter I had written—the one asking for the phone number—was later returned by the post office. W. J. ——— had moved without leaving a forwarding address."

"What do you think is going on?"

I shrugged. "My hunch is this W. J. ——— knows me, or knows of me, but I don't know him. At least I don't know him by that name. Because of the darkness, I couldn't really tell if I knew the guy at the house."

"But why would somebody do this?" asked Brian.

"I don't know. Somebody who hates gays. Me. Or the fact that I work for the bureau. I've been going over all my cases trying to remember something, anything, that might help—"

Brian interrupted. "Do you think it's Mitrione?"

I had told Brian a few weeks before that Mitrione had been released from prison.

"I don't think so. I don't think he's got a grudge against me personally. Besides, I doubt he even suspects I'm gay. I'm always so careful."

We talked late that night and started all over again with coffee the following morning. Throughout, I sensed something else was on Brian's mind. I'm sure he wondered, as I did, if W. J. was planning anything else.

Back at work I used office resources, trying to identify W. J. I checked our nationwide computer system to see if he had an outstanding arrest warrant or criminal history. I submitted his name to local law enforcement agencies to determine if he had been arrested locally. I went through office indexes to see if a W. J. ——— was part of any investigation, past or present.

I had ethical qualms about doing this, but it wasn't all that uncommon among FBI agents. Retired agents working in security called to check driver's licenses or license plates. Agents themselves used office resources for personal reasons. I did want to make sure W. J. ——— was not involved in a current or past investigation, and so despite my reservations, I took a chance here.

I hoped a photograph of W. J. ——— would turn up, but none did. In fact, the only significant information that came from these searches was his forwarding address. He had moved to ——— , a city in the Midwest. I contacted a friend who had access to a data base, but we didn't find out anything more.

August arrived, and nothing further happened. I wondered if perhaps that was the end of it—a one-time thing. There was nothing further I could do but wait. At times that was a very hard thing to do.

■　■　■

In late September I returned home for a weeklong vacation. My older brother Tony, who had moved to San Diego recently, flew back with me. Lou joined us, and it was the first time in several years just the three of us were alone with our parents. "It's good to have my boys home again," my mother said.

It didn't take us long to settle down at the kitchen table that first night. While our mother was busy at the stove, Dad took out some beers, opening one for himself.

"We were wondering if you were going to leave us dry," Tony remarked with a grin.

"Your father would never do that to his sons," my father answered, raising his can of Old Milwaukee. "C'mon, *salut'*," he said, but none of us moved.

Lou shook his head, looking at Tony and me. "Dad's still drinking Old Milwaukee?"

"A dollar a six-pack," I said on cue, knowing it would get a rise out of my father.

"What do you mean?" He laughed. "On sale this week for ninety-nine cents!"

"*Salut'*," we said almost in unison, and began to drink.

Lou pretended to gag. "Dad's the only one in Canastota who drinks Old Milwaukee."

"They stock it just for him," Tony said.

"I should have bought stock in the company a long time ago," I added. "I could have retired a wealthy man by now!"

My father was not about to let us get the best of him. "For guys who don't like it," he said, saving his best—and highly expected—line for last, "you do a pretty good job of drinking it!"

My mother made three pizzas and set them down on the table. Tony reached for a slice.

"Tony didn't get enough airplane food," I said while helping myself to a piece.

"They had lasagna, but it didn't taste anything like Ma's," Tony commented.

Lou asked, in mock righteousness, "We don't say grace anymore?"

We made the sign of the cross with our mother, and she said grace.

"You know, it's been a long time since just the five of us have been together in this house," I said as we ate.

Lou looked around. "And we're all sitting in exactly the same places we did when we were kids."

My mother and father brought us up-to-date on events with family and town, and then my father said he was disappointed that nobody could be home for his birthday the week before. "But I got cards from everybody but Mr. Louie."

"Absentminded professor," I commented.

"Actually, Dad," Lou said, "I bought the card but then mailed it to myself by mistake!"

That got a laugh out of all of us.

"I was pretty nervous," Lou continued. "You see I just found out I was going to be a father!"

We cheered and hugged him, and there were several minutes of excited congratulations and comments. My father looked overjoyed, but my mother seemed a little sorrowful. I'm sure she was thinking about me. I wondered if my parents had told my brothers about the correspondence from W. J.

■　■　■

On Sunday Tony visited his in-laws and Lou returned to Rochester. I took my mother for a drive, and when we returned, my father was working in his large garden behind the house. Mom called to him, and he waved to us.

"He's trying to get all the vegetables in before the frost," she explained. "He's out there all day during the summer. I think he would stay out there all night, too, if there were lights on the garden!" I helped my mother walk out to the garden, and we stood, holding hands, watching my father pick the last of the peppers. I always felt his garden was his church.

A little later, as I was lacing my running shoes, he came onto the breezeway, carrying a basket of peppers. My mother had gone into the house.

"I'm almost through with the garden for the year," he said. "The vegetables I'm storing should last us a long time. I'll pack some peppers for you and Anthony to take back with you."

I nodded.

He put the basket down, saying, "Going for a little run?"

"Only six miles," I answered with a smile. I began to stretch. "The older I get, the more time I spend stretching. Someday I'll probably spend more time doing that than running!"

"You're just a young kid!" he said with a laugh.

"I don't know about that. The new agents in the office are young enough to be *my* kids now!"

"Yeah, but you're in better shape than they are. You can still give them a licking—just like Carmen Basilio."

He walked over and closed the kitchen door. I realized it was the first time we had been alone since I arrived home. I sensed his next words.

"Did you ever find out who wrote that letter?"

"I did some checking when I got back to San Diego but didn't have much luck."

"I still don't understand how he got our address."

He didn't seem as worried as the first time, only puzzled. I asked him if he had received any more letters, but he shook his head no. I felt uncomfortable bringing all this up again. I got up. "Well, I wouldn't worry about it. There are a lot of flaky people out there, and the things they do often don't make any sense."

"I wish you would leave that job," he said. "Your mother and I worry about you."

I was nodding but didn't respond. I had started making my way to the back door of the breezeway when I heard him say, "I didn't say anything to your brothers about the letter."

I turned.

"Be careful. Don't overdo it," he cautioned, as he always did.

"No problem," I said exaggeratingly, and smiled.

I walked outside and began my run. I glanced back, and he was watching me. He waved, and I waved back to him.

I headed north down the dirt path toward the railroad tracks. I could still picture my father on the sidelines, following the football up and down the field, shouting encouragement and cautions to me. Before taking to the mat, during wrestling, I'd look up to find him, on the crowded balcony, his work clothes still on.

My father raised his sons by example. He taught us to think through problems, give our best, and to draw strength simply from having the name Buttino. He and my uncle Milton would tell my brothers and me, whenever the shadow of self-doubt crossed our lives, "But you're a Buttino."

Canastota is so small that during a six-mile run I could pretty much cover the entire town. I made my way past the homes of many people I knew. Others, driving by, recognized me and blew their horns or waved.

I passed St. Agatha's Catholic Church, where my brothers and I had been altar boys. I crossed Peterboro Street and headed for Schmidt Field, named in honor of Pinky Schmidt, a coaching legend in Canastota. Pink had the reputation for turning out gritty, championship-caliber teams year after year despite the fact that other schools in the league were much larger. Nobody liked to play us in the fourth quarter. We seemed to get tougher as the game wore on. I ran the hundred yards of the old high school field where I had once played defensive halfback. It was hard to believe that twenty-six years had gone by.

I hadn't run for several days and glanced at my watch. I was at about the three-mile mark and beginning to feel good physically. The running also became easier. I started to feel some of the mental peacefulness I experienced from running.

I took my customary pass by our old house on Roberts Street. We moved from the house when I was fourteen, and as I saw the faded brown shingles, I wondered what was inside from my past. Who was I then? I remembered being told I used to sleepwalk a lot, but I don't know why.

A chill that wasn't from the wind ran through me. Who was I really? Was I put together with layers of defenses and rationalizations? I didn't remember always having been like this. I was more vulnerable then. "The child is father of the man," Wordsworth had written, and I wondered if I would ever have to revisit that house in my mind.

The wind blew stronger against me as I turned in the direction of the Erie Canal. It cut through the center of town, and I ran along its towpath for a short distance. I headed south on Peterboro Street, the main street in town, running past the few short blocks that constituted "downtown" Canastota.

It was all so familiar: the post office; the now-vacant Avon Theater;

the old Chatterbox restaurant, which had been remodeled and renamed. I thought about all the time we spent there, during high school, talking and laughing and believing that the world we knew would go on forever.

Few had stayed. Unlike generations before, most of us had scattered to places unknown, away from roots, from smells and faces and places as familiar as our own skin. Canastota had got into us—into the way we walked, talked, held our heads, and prayed. It was always home to me.

The last part of the run consisted of a long, slow climb up Rasbach Street. I always tried to think of something pleasant during this part of a run, and memories returned of the previous Friday night, when my brothers and I were with our parents. It had seemed like old times. And I had felt strong then and happy.

9.

It was midmorning on Monday, October 31, 1988, and just as I was about to leave the office, I received a call to see the assistant special agent in charge. Tom Kuker was responsible for administrative and personnel matters. Being asked to see him was highly unusual. It often meant there was a problem.

The offices of the SAC and ASAC are separated by a small reception area which is shared by their respective secretaries. Both women were typing when I entered the area. I greeted them as Kuker came out of his office. He asked me to join him in the SAC's office.

"Good morning, boss," I said as we entered the room.

Tom Hughes was seated behind his desk and said hello. He motioned me to one of the chairs. Kuker pulled up another chair and also sat opposite me.

Hughes had spent much of his career working on the bureau's budget; Kuker had been a street agent. Though both were a little over six feet tall, Hughes was thin while Kuker looked like a college fullback. Agents knew Hughes had a temper, but he seldom raised his voice. Kuker was also not one to holler or yell, but he could be very cold at times.

There was FBI memorabilia on Hughes's desk and numerous plaques and photos on the walls. The American flag and the California flag were on stands behind him.

Kuker had some papers in his hand, and I sensed that Hughes was acting either as an observer or as a witness. "Frank, I want to show you something we received recently," Kuker said, and with that handed me a clear plastic envelope sealed with FBI evidence tape.

The plastic envelope meant that the materials inside were considered evidence. I recognized the letter inside as my own. I had also received a postcard from a James W. in June 1988, and that was in the envelope, too. There was a handwritten note that said:

MR. BOHLENBACH—

Recently received this letter from one of your agents . . . Frank Buttino . . . in response to an ad.

Was not aware that homosexuality was tolerated in your dept. Just thought you would care to know what is going on, for future reference.

W. J.

The handwriting looked the same as in the note sent to my parents. But I had written to two different addresses in San Diego. How could W. J. have received both letters?

I was shaken but tried to remain calm. I hadn't actually prepared for something like this happening, and that wasn't like me. Hughes and Kuker were observing me carefully.

Kuker handed me an FD-645. It stated that an official inquiry was being opened "pertaining to allegations of misconduct or improper performance of official duties." The sentence "This inquiry pertains to an anonymous allegation of homosexual activity" was typed on the blank lines near the top. The document said I had to answer all questions fully and truthfully or face possible dismissal.

I signed and dated the form and gave it back to Kuker without comment. He signed it and gave it to Hughes for his signature. Meanwhile, I tried to figure out what was going on.

Jim Bohlenbach was our media coordinator, and his name often appeared in the news. This could have been the reason why W. J. had written to him. The phrase "your department" made it sound like somebody unfamiliar with the FBI.

Kuker began to read from an Executive Order 10450 form. Though I wasn't familiar with it, I did remember seeing it on a case once. The 10450 deals with security requirements for government employees. It also outlines procedures used in investigations to determine whether such employment is "clearly consistent with national security." I became anxious. This had to do with bureau concerns about my being a spy.

Kuker finished and then informed me that the correspondence from W. J. had been received in July. He asked if the letter addressed to James W. was mine.

The bureau had held on to the letter three months before saying anything. I didn't know what that meant.

"No," I answered.

"It looks like your handwriting," Kuker responded.

I didn't know if he was giving me another chance. He looked over at Hughes.

"The bureau could ask you for handwriting samples or conduct a fingerprint examination of the letter," Hughes said. His voice, like Kuker's, was without any hint of emotion. Both were often like this.

Perhaps I had judged wrong; maybe they were going to pursue it.

"Would you be willing to take a polygraph on it?" Hughes asked.

I hesitated before answering. "I don't know, boss. I've been told law enforcement people don't do well on them."

Kuker asked a few more things and then said a statement would be ready for me to sign that afternoon. Hughes added that only he, Kuker, and Bohlenbach knew about the correspondence. "Let me know if anyone else says anything about it," he said.

I thought it a curious thing to say but let the remark pass.

I left the room and walked back to the squad area. Though I tried to act as normal as possible, I felt as if I were in a trance. Most of the agents on my squad had left. I took off my jacket, picked up the file I had been working on, and turned my chair toward the window. Anyone observing me would assume I was reviewing the file, but I was focusing on maintaining control.

I turned back toward my desk. I took out a notebook and pen and began to write down the details of what had just happened.

The FBI's employee manuals were constantly being revised, and I thought maybe I could find something in them about bureau policy with respect to the hiring and retention of homosexuals. The squad supervisor was not in his office, and I located the appropriate manual. I couldn't find anything in the table of contents or index about homosexuals or homosexuality. I looked through other manuals but still couldn't find anything.

I returned to my desk and picked up the file again. If the bureau thought I was a spy, then it could have been monitoring my activities since the correspondence arrived at the office. This would explain why my bosses hadn't told me right away. They could also be tapping my office and home telephones. It was extremely difficult to get authorization to tap someone's phone except when national security was involved. More than likely they were reviewing my telephone toll records.

The bureau might have been watching my house from a van or neighbor's house. If it had conducted a surveillance, it would know about Brian and that he sometimes stayed the night. I thought back but couldn't remember anything that seemed out of the ordinary either at work or at home.

If the bureau was surveilling me, it would probably use out-of-town agents so that I wouldn't recognize them. The cars, too, would be nearly impossible to detect as bureau cars. It was also possible the bureau would use an airplane. These surveillance planes fly so high they are extremely difficult to detect from the ground. Agents in the plane would monitor my movements and direct ground surveillance units. A private radio channel would be used, and the voices "scrambled" so that no one could monitor the transmissions. A great advantage of using an airplane was that surveillance vehicles on the ground could follow me and remain out of sight.

If all this were going on, the bureau would be especially interested in knowing whom I would contact after the meeting with Kuker and Hughes. Yet no one seemed to be watching when I returned to my desk. Even now no one else was in the squad area.

I still had my undercover assignment and was working other highly sensitive FCI investigations. If the bureau really considered me a security risk, wouldn't it have removed me from these or suspended me outright?

I dialed Brian's number. His school and work schedule was different from day to day, and I could never remember exactly where he was at any given moment. I got his answering machine but didn't leave a message. He'd be able to tell that something was wrong.

I dialed the number of a close friend who worked for another branch of the federal government. I was trying to decide whether I should tell Hughes and Kuker I had lied before signing the statement being prepared. I needed advice.

"Something's come up, Robert," I said. "I need to talk to you right away."

We had always been guarded in our telephone conversations from work, and we were now. Robert told me to come right over.

I drove my bureau car out of the garage onto the busy street. My mind was still racing with possibilities and concerns, and I had to remind myself to concentrate on my driving. The last thing I needed at that point was to get in an accident with a bureau car. I told myself not to be paranoid but knew I had to be careful. I did not want to jeopardize Robert's career.

I tried to make certain I wasn't being followed. I took in everything around me. I stopped at a red light, looked up at the sky, but didn't see an airplane. As I reached the top of a long hill, I quickly pulled into a side parking lot and waited. No other cars came up the hill behind me. Several minutes passed before I got out. I walked the remaining distance to Robert's office.

I identified myself to the receptionist and sat down in a chair. Robert came out and greeted me with a handshake while the receptionist looked on. We went inside his office, and he closed the door. He also pulled the drapes shut.

Robert was about fifteen years older than I was, and we had been good friends for nearly a decade. Part of his professional responsibility was counseling people, and he was good at it. He was easy to talk with and patiently listened before offering his opinion. We had shared many confidences over the years, and I trusted him a great deal. Since he also worked for the government, I knew he would understand.

"Are you all right?" he asked.

I shook my head. "Not really."

"Do you want to get something to eat?"

I shook my head again.

I had told Robert about the W. J. note to my parents. "He wrote to the bureau," I said. Robert's face turned ashen. I told him what happened that morning.

"You know, I thought I was pretty comfortable about being gay, but I guess I'm not," I said. "I should have told Hughes and Kuker the truth this morning."

"But you're talking about your career, Frank. The bureau is not known for its tolerance toward us. If you told them you were gay, I don't think they would let you continue to work there—in spite of your record."

We talked about what the bureau might do next and what I should do. I told him I was considering telling the truth when I got back to the office.

"Only you can make that decision," Robert said. "Perhaps they don't want to know the truth, and this thing will just pass."

I nodded. "But if they do pursue it, it means I'm going to lose my job."

I got up to leave.

"Whatever happens in the meantime," he cautioned, "don't let your job performance suffer."

My last performance rating had been "superior," but I knew what Robert meant. The bureau could use poor work performance as a reason to fire me. It could argue that I was no longer effective as an agent once my homosexuality had become known.

I returned to the office and a short while later was called in to see Hughes. Kuker had prepared a three-page statement, and I examined it carefully. Kuker swore me in. The place for my signature was just below a line which read: "I have read this statement consisting of this and two other pages and it is true and correct to the best of my knowledge."

I knew that the most important part of the statement wasn't true and that this was my chance to set the record straight. But I signed my name anyway. I had lied under oath. That lie haunted me in the weeks and months ahead.

I remained at my desk that afternoon, dictating case work. Most of the other agents returned around 4:30 P.M., and there was the usual light-hearted banter. I normally stayed beyond the required 5:00 P.M. but decided to go home on time that day.

Rusty, the new dog I had obtained from the Humane Society, was glad to see me. I called Brian but got his answering machine again. This time I left a message.

I wanted to talk to somebody who might be in a position to know about FBI policy in regard to homosexuals, but I wanted the conversation kept confidential. I dialed Dr. David Soskis's number. He was a Philadelphia psychiatrist on retainer by the bureau. I had never talked with him before, but he had a good reputation for assisting FBI employees on a confidential basis. His wife answered and said the doctor was out-of-town. He would return the second week in November.

Brian called around ten o'clock. "What's up?" he asked in a cheerful voice.

"Are you sitting down?"

"This sounds bad."

"It is," I said, and then told him what had happened. There was a very long silence afterward. He asked if I wanted him to come over.

"How tired are you?"

"I just finished a lab project, and I've got an early class in the morning. But if you want me to, I'll come over."

"That's all right," I said. "You sound tired. Besides, it's getting late."

"What do you think is going to happen next?"

I told him that I didn't know but that I wasn't very optimistic.

"You don't think they'll fire you, do you?"

"If they pursue it, I'm history."

I rarely felt lonely, but that night was different. Then Rusty suddenly jumped up onto the far corner of the bed and lay down with a slight groan that sounded like contentment. "You're a good boy, Rusty," I said, reaching over to pet him. He was also a good watchdog, and I kept him in the house at night.

I went to work the following morning knowing I could be fired. I saw Hughes and Kuker a few times, but they didn't act any differently toward me. I even ran into Jim Bohlenbach, and he didn't mention anything. Neither did anyone else at the office. No changes in my work assignments occurred, and I began to feel I might have overreacted. I was a good agent, and perhaps the bureau wasn't going to give any credence to an anonymous letter writer.

I didn't see Brian until the following Friday. I cooked him Italian sausage and peppers, one of our favorite meals, and we made sandwiches from the long Italian rolls I bought at Solunto's Bakery. Neither of us talked about the bureau during dinner. After we finished, I poured two small glasses of anisette. "Cheers," Brian said, and I responded with *Salut'*.

Despite my revived optimism, I felt the need to fill Brian in on some things he might not have considered. It seemed only fair. "You know," I said, "the bureau might be tapping my phone. I seriously doubt it, but it's possible. The national security issue gives them great latitude in such matters."

Brian was nodding, watching me.

"The bureau received the letter three months ago, which means they may have been watching me since then. And if they have, or reviewed my telephone tolls, then they know most of our gay friends. They would, of course, know about you."

Neither of us spoke for a few moments. He cleared his throat. "What do you think is going to happen now?"

I shrugged. I told him that if the bureau pursued the matter, he would probably be interviewed.

"What should I say if they ask me if you're gay?"

"That's a decision only you can make, Brian. But you should know you have the right not to talk to them. And unless they have a search warrant, they can't enter your house."

Brian got up from his chair to carry his dish to the kitchen sink. He stopped, his back toward me. "This is bullshit!" he said angrily. "They're just like the military in their attitude toward us. It's none of their business what we do in our personal lives!"

I walked over and put my arms around him. His voice was calm when he spoke again. "You're a good agent, Frank. What does your being gay have to do with your job?"

"I'm sorry, Brian," I said. "I'm sorry any of this had to include you."

■ ■ ■

One mid-November morning, before work, I reached Dr. Soskis by phone. I did not identify myself or the office I was assigned to. I told him I was a veteran agent and briefly explained my situation. I asked him if he knew what bureau policy was regarding the employment of gay agents, but Soskis delayed his answer. He asked, instead, very specific questions about bureau procedures. I knew he was trying to determine if I was really an FBI agent.

Apparently satisfied, he said he didn't know if the bureau had a policy regarding homosexuals but added, "With your length of service you know FBI agents and their attitudes. And you know the attitudes of the upper echelon of the bureau." He paused before continuing: "This is not a liberal period of time in our country, and working foreign counterintelligence will be a major consideration for the bureau."

He spoke more slowly, pausing more frequently. "From a psychological point of view, you need to prepare yourself for what could happen to you . . . from being suspended to being fired. At this point you should not be making any career decisions, and you should not resign, though the latter might be an option in the future."

His voice grew more serious at that point. "As a medical health professional, my most immediate concern is your health. You're in a high-risk group for AIDS."

I told him that I did not engage in high-risk behavior and that I was healthy.

I said I had close gay friends I could count on. He seemed pleased to hear this and encouraged me to maintain these relationships.

"Filter your sexual life now through the eyes of the straight bureau," he advised. "I would recommend you clear your house immediately of any sexual material the bureau might find offensive. You must also be prepared if they ask you again about your homosexuality. Don't lie to them a second time. But you don't have to do their job for them. And you don't have to volunteer information to them. You must, however, assure them of your loyalty to the country and the bureau. Emphasize your desire to finish your career and that you're not interested in becoming a test case for gay rights."

I was taking notes as quickly as I could.

"Assure them that you have eliminated letter writing as a way of meeting others and that you don't frequent gay bars, nor are you "out" to the gay community. Make clear to them you don't belong to any gay rights organizations."

He stopped then, and this gave me an opportunity to catch up with my notes. I started to thank him, but he wasn't finished.

"I am troubled about the letter to your parents," he said. "From a personal point of view, I'm concerned about this W. J. How did he get the address of your parents? Does he have access to some data base of information? Why is he doing this to you?"

I told him I had thought about these things but didn't have any answers.

"Perhaps it's someone you know," he said. "Or maybe it's someone in the FBI. Whatever the case, this W. J. certainly knows you. You may meet him in the future. Be aware of anyone who tries to befriend you or shows unusual interest in you. But whatever you do, don't take revenge against him."

I started to say something, but he interrupted. "I would personally be concerned about my safety if I was in your position—"

"I'm not afraid of this guy," I said sharply.

"Think about it," Soskis responded. "This guy knows that you're an FBI agent and that you can probably find out who he is. He knows you carry a gun and would probably use it if necessary. He knows all this, and he still did what he did? This guy's a loose cannon."

■ ■ ■

I decided to take Soskis's advice and remove certain materials from my house. There was nothing pornographic or illegal, but I did have back copies of the *Advocate* and some local gay newspapers. I kept this literature hidden in a couple of places.

I saw the postcard I had received from James W., but the letter and note sent to my parents' house were missing. There was no way I could have thrown these out. I went through all the materials again but still couldn't find the letter or note. I got up to search the closet and every other conceivable place.

I knew then that W. J. had been in my house. He had broken in and taken possible evidence. I tried to think rationally. Why would he want the letters back? Why did he also take the magazine in which his ad appeared—and the second letter I wrote him? The letter that had been returned? Was he afraid it contained something I could trace? I thought about Dr. Soskis's comment about this guy being a loose cannon.

I also thought about the doctor's remark about the FBI possibly being involved. Undetected entry into somebody's house isn't all that easy. My attention to detail, especially in my own home, would have alerted me to anything amateur. Moreover, the person or persons who broke in knew exactly where the material was or knew they had plenty of time to look for it. Only the bureau knew where I was on an hour-to-hour day-by-day basis.

It was late, but I decided to call Brian anyway. I asked if he could come over.

"What's the matter, Frank?" he said, after arriving.

I had difficulty speaking at first.

"Frank, tell me what's wrong."

"W. J. has been here."

Brian froze. He put his hand on the back of his head the way he did when he was nervous. I told him about Soskis.

We went through the house again, turning it upside down in our search. The materials were definitely missing.

"You should tell the bureau," Brian said.

I shook my head. "If I do, then I'm admitting I'm gay. They'll fire me for either being gay or lying to them about it the first time. Besides, they could use all this against me. They could say it's a reflection of me, the kind of people I associate with, and the reason why they don't want gay people in the bureau. No matter how much I try to explain, I'm going to look bad. No, I can't tell them."

Brian persisted. "But this is a crime. Someone broke into your house and stole things from you. You're an FBI agent, and the bureau needs to do something about it. If they won't do anything, you should call the police."

"I can't do that, Brian," I said, slowing myself down. "If I call the police, I'll have to explain everything to them. Then they're going to contact the bureau, and the word will get out that I'm gay. No, I can't take that chance."

Brian was looking at me and seemed to be shaking slightly. "I'm worried about your safety, Frank. This guy tried to hurt your relationship with your parents. He's trying to get you fired. And now he breaks into your house. You even said the doctor called him a loose cannon. Frank, you can't be sure what he might do next."

I was exhausted and sat down in a chair. I leaned back and closed my eyes. Brian came around behind me and put his arm around my neck.

"I know how you feel about the bureau," he said in a soft voice. "After all these years I can't believe this is happening to you."

I could feel tears form in my eyes.

"Every time I needed your help, in the Navy or finding a place to live, or with school, you were always there for me. If there's anything I can do to help you, I will."

I turned toward him. "This has become a nightmare, Brian. I'm just glad you're here."

"Do you want me to stay tonight?"

"Yes," I said.

I got up and turned off the kitchen light. Brian followed me.

"Frank, I don't want to upset you any more than you are," he said, "but do you think the bureau is behind all this?"

part three

to go on anyway

10.

A few days later an audiotape of a speech my brother Lou had given arrived in the mail. Although he'd given speeches before, this was the first time he ever sent me one. I was curious why. Brian and I were going out to dinner that night in Ocean Beach and decided to listen to it along the way.

The speech was delivered in our hometown of Canastota, and my parents, aunts, dozens of townspeople, and members of the historical society were in attendance. The point of the speech was that because of prejudice and low self-esteem, Italians and Italian-Americans hadn't truly arrived in America yet. Lou mentioned my parents, the names of some of the people in Canastota, and Carmen Basilio.

Brian and I arrived at the restaurant as the speech was about to end. I parked the car, and we sat listening as my brother described a dream he had about an old man sitting across the campfire from a much younger man. Though it was very dark, Lou said he could see the old man's face. It was worn and wrinkled. He couldn't make out the younger man because his back was turned, but he had just finished telling a terribly sad story. There was no way of knowing what he said, but there was a feeling of sadness, even despair in the air.

The old man poked at the fire, and embers flared. He looked worried. He had to choose his words carefully, for the young man was without hope.

The old man said to the younger man that no matter what, he had to go on. "You don't know how it's going to turn out, and so you've got to go on anyway. Despite the pain and sadness and the fact that you can only see darkness ahead, you must go on. Go. Go on anyway."

Brian cleared his throat. "He's talking about you, Frank."

Late that night, when I was alone, I listened to the speech again. When

Lou came to the words about going on anyway, I wrote them down, and I carried them with me in the days ahead.

■ ■ ■

On December 5, 1988, Kuker's secretary called me at my desk. "Frank," she said, "the ASAC would like to see you."

I told her I'd be right over.

Five weeks had passed since Hughes and Kuker questioned me about the letter and note. I sensed that the other shoe was about to drop.

Kuker's door was ajar, but I knocked anyway. He looked up from his desk. "Come in, Frank," he said.

I closed the door and walked to the front of his desk, remaining standing.

"OPR wants to interview you in Washington," he said. OPR is the abbreviation for the Office of Professional Responsibility, the FBI's internal affairs unit. "They've made airline and hotel reservations for you, and your flight leaves at two-thirty this afternoon."

I nodded and left the room. I told the secretary and my supervisor that I had to go out of town. They both wished me luck and kidded me about doing a "good job." No doubt they thought I had been assigned another special.

A contractor and his crew were at work when I arrived home. Brian and I had spent months tearing down my fireplace, chimney, and an outside wall. We had dug up the patio, and a large concrete slab had been poured. The final stage of the twenty-thousand-dollar project, a solarium addition, was now nearing completion.

I called Brian from the back bedroom and told him about having to fly to Washington that afternoon. His voice was more sad than angry. "I knew they wouldn't let it drop."

I asked him if he'd watch the house while I was gone.

"Sure," he said, and wished me luck.

I packed, stopped at the bank, then rushed to the airport. I would barely make the flight. I was feeling tense waiting in line. When handed my tickets, I asked when the reservations had been made. She queried the computer. "Last Thursday, Mr. Buttino."

The bureau had known four days ahead of time and had given me only a half day's notice. The flight was also nondirect. It would put me in Dulles International Airport sometime after midnight, and the OPR interview was scheduled for first thing the following morning. My treatment reflected bureaucratic ineptness or was planned. Maybe the bureau wanted me tired and feeling anxious.

En route to Washington I thought about the statement I planned to make. I had thought about it before and began writing it down now. I hoped it wasn't a mistake.

I thought about the questions OPR might ask and how best to respond. It would have reviewed my personnel file. Its main concern would be that I was a spy.

The tenth anniversary of the murders of San Francisco Mayor George Moscone and gay Supervisor Harvey Milk had just passed, and articles in gay newspapers discussed the event and its significance to lesbians and gays. Milk had come to power in San Francisco just when I was coming to terms with my own sexuality. He had paid the ultimate price for trying to improve the self-respect of gays and lesbians.

While I greatly admired Milk's courage and accomplishments, I felt his confrontational approach would be ineffectual with the bureau. You simply didn't challenge headquarters. I thought it best if I tried to convince HQ that I was not a security risk and that my record supported this. The last thing I wanted was to become a cause for gay rights.

My father always told his sons to be careful. Though he tended to give others the benefit of the doubt, he had many reasons for mistrust. His own parents, Italian immigrants, had passed on to him their view of America as strange and threatening. He was also aware of discrimination. He and my mother had been called "wops" and "dagos" when they were growing up.

I would have to be careful with my answers. Honest—but careful.

The plane arrived past midnight, and I took a cab to the hotel. It was in Crystal City, Virginia, a short distance from downtown Washington. The time difference made me restless. I didn't sleep much before the wake-up call came at 6:30 A.M.

The cabby dropped me off in front of the main entrance of the J. Edgar Hoover Building. I hadn't been back to FBIHQ since the Mitrione case, and the only difference I noticed was an increase in the number of homeless people. It was a cold morning, and some slept on grates to keep warm. I needed a cup of coffee and walked to a nearby McDonald's.

I went back to FBIHQ, identified myself to the security people, and was handed a visitor's badge. I was given directions to the OPR offices and walked alone to them.

The secretary opened the door for me, and I went inside.

I told the secretary I had an appointment with Special Agent Raymundo Arras, and in a matter of moments he came out and introduced himself. Arras was younger than I was, a little taller, and Latino.

Special Agent Sandra Fowler, another OPR investigator, joined us. She looked to be in her late thirties and seemed less friendly than Arras. As they led me to an adjacent room, I was struck by the irony of being questioned by two minority agents.

The decor of the room we entered surprised me. It was the nicest bureau room I had ever seen. It contained a small couch, comfortable high-back chairs, and end tables. A coffee table was at one side of the room; at the other, a desk with chairs. It seemed like somebody's living room.

Ray Arras motioned me to the couch. I took out my notebook and pen and sat down. Arras and Fowler sat opposite me in the high back chairs.

Sandy Fowler was the lead agent. This meant she would be responsible for the questions, notes, and statement I was to sign. Arras served as an observer and witness, though he, too, could ask questions. He would also assist with the statement.

Fowler said that this was an official administrative inquiry and that there was a potential criminal problem if I had lied under oath in the statement I had signed for Hughes on October 31. Fowler explained OPR's function and said my case would ultimately be decided by headquarters and the Department of Justice. "OPR's function is to prepare an investigative package so that they can make their decision," she said.

I listened carefully because all this was new to me. When she was done, I asked when the interview had been scheduled.

"That's not important!" she snapped. "Besides, we'll be asking the questions. I won't allow you to take over the interview!"

Her response caught me off guard, and I thought of responding in kind. But I felt it would be counterproductive. I said, instead, "I was just curious, Sandy. The ASAC told me yesterday morning I had to be here today. My house is under construction, and it was difficult to leave on such short notice."

Fowler didn't respond. She handed me an FD-645 form, which outlines an FBI employee's rights and responsibilities during an administrative inquiry. She said the inquiry had been initiated "because of the allegations of homosexual conduct contained in the letter to the San Diego office."

I signed the form, and Arras witnessed my signature. As we were doing so, Fowler added that the bureau was "concerned about this because of the potential security issue and the potential for compromise in the foreign counterintelligence field and the criminal field. The bureau's policy is that homosexuality has been a potential for compromise—if it is not known. The bureau is concerned about what you do and how it impacts on your job. We would also ask that you take a polygraph regarding these issues, but the polygraph is voluntary."

Fowler picked up her pen, signaling the formal start of the interview. She handed me a copy of my October 31 statement. I looked it over as she highlighted my bureau assignments. This was for the record. When she finished, I said there was something I wanted to say.

Fowler stared at me, perhaps wondering if I was going to be uncooperative, even confrontational. In either case her work would be a great deal more difficult. Arras's expression didn't change at all.

"First," I said, my voice calm, "I was not fully candid in the statement I provided Hughes and Kuker. I did in fact write the letter which begins 'Hi James' and is signed 'Frank.' Second, I am homosexual. Third, I will cooperate fully in this investigation."

It was the first time I had ever told nongay people I was "homosexual," and the words sounded strange. But I didn't feel uncomfortable and was glad for that.

Fowler became noticeably more relaxed, and I briefly explained that I didn't know I was gay when I first joined the bureau in 1969. I said I had my first homosexual experience in 1974 and since then had come to accept my sexual orientation. I told them I kept this secret from the FBI because I thought the bureau would fire me.

Fowler leaned forward in her chair, her voice very empathetic now. "We investigate one case involving a homosexual FBI employee each week. Some have to do with criminal conduct by employees, such as pedophilia, but your case is different. We've never had this situation before: an agent with nineteen years in the bureau, a good record, and we find out he's homosexual. You could be a test case in the bureau, Frank. Bureau policy may be established on the basis of this case."

I appreciated her words, but I didn't want her to mistake my intent. "Sandy," I said, shaking my head slightly, "I'm not looking to be a test case. All I want is to keep my job."

"It might be difficult for you to continue working in the bureau. I mean, if the word gets out. You know how the bureau is."

Professionally the FBI operates on a need-to-know basis. But in personal matters secrets did not remain secrets long inside the bureau.

"I'm pretty well liked and respected in San Diego," I responded. "I think I can deal with the people there. My main concern is with headquarters and losing my job."

Fowler looked at me a moment longer, then down at her notes. "Let's begin, Frank," she said. "First, the lab [FBI laboratory] didn't find your fingerprints on the letter received by the San Diego office about you, but it did identify the handwriting on the letter to James as yours. They have concluded you did not write the cover note signed with the initials W. J."

I didn't react but thought the hypothesis odd. Did the FBI really think I planned all this? That I wanted it to find out I was gay? I started to wonder just how naïve the bureau might be in matters concerning homosexuality.

Fowler asked me to talk in detail about my homosexuality, beginning with adolescence. I nodded, explaining that until I was in my late twenties, I thought I was heterosexual. I had dated women and was sexually intimate with some of them. But at age twenty-nine, I said, I had my first sexual relationship with another man. I hoped at the time it was just a passing phase in my sexual development and wanted to believe I wasn't gay despite the experience. As time went by, however, I said I began to date women less and less. Eventually—by the time I was thirty-seven—I accepted the fact that I was gay and stopped dating women altogether.

I told them that during this period I had read a lot about homosexuality and had made some close gay friends. I said I met gay people through mutual friends or the personals in gay publications. I thought that the personals were more discreet than gay bars and parties. I explained I used either an alias or only my first name when responding. My return address was a post office box number. I said I only revealed that I was an FBI agent after I knew and trusted someone I met.

I went on to say that I was by nature a private person and that if I were heterosexual and single, I would conduct my personal life in a similar manner. I said I was not promiscuous and not known or active in the gay community. I noted that occasionally, while traveling, I might go to a gay bar in a city where no one knew me. I said being gay had never adversely affected my job performance.

I continued along these lines until we took a break for lunch. I felt drained by then. I was allowed to leave the building, and as I walked through the courtyard, I stopped at a public telephone. I hadn't noticed anyone following me but knew it was still a possibility. I tried to reach Brian but got his answering machine. I had been thinking about calling someone I knew and trusted in Washington. Though it was a local call, the bureau could find out the number from the telephone company's computerized records. But I had nothing to hide anymore. I dialed Everett Waldo's number.

I had met Everett a few years before in Washington through mutual friends and had never told him I was an FBI agent. He had been married with children, but his marriage dissolved when he realized he was gay. Everett was an ordained Methodist minister who had served for many years on the staff of the U.S. Civil Rights Commission before retiring. He was smart, honest, and a good person.

Everett answered on the second ring, and we exchanged greetings. I told him I was in town on business for a few days. He must have suspected something was wrong because he insisted I stay at his house. After hanging up, I lingered over a cup of coffee. I didn't feel hungry. Although I felt some relief at finally revealing my secret to the bureau, I knew my disclosure could very well cost me my career.

The FBI was not aware of the letter to my parents, and I offered this information to Arras and Fowler at the start of the afternoon session. I detailed the sequence of events beginning with my correspondence with "W. J. ——" and later "James W." I could see by their expressions that they either were confused or didn't believe me.

"Did you ever meet W. J.?" Fowler asked.

I shook my head. "I didn't meet him as a result of my correspondence with him, but I may have met him some other time. I just didn't know him by those initials. . . . Sometimes gay people use pseudonyms, so he might have used another name. I can't be sure."

They waited, and it made me uncomfortable. "W. J. might be the agent sitting next to me in the San Diego office for all I know," I said.

They continued waiting, and I probably should have remained silent but didn't. I was going to go out of my way to prove to them I was trying to be cooperative. "Certainly this guy knows who I am, but it doesn't necessarily mean I know him. If I knew who he was, I would tell you. But it doesn't make any sense, does it? I mean, if a person was blackmailing an FBI agent, would he bring attention to it by contacting the FBI and identifying the agent as a security risk?"

I knew there were a number of possibilities for the person's motivation and offered what I considered the prime one. "Isn't it possible that this is a person who hates homosexuals? A person who found out I was gay and an FBI agent and decided to try to ruin my relationship with my parents *and* get me fired from my job?''

There was more silence; only this time I felt I had said enough. A few additional moments passed before Fowler returned to her prepared questions.

At first the questions focused on bureau concerns about national security and blackmail. I explained I had never been approached by anyone associated with a non-U.S. intelligence service, nor had I provided information from bureau files or records to a member of a non-U.S. intelligence service. I said I had never been threatened with exposure about my homosexuality and never had homosexual contact with any foreign individual with questionable motives.

"As an FBI agent I have always been alert to the possibility of some kind of approach and would have reported that contact immediately— even if it meant revealing my homosexuality to the FBI."

Fowler asked about travel outside the United States, and I told her that I didn't have a passport and that my only foreign travel was to Canada and Mexico. These trips were infrequent and of short duration, I said, and were for sight-seeing and vacationing purposes only.

Fowler then moved on to a different set of questions. These began with "Have you engaged in sex in rest rooms, parks, on beaches, and in other public places?"

I had expected they would ask such questions, and I answered no.

She asked if I spent off-duty time looking for casual sexual encounters, and again I answered no. I also repeated what I had said before: that I was a discreet, private person who did not conduct my life in that way.

"Have you ever paid for sex or ever been paid for sex?"

"No."

"Do you engage in sex with children?"

The question angered me. "I have no interest in sexual activity with young children—either boys or girls," I said coldly. "I have done volunteer work with children for several years. I have no sexual interest in children whatsoever."

I glanced at my watch. It was nearly 5:00 P.M. I anticipated several other questions and wondered if they were going to get to them or if I'd have to come back. They looked tired, too. My head began to throb.

"Have you ever had sex with another FBI employee?" Fowler asked, and shifted slightly in her chair. Arras glanced down.

What were they thinking? What was on the bureau's mind? Did they think there was a gay sex ring in the FBI? Were they worried about such a story reaching the media?

Fowler asked the question again, and I thought of "Doc" Reading, a history teacher I had had at Colgate. "If I don't laugh, I'll cry myself to death," Doc often said.

I began to nod slowly. "But I'm not going to give you any names."

She looked at Arras for support. "We need to know the full details. When and where and how often. The bureau will want to know everything about it."

"I've had sex with only one other FBI agent, Sandy. And it happened in 1982."

Fowler made a note of the date and waited for me to continue.

"The agent was female," I said.

Though I sensed they both were relieved, in my notes I wrote that Fowler was no longer interested in when, where, and how often.

It was nearly six o'clock, but Fowler pressed on with her questions. "We need to know the kind of sex you engage in with other men."

"What is the relevance of that question?" I asked angrily. "What does it have to do with anything?"

Fowler fired back. "The bureau will not be satisfied unless we cover this area. We ask similar questions of heterosexual employees in similar situations."

I didn't believe her. "I've already told you I'm homosexual and I engage in homosexual sex. Why do you need to know these details?"

She didn't answer.

"You're single, Sandy," I said. "Is there anything about your sex life or personal life that you would not want your parents or the FBI to know?"

I turned to Arras. "And how about you, Ray? Is there anything about your sex life with your wife that your parents, or the bureau, don't know about? Have you ever had an affair? Do you have any secrets?"

Addressing them both now, I added, "Don't we all live a secret life to some extent? Aren't there some things we don't share with others not because they're bad but because they're personal? Isn't that why we call it your personal life?"

It was quiet only momentarily. Fowler then advised me that the bureau would look upon my refusal to answer as being uncooperative. She proceeded with specific questions: "Do you engage in oral sex with other

men?''; ''Anal sex?''; ''Masturbation?'' She asked if I took the ''active''
or ''passive'' role in these acts.

''Is there nothing about my personal life that is sacred to the bureau?''
I shot back.

Both Fowler and Arras continued to demand and insist I answer these
questions. The arguing became even more intense. I was becoming nauseated as my privacy was more and more invaded.

I knew some of these acts were illegal in certain states and wondered
if that was the reason I was being asked them. The FBI could say I had
engaged in illegal sexual activity.

But these laws remained largely unenforced. People forgot that they
were applicable to heterosexual conduct, too.

I was aware that all I was saying would be put in the statement I
would sign and become part of my permanent record in the FBI. A sick
feeling came over me. Was the bureau asking me these things to get me
to quit? How long were they going to keep me there? Until I threw in
the towel?

''What kind of sex acts do you *not* engage in with other men?''

''I'm not going down a shopping list so you can check off all the
things I don't do with other men!''

We argued, but I wouldn't back down. The compromise we reached
was that instead of specific answers to these questions I would be allowed
to say, ''I have never been involved in bizarre sexual activity.''

■   ■   ■

It was cold and dark when I got off the metro. I was grateful to be able
to stay with somebody I knew.

Everett's house was farther than I remembered, and I had to set my
suitcases down a few times along the way. When I arrived, the porch
light was on and the house was well lit. It was warm and inviting.

I knocked, and in a few moments Everett appeared. Even in the dim
light I could see there was more white in his hair and beard than when
I last saw him. Though he was of medium build and height, he always
seemed bigger to me. I think it had to do with his intellect. I extended
my hand, but he moved to hug me instead.

Everett showed me where I would be sleeping, and I changed into
Levi's and a sweat shirt. When I went back downstairs, he was preparing
dinner. ''This is a great house, Everett,'' I said. ''It must be difficult for
you to move.''

He was selling the house and planning to move to California. "There are a lot of wonderful memories here," he said wistfully. "I raised my kids in this house."

He asked if I wanted a drink.

"I could use one right now."

He pulled a dusty bottle of wine out of the cupboard, opened it, and poured me a small glass. "Something's wrong, Frank," he said, handing it to me. "You look like hell."

I managed a smile. I had forgotten how direct Everett could be. "It's been a long day," I answered. "I have something I want to talk to you about later on."

After dinner I called Brian to tell him what had happened. I could tell all the personal questions I had been asked disturbed him.

"What do you think is going to happen next?" he asked.

I told him it was up to the bureau now.

"From what you described today, it doesn't sound good, Frank." He asked when I would be coming home.

"I hope by Friday."

Everett was writing in his study when I knocked on the door. "Ready to talk?" he asked.

I sat opposite him in a lounge chair. I thought about where to begin. "Everett, I have something I want to share with you. I hope you won't be offended that I have not told you this before, but I'm sure you'll understand why."

He didn't respond, and I continued.

"I'm an FBI agent and have been one for nineteen years. The problem is that someone informed the FBI that I'm gay. I got called back to Washington for questioning yesterday. Today I told them that I'm gay."

Everett must have been a good poker player because I couldn't tell what he was thinking. I explained the W. J. letters and told him of the bureau's concerns. We talked until nearly midnight. At that point I was too tired to go on.

"You know, Frank," he said finally, "you have to realize you'll never be able to answer all their questions or satisfy all their concerns about you and homosexuality. That isn't to say that what you're doing isn't a very brave thing." He added, almost as an afterthought, "But you're not going to keep your job."

I laughed. "Thanks for the encouragement."

"Listen to me," Everett said. "You made a contribution to this country as an FBI agent for nineteen years. You now have an opportunity to make a contribution to this country in another way.''

I knew what he meant. The thought of challenging the bureau if it fired me had crossed my mind. But after that day's inquisition by Fowler and Arras I wanted no part of the public spectacle my challenge would generate.

11.

OPR questioning began promptly at nine the following morning. Fowler must have worked late because she said the statement I was to sign would be ready shortly. We talked a little, and then the statement was brought in. Haggling began over word choices and what should be added and deleted. This went on for nearly two hours.

The bureau would view the statement as my "confession." It would provide the basis of the case against me if the bureau decided to pursue it. I also knew I might not get another opportunity to defend myself. As a result, I had Fowler add that my real estate investments made it possible for me to quit my job without financial hardship and that if I had something to hide or was guilty of criminal wrongdoing, I certainly wouldn't be proceeding with the inquiry. I put in that I loved my job, enjoyed making a contribution to the betterment of the country, and had great respect for my colleagues in the FBI. I explained that I had shared many personal matters because I wanted to continue with my career and that I was not seeking notoriety or to become a gay cause.

I wanted to insert that I might resort to legal action if I lost my job, but Fowler and Arras advised against this. They thought it would be counterproductive. So, instead, I had the final paragraph in the statement read: "I am proud of my record in the FBI and it is my desire to continue my career in a dedicated, professional manner until I retire. I do not intend to resign from the FBI."

Fowler brought the statement into the secretary's office to be retyped. When she returned, I consented to take a polygraph. I also said I was willing to have the FBI conduct an updated background investigation on me. My only condition was that I be able to tell my parents and family first about my homosexuality. The investigation, I knew, would prove that I had never been blackmailed or coerced by anyone to reveal classified information.

I advised them I was willing to submit to a "psychological fitness for duty" examination. This was a relatively new psychological screening process for applicants. It was Everett's idea. He said some in the FBI would view homosexuality as a mental disorder.

I returned to Everett's house, and we discussed the statement. It would be ready for signing the next day, and after that I would take the polygraph. I had little familiarity with the polygraph but believed it would vindicate me. Refusing to take it might make me look as if I were lying or had something to hide.

FBI regulations forbid an agent from having an attorney present during the inquiry and at the signing of the statement. Everett felt very strongly that it was unwise to continue any further without advice from counsel. He also vehemently opposed my taking the polygraph, and the more we talked about these matters, the more my confidence began to wane. Everett knew a man in Washington named Franklin Kameny who was very familiar with government inquiries into homosexual conduct. Kameny was a longtime gay rights activist.

"But I'll tell you something, Frank," Everett cautioned. "Kameny is tough and combative. If we call him, I know he'll tell you not to sign the statement *and* not to take the polygraph."

I was frustrated. "But if I don't sign it, they will fire me for being uncooperative."

"And if you acquiesce, they'll fire you anyway for initially denying you wrote the letter."

In the course of our conversation Everett also suggested I begin seeing a therapist upon my return to San Diego. He said I needed somebody with an objective and sympathetic ear.

I told him then about calling Dr. Soskis, the psychiatrist on retainer by the FBI, and he reacted with great alarm. "How can you trust somebody paid for by the FBI?" he said.

I felt a little uncomfortable by his reaction and the suggestion I needed to see a therapist, but I let these things pass. There was enough to deal with at that point.

I called Brian. He thought it appalling I wasn't allowed to have an attorney. "Frank, criminals have a right to a lawyer, and the FBI won't let you have one?"

Brian was a science major in college and also adamantly opposed to the polygraph. "It's ridiculous to think you can put wires on somebody to determine if he's telling the truth."

After hanging up, I called Tom Homann, a San Diego attorney. I had seen his name mentioned in gay newspapers and knew he had an outstanding reputation in civil rights matters. Homann had successfully challenged Navy policy which dismissed sailors who tested HIV positive. He had also sued the San Diego County sheriff, who refused to hire gay and lesbian deputies. (The sheriff later agreed not to discriminate on the basis of sexual orientation.)

From these news stories I suspected he was gay. It was about 6:00 P.M., Pacific Coast time, and I hoped to catch Homann at his office.

I dialed his number after obtaining it from directory information. The person on the other end of the line said, "Law offices," and I asked for Tom Homann.

"This is Tom" was the reply.

I introduced myself and asked if he had time to talk about an important matter concerning my job. He was friendly and said for me to go ahead. I briefly explained my situation and asked for his advice regarding the statement and polygraph.

Homann also didn't think I should sign the statement without an attorney present and began to give me the names of lawyers in Washington. I interrupted him, saying that if I didn't abide by FBI regulations, I could be fired. We decided that I would add another paragraph to the statement, and we talked about its wording. Afterward Homann stated he had absolutely no faith in the polygraph, but that, too, was something *I* had to decide.

Even though exhausted, I had trouble getting to sleep. Was there any way of knowing for sure what to do? What was right? Was it possible to keep my job and protect myself at the same time?

■ ■ ■

The statement was ready for signing as soon as I arrived at OPR the following morning. We made some minor changes, and then I asked, for the record, what FBI policy was toward my having a lawyer present. Fowler restated the bureau's position, and I said I wanted the following added:

During the three days I was interviewed regarding the information contained in this statement, I was informed by the interviewing agents that, according to Bureau policy in an Administrative Inquiry, I was not entitled to have an attorney present with me

*during the questioning. I was also informed that I was not allowed
to have an attorney review this statement with me prior to signing
it. I expressed to the interviewing agents and am stating it now
again that I would prefer to have an attorney review this statement
with me prior to my signing it. I am signing this in spite of my
reservations about not having an attorney review this statement
with me.*

Neither Fowler or Arras objected, and we took a short break while this
was being typed.

I went to an employees' lounge near the OPR offices with the intent
of reviewing my notes, but I was too tired to concentrate. About twenty
minutes later Arras came in to get me. I read the statement over again,
initialing each page at the top and bottom. It was fourteen pages long,
and I signed at the bottom of the last page.

I had about two hours before the beginning of the polygraph. The
polygraph unit was in a separate building and Arras gave me directions.

I had come to respect Fowler and Arras for their professional handling of a difficult task. I knew they were getting their orders from
their superiors. Before I left that day, I told them I appreciated their
efforts. I also added, in jest, that I would go easy on them when
Mike Wallace interviewed me on *60 Minutes*! Later, when Wallace
did interview me for the program, I wondered if Fowler and Arras were
watching.

I ate a sandwich and went for a walk. It was a nice day, and I headed
toward the Old Post Office Building on Pennsylvania Avenue. The OPO
was where new agents primarily trained prior to construction of the new
FBI Academy in Quantico, Virginia. I had trained at the OPO as a new
agent in the summer of 1969. It had been a typically hot, muggy summer
in the nation's capital, and the building didn't have air conditioning. The
once dark granite exterior had been transformed into an attractive gray.
I'd heard the interior had been converted into shops, restaurants, and
offices.

I didn't think the FBI was following me, but there was no way of
being sure. Some FBI field offices have surveillance squads comprised
of nonagent personnel. They look like ordinary people.

If I were being surveilled, they would be conducting a background
investigation on Everett. I had warned Everett about the possibility.
"From my work for the government and my political activism, I'm sure

FEDERAL BUREAU OF INVESTIGATION

FRANK BUTTINO
SPECIAL AGENT

880 FRONT STREET
SUITE 6-S-31
SAN DIEGO, CALIFORNIA 92188   (619) 231-1122

*Me, 1990, after filing my lawsuit. It was a tense
time.* INSET: *My FBI business card.*

In new-agent training class, Washington, D.C., 1969. I was twenty-four years old and excited about beginning my new career.

My first FBI credentials, signed by J. Edgar Hoover

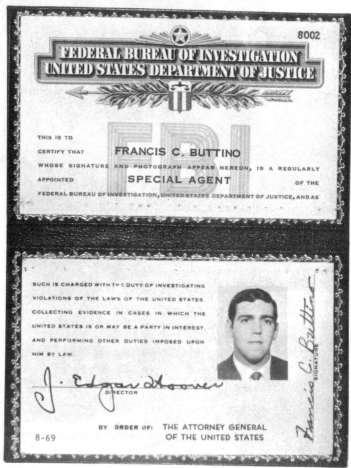

*My February 7, 1972, meeting with FBI Director
J. Edgar Hoover—three months before he died.
Hoover served as director for nearly forty-eight
years, under eight presidents.*

I saw a program in the television series The FBI
*being taped in 1972. I'm with the actor Efrem
Zimbalist, Jr. (LEFT), and another agent (CENTER).*

Working undercover in the 1970s

Meeting FBI Director William S. Sessions in San Diego, 1988.

I'm already in their files," he said with a mischievous grin. "They won't have to look very far!"

I stopped in front of the Old Post Office Building. It had changed a great deal in nineteen years, just like my life. If I had known I was gay back then, I never would have joined the FBI. I wondered what my life would have been like.

I turned and walked back along Pennsylvania Avenue toward FBI headquarters. I located the private office building which housed the polygraph unit and took the stairs to its second-floor suite. The reception area looked like a typical business office, and I identified myself. It was 12:40 P.M.

I watched as several people entered and exited the offices in back. A few made eye contact with me, and I wondered if they knew who I was and why I was there. One such person was a polygraph examiner I had met once. He seemed to recognize me, so I said hello and identified myself. We shook hands. I'm sure he realized that my being there meant there was a problem. I told him briefly what it was about.

He shook his head. "It's an area the bureau has never really dealt with." We shook hands again, and he wished me luck.

A few minutes later a heavyset man about my age came out of an office and introduced himself as Frank Morgovnik. He wasn't very friendly and led me, without speaking, to a small room in back. I noticed similar such rooms along the way.

In the middle of the room was a table with a built-in polygraph machine. A chair was on each side of the machine. There was a video camera in one corner of the room, near the ceiling, and three of the walls as well as the ceiling were painted a glossy white. The fourth wall was mirrored, and I assumed it was one-way. The room contained no pictures or other personal items. The fluorescent lighting overhead made me squint.

I reminded myself to be careful about what I said or did, even if left alone. I had always been a little claustrophobic, and I was beginning to feel that way now. I tried to calm myself. I took out my pen and notepad and asked the examiner to spell his last name. I recorded it along with the date and the time.

I filled out and signed several forms. One was an FD-540. Titled "Warning and Assurance to Employees Required to Provide Information," it was the same form I had signed for Hughes and OPR investigators. Morgovnik handed me an FD-328—a consent to interview with polygraph form outlining my rights. It said I could refuse to take the polygraph, stop it at any time, or refuse to answer any of its questions. The form also stated that the polygraph would focus on foreign counterintelligence issues as well as the contents of my signed statement. Beneath my signature on still another form were the words ''No threats or promises have been used against me to obtain my consent to the use of the polygraph. I understand that the examination room does contain an observation device and the examination will be monitored and recorded.''

Morgovnik took out an FD-497 and began filling it out. This was a polygraph examination worksheet. It contained information regarding my background and other administrative information.

As Morgovnik was working on this form, I looked over at the wires and straps. These would be attached to me and to the polygraph machine. Their purpose was to measure my biological response to questions. The machine technically could not determine if a person was lying; it only recorded changes in breathing, heartbeat, blood pressure, and sweat. These changes were recorded as squiggly lines on a roll of moving graph paper. Variances in the height of lines supposedly indicate whether or not a person is being truthful.

Morgovnik was finished and moved his chair directly opposite, and very close to, mine. Referring to my notebook, he asked what I was doing.

''I'm taking notes about what's going on.''

He asked why.

''Why?'' I repeated. ''Because I'm going to get fired from my job, and I want to keep track of everything that is happening to me.''

He told me to put the notebook away.

I thought about fighting him on this but decided against it. I had come too far. Yet I was also getting tired of backing down every time the bureau wanted its way.

Morgovnik had been briefed by Fowler and Arras. He now went over the statement I had signed. He then asked my help in phrasing questions. Such collaboration is not uncommon.

Polygraph questions are phrased to elicit yes or no answers so that physiological responses can be measured. I was comfortable with the questions we drew up and anxious to begin the examination itself.

Morgovnik strapped metal electrodes to my fingertips. He wrapped a rubber tube around my chest and an inflatable pressure cuff around my arm. He moved his chair back behind the polygraph machine, telling me to sit absolutely still. He said the slightest movement or variation in my breathing could invalidate the test.

My claustrophobic impulses reemerged, and I felt like ripping off the wires and fleeing. I felt as if I were being strapped into an electric chair.

Instead of panicking, I tried to picture myself running along the canyon trail near my house with Rusty, just as we had done so many times before. I imagined that it was a sunny day, in early autumn, and beautiful oaks and sycamores were cooling the air. I told myself I would be back there again soon.

The exam began with what are called control questions. Their purpose is to establish the height line for responses that are factually true, such as "Is your last name Buttino?" and "Are you a special agent of the FBI?"

The polygraph covered three major areas. First it focused on foreign counterintelligence. That part of the test consisted of two control questions and eight noncontrol questions. The most significant of the latter were: "Have you ever had any unauthorized contact with a representative of a non-U.S. intelligence service?" and "Have you ever passed any classified or sensitive information to a representative of a non-U.S. intelligence service?"

I answered no to these and the other questions. This entire set of questions was repeated two more times, with short pauses between. Afterward the wires were not taken off, nor was I allowed to stand or even move much in my chair.

It seemed bizarre. I had interviewed hundreds of suspects in the course of my career, and it was virtually impossible to know if a person was lying unless you knew beforehand. If the polygraph was so accurate, why didn't we save a lot of time and taxpayer's money and simply polygraph every suspect? And if the tests were trustworthy, why weren't the results permissible in federal court?

Morgovnik was ready to administer the second part of the test, and again I tried to picture myself in San Clemente Canyon running with Rusty. But this time I could conjure up no images. I looked at Morgovnik. He seemed indifferent—as though it were only a job and I were no different from others the FBI brought in.

I explained to Morgovnik during the pre-polygraph that a couple of times in my career I had checked a name or license plate number for a retired FBI agent. Morgovnik would know this was not uncommon and probably had done it himself before. I didn't think this would pose a problem in the second round of questioning, which focused on my signed statement. Key questions here were: "Have you lied on your sworn statement?"; "Besides what we've discussed, have you provided any unauthorized person information from a bureau record system?"; and "Are there any other unauthorized disclosures of bureau information that you are now concealing?"

My answer to all the questions in the second part was no.

The third and final portion of the test involved questions about W. J. Morgovnik was to ask me, among other things, "Did you ever meet the person you wrote those letters to?" and "Did the person you wrote those letters to ever threaten to disclose them to your employer?"

I answered no again, and Morgovnik unstrapped me. He told me he was going to review the results, and he allowed me to leave. The whole test had taken three hours.

I called Everett. He was still concerned about my taking the polygraph. "It doesn't work," he said flatly. "There's no way you can look inside somebody's mind."

We planned to go out for dinner that night, and I told him I thought I'd be back around six o'clock. I grabbed a cup of coffee and returned to the waiting area of the polygraph office. Despite Everett's warnings, I felt optimistic as Morgovnik led me back to the examination room.

He again moved his chair opposite, and close to, mine. "In my opinion," he stated without emotion, "your reactions to the questions about contact with—and the passing of—information to non-U.S. intelligence services were not indicative of deception."

I was happy but didn't let it show.

Morgovnik then said my reactions to the second and third set of questions were inconclusive or indicative of deception.

He went on to talk about the charts and offered explanations as to why I might not have passed. He started to go over my signed statement again, beginning with the correspondence to W. J., but I got up at that point. I was too exhausted to go back over it all again. "I told you the truth," I said angrily. "I don't know who this person is. If I did, I would tell you."

Tears started in my eyes, and I rubbed them away. My father always told us to be honest. He said be honest and everything else would work out. Well, nothing was working out.

I began to pace. I was sweating now and frustrated and furious. I clenched my fists. "Who is this person? Why is he doing this? Why is he doing this to my parents? They're elderly people, and this idiot is causing them to be afraid. What kind of person would do this to them?"

Morgovnik, his voice low, said, "You'd like to get even with him, wouldn't you, Frank?"

I turned. "Yes. Yes, I would. I'd like to grab him and push him against the wall and say, 'Who the fuck are you and why are you doing this to my parents? What did I do to you to make you do this to me?' "

"You'd like to get even with him, wouldn't you? Do to him what he did to you?"

Something in his voice stopped me. I looked at him. The son of a bitch wanted me to lose control. "Stop!" I shouted, holding up my hand. "Stop asking questions! No more comments!"

Morgovnik remained still, observing me closely. I remembered the video camera; I glanced over at the one-way mirror.

"Yeah," I said with control, moving back to the chair. "I'd like to get even with this guy. There are a lot of things I'd like to do to him, but I'm not that kind of person."

Morgovnik asked if I would be willing to take another polygraph.

"I'm telling you the truth. Why isn't the bureau concerned that this is happening to one of its agents and his family? Why is it concerned only with me?"

Morgovnik, his face expressionless, remained silent.

"Sure. I'll take another exam."

Morgovnik told me to think about all the information I had provided OPR and try to figure out what was preventing me from passing the polygraph. He asked me to work on new questions for the next day's polygraph. I doubted his sincerity but let it pass. I was too tired to fight anymore.

Everett and I returned to his house after dinner that night and sat in his study discussing the polygraph. I took out my pen and notebook and wanted to begin drawing up questions.

"I'm really frustrated, Everett. I've told the truth, and they say I'm lying. Those were my own questions. Why would I make up questions I couldn't truthfully answer? It doesn't make any sense."

Everett shook his head. "Frank, listen to me. Don't you understand this has nothing to do with the truth? You've told them you're gay, and they're not going to let you continue working for them.''

"Maybe you're right," I said, "but I've still got to try.''

■ ■ ■

The second polygraph included some of the new questions I had developed. When it was over, Morgovnik told me again the results indicated that I was lying.

12.

Emerson wrote: "Things are in the saddle,/And ride mankind." This was true for me personally at that juncture in my life. The organization I had dedicated my life to was now in control of that life. As an agent and a closeted gay man I had learned to take charge and make choices—to monitor carefully every word, action, and emotional reaction. Having to explain and defend myself was a new experience, and I didn't like it much. My hope was that a break in the case would shift the burden elsewhere—perhaps to W. J. himself.

■ ■ ■

I scanned the directory at the old gray stone building at the corner of Fifth Avenue and E Street in the Gaslamp District of San Diego. I noticed that the pawnshop which used to be at ground level was gone. The entire area was being restored.

I pressed the buzzer, and a male voice answered. I gave him my name, the door clicked, and I took the stairs to the second-floor landing. I didn't see or hear anyone else as I approached the office door I was looking for. I smelled cigarette smoke.

The door was ajar, and I could see a man inside seated at a computer, typing quickly, a cigarette dangling from his mouth. He saw me and smiled. "Ah, Frank, be with you in a minute," he said, taking a drag from his cigarette. He blew the smoke toward the high ceiling and went back to his work.

In a small room to my right a man sat working at a table with his back to me. The room to my left was the largest of the three and had a couch, chairs, and table. Corner windows overlooked the street below. Unlike the outside of the building, the three rooms looked as if they hadn't been changed in years.

The man butted his cigarette and got up to shake my hand. "I'm Tom

Homann,'' he said, then directed me to the larger room.

Homann was about my age, much taller than I, with light brown hair and a full beard, both of which were turning gray. I had often seen his photograph in gay newspapers, yet he seemed thinner than I remembered. From our phone conversation I knew he chose his words carefully. I had also detected a degree of sarcasm when he talked about FBI attitudes toward gay people.

Perhaps I had become accustomed to government prosecutors dressed in conservative business suits. Homann's appearance surprised me. When I worked in Detroit in the early 1970s, I had seen William Kunstler and other attorneys who represented New Left radicals. Wearing a light blue shirt, Levi's, and sneakers, Homann reminded me of some of these attorneys.

I gave him a copy of the statement I had signed for the FBI, and we sat down at a large oak table. Homann leaned back in his chair, stretching his long legs out on the table. He shook his head several times. Finishing, he exclaimed, ''They seem to have a preoccupation with your sex life, don't they?'' He was looking at me over the top of his glasses. ''Why don't we call a press conference and invite the media and the FBI? You'll announce that you're gay and that you're being investigated by the FBI because of your homosexuality.''

I couldn't tell if he was serious or not. It also concerned me that the man in the far room might be able to hear us. I asked Homann to close the door, and he did.

''I know a producer who works for *Sixty Minutes*,'' Homann continued, ''and I'm sure they'd love to have you on their show.''

He *was* serious.

''The last thing I'm looking for is any publicity about this,'' I said. ''I just want to continue working for the bureau.''

His expression changed slightly, and he became more grave. ''The federal government and especially the FBI are not known for their tolerance toward gay people. Publicity might be the only way to keep your job.''

I shook my head. ''That's not what I want, Tom. I'm scheduled to return to headquarters for more questioning, and I've come to ask your advice about that.''

He nodded, and I brought him up-to-date. After a brief discussion we agreed there was nothing I could do but wait and see what the FBI would do next.

I asked Homann not to discuss my situation with anyone else, and he nodded. I wanted to pay him for his time, but he waved me off, saying, "Don't worry about it." I thanked him and told him I would contact him when I returned from Washington.

It was a short walk back to the San Diego FBI office. The meeting left me unsettled. While I knew and respected the fact that Homann had a reputation for being bright, aggressive, and unafraid of the government, his remarks about contacting the media were bothersome.

I was already worried that someone might leak information about my situation. That kind of publicity might trigger the bureau's immediate firing of me. Homann was a strong advocate for gay rights, yet I wondered if I should have contacted an attorney who wasn't gay. I had to be careful about allowing anybody to use my case to further their own gay rights agenda.

I remembered Fowler's saying that OPR investigated one case per week involving a homosexual. But she never said what the bureau did afterward. If the employee had not been compromised, was he or she allowed to continue working?

I had passed the foreign counterintelligence portion of the test, my case assignments had not changed, and there was no indication that my squad supervisor or anyone besides Hughes and Kuker knew what was going on. Had I overreacted again? Still, Fowler's comment about my becoming a possible test case bothered me.

I tried to arrange a meeting with Hughes and Kuker, but Hughes was out of town. I wanted to apologize to them for denying I had written the letter to James W. Kuker said he had talked with OPR and was of aware of what I had said. He also knew I was to return to Washington for further questioning the following week. He said the three of us could talk when I got back.

■   ■   ■

My questioners were again Fowler and Arras, and the session began with Fowler restating the results of the polygraph: first, that I was not deceptive regarding foreign counterintelligence issues; secondly, that the results were inconclusive in regard to my giving sensitive information from FBI files to individuals outside the bureau; and thirdly, that I was deceptive about knowing the identity of W. J.

She was about to go on when I interrupted. I said I disagreed with the latter two findings and was willing to discuss them at length if they so desired. She told me no, not at that time and began asking questions of an increasingly personal nature. I realized that the more I told them, the more they could ask me about. And all this was making them suspicious that I had withheld information.

I signed another statement at the end of two days of questioning but was not asked to take a polygraph. I asked Fowler how long she thought it might take the bureau to decide my case, and she answered, "Several months."

I returned to work in San Diego the following morning. People were curious about my mysterious trips, but no one asked me anything specific about them. The following week I met with Hughes and Kuker and apologized for denying I had written the letter.

Hughes's anger surprised me. "I am concerned about the security of our investigative records," he told me.

I tried to assure him that I had never compromised an FBI investigation or given information from our files to anyone. "And I give you my word that it will never happen in the future either, boss," I added.

"I am also concerned with the candor issue and the fact that there was a second letter to your parents that you did not tell us about."

I explained, as I had to OPR, that I viewed the letter to my parents as mean, but not threatening, and that was why I had not reported it.

Hughes also expressed concern about the investigative effectiveness of the FBI if information about me became public. He offered a new piece of information that made me hopeful. "OPR has initiated an investigation to identify W. J. and to determine his motive in writing the letters."

Hughes wondered if W. J. would go to the media next, but before I could comment, Kuker began to question me about my correspondence with W. J. Because it was complicated, I said I'd prepare a 302 report for him as soon as possible. I told them both that I would be willing to assist OPR in the investigation in any way I could.

"Let me know if anyone says anything about this," Hughes said.

"Everyone is treating me the same as before," I told him. I also said I did not have a problem with my sexual orientation but understood how that might not be true for others.

"We'll take this one day at a time," Hughes said reassuringly.

I thanked them and left the office. Though Hughes's reaction troubled me, I was glad about the OPR investigation. I was confident that it would not take long to prove I had never met W. J.

I returned to my desk and immediately began preparing a chronology of my correspondence with W. J. I finished in about an hour and brought it in to Kuker. He asked me if I would sign a form giving the FBI permission to examine my bank accounts, credit reports, and other financial information.

I expected, and welcomed, the request. If the bureau thought I was a spy, then it would want to know if I was in financial difficulty or if any large, unexplainable sums of money had been deposited into my account. It also would want to determine if my assets were in line with my income.

I signed the form. Though I had extensive investments, they had been honest and meticulously conducted.

■　■　■

Brian and I prepared for my annual New Year's Eve party with our usual care. The Christmas tree was trimmed, and it looked beautiful sitting in the center of the new solarium. There were poinsettias, lights, and other holiday decorations, and we prepared a grand feast for our twenty-five guests.

A few friends were not yet aware of my situation at work, so I took them aside individually to tell them. I assured them I would not disclose anybody's name to the bureau. Other than that, I tried to block out what was happening to me, concentrating instead on having a good time. It turned out to be one of the best parties we ever had.

I always felt a little sad during the holidays not being with my family. After talking with them on the phone on Christmas Day, I felt even more sad. It was hard to tell them everything was fine when I was facing the most important crisis of my professional life. But knowing how upset and worried it would make them, I wasn't ready to tell them yet.

Brian and my close friends were an extended family, and I wasn't sure how I would be doing without their support. Earlier in the evening I had also called Everett to thank him for his help.

As the clock neared midnight, and in the midst of noisemakers and champagne, I couldn't help but wonder what the new year would bring. What would be lost and what would be gained. Who would be with me and who not. And if I'd be an FBI agent anymore.

■　■　■

I was certain that Tom Kuker was supervising the W. J. investigation. As the office ASAC he also had considerable other administrative responsibilities. I didn't know how many agents might be asked to assist him, but I thought John Dolan would be one of them. John was experienced, capable, and trusted by both Kuker and Hughes.

My foreign counterintelligence assignments remained the same throughout January and February 1989, and I continued to view this as a positive sign. Then, in late February, a startling piece of new evidence came to light. Tom Kuker had called me in to go over my credit report. I identified the banks and lending institutions that held mortgages on my properties, the loans I had taken out, and the purchases I had made. The credit report also reflected inquiries from companies with whom I had done business. Kuker asked about an entry listed for May 1988. It was a credit inquiry by a San Diego company I had never heard of.

I had sent my first letter to W. J. ———— in late January or early February 1988. In June I sent the letter to James W. W. J. wrote to my parents and the FBI, respectively, in June and July. May was a pivotal month.

"W. J. could have found out my name from my post office box or in some other way," I said to Kuker. "Then he runs a credit check to find out more about me. From this he learns I'm an FBI agent and where my parents live."

Kuker didn't say anything, but my optimism soared.

Still, in the days ahead I wondered why the bureau had decided against conducting the background investigation on me that I had suggested to OPR. I knew OPR hadn't done this because word would have gotten back to me from family, friends, and co-workers. Was the bureau afraid that others would find out? That the word would get out that the FBI had a gay agent working for it? And if this was true, had the bureau put its reputation ahead of the truth?

13.

Though the cases of most agents are fairly routine, once in a while an event occurs that transforms the bureau and the lives within it. This happened on Friday morning, March 10, 1989.

The day started routinely enough. Martin Hernandez waited at the curb as I drove up. I was Martin's training agent, and he also car-pooled with me.

New FBI agents are normally assigned an experienced agent to work with them during their first few months in the field. I remembered how awkward I had felt in my first-office assignment. I had been fortunate to have a savvy training agent to guide me through the thicket of FBI rules, regulations, and procedures. I believed being a training agent was even more important today than when I had been a rookie. The job was much more difficult and dangerous.

Not all experienced FBI agents serve as training agents. Some don't want their daily routines disrupted; others don't want to invest the extra time it takes. Squad supervisors also don't select certain agents because they are not particularly good role models.

"*¿Qué tal, amigo?*" I said when Martin opened the car door. It was about the extent of my Spanish, and Martin knew it. He answered me with a shake of his head.

He seemed preoccupied. He and his wife recently had a baby girl, and Martin said the infant had cried most of the night.

Though it was a Friday, I kidded, "Think you're going to make it through the week?"

Martin was evidently too tired to get the joke. "I don't know," he mumbled.

Martin, who had been born in Mexico, spoke Spanish fluently. He was a quick learner and a hard worker, and he had a good sense of humor.

We often ran together and occasionally socialized after work. Martin was going to be a good agent.

We drove in silence for a while. When I glanced over, I noticed he was wearing a new suit. "Nice suit, Martin," I said casually.

"What? Oh, yeah. Thanks."

Martin was shorter than I was.

"Does it come in men's sizes?" I asked, shooting him a glance.

He laughed, shaking his head. "That was a good one . . . *old-timer!*"

It was one of Martin's familiar rejoinders. FBI agents can retire after twenty years of service once they've reached the age of fifty. Because of this, most agents are in their twenties and thirties. I had just turned forty-four and was beginning to be called an old-timer.

"You know what they say about being over the hill?" I asked.

Martin hadn't heard this one before. "Go ahead," he answered, knowing I would anyway.

"You pick up speed!"

Martin and I sometimes talked about homosexuality. His cultural heritage and religion predisposed him to look upon it negatively. Yet I sometimes wondered if Martin suspected I was gay because of my interest in, knowledge of, and positive attitude toward the subject. He never asked me about it. It seemed that heterosexual men, especially male FBI agents, were usually uncomfortable talking about their personal lives. Many of my gay friends, by way of contrast, were much more at ease discussing these matters.

Since it was a Friday, Martin and I planned to tie up loose ends. Yet shortly after our arrival at the office, a voice came over the PA saying, "Attention! Attention all employees! Please do not leave the office until further notice!"

I put down my coffee cup and spotted a relief supervisor coming out of her office. She looked tense. Our squad gathered around her.

"There's been a bombing," she said. She also wanted to know if all of us had heard of Captain Will Rogers III and what happened in the Persian Gulf the year before. It would have been difficult to live in San Diego and *not* know about Rogers or his ship.

Captain Rogers was skipper of the USS *Vincennes,* an Aegis-guided-missile cruiser on patrol in the Persian Gulf in July 1988. Iran and Iraq were at war, and the ayatollah Khomeini was making bellicose statements about the United States. Tensions were at a fever pitch, and everybody was edgy. Suddenly the captain and crew thought a Iranian fighter plane was dive-bombing toward it. The *Vincennes* opened fire and scored a direct hit. Within hours the world was shocked to learn that the plane was civilian and all 290 people on board had been killed.

The *Vincennes* returned from the Persian Gulf in October 1988 and docked at its home port of San Diego. The captain and crew were immediately besieged by reporters, and interest further intensified. Pan Am Flight 103 exploded over Lockerbie, Scotland, in December. All 270 people, including a large number of college students returning home for Christmas vacation, were killed. It was suspected to be the work of terrorists linked to Iran.

Our supervisor now advised us that shortly after 7:30 A.M. a van had caught fire at the intersection of La Jolla Village Drive and Genesee Avenue. The driver was Sharon Rogers, en route to her teaching job. "The San Diego Police Department initially thought it was a routine vehicular fire," the supervisor said, "but after they determined the identity of Mrs. Rogers and examined the van more closely, they now believe the fire was caused by a bomb."

Our squad was handling terrorism investigations. I thought about the Sandini car bombing.

We were told that San Diego police had contacted both the Naval Intelligence Service and the FBI. The NIS was contacted because Rogers was in the Navy; the FBI because the bombing could be the work of terrorists.

Somebody asked if Mrs. Rogers had been injured.

"She heard a loud noise and got out. That's when the van went up in flames. She and her husband are together and under the protection of the police department."

We were told to stand by for further instructions. I walked over to Martin and put my hand on his shoulder. "This is serious," I said.

I explained to Martin that headquarters might put our office in charge of the investigation because the crime occurred within our jurisdiction. And if it did, we would have to coordinate the investigation among the State Department, the Department of Defense, the CIA, the rest of the intelligence community, and perhaps even the White House. President Reagan had responded to Libyan-sponsored terrorism by bombing Libya. If the van bombing could be linked to Iran, we might possibly expect the same kind of response.

Support staff personnel hurriedly carried supplies and equipment to the command post, which was a large conference room easily converted into the office crisis center. I stayed at my desk awaiting assignment. Before long I was told to report to the command post.

The looks on people's faces and the noise there demonstrated the gravity of the situation. Questions, information, and possible leads poured in from other law enforcement agencies and the public. I was reaching for one of the many ringing phones when I felt a hand on my shoulder. It was Tom Kuker. Though he seldom showed any emotion, there was intensity in his eyes, too. "Frank," he said, "Keep track of all the information that's coming in, and get it organized. We'll need to prepare a summary teletype for headquarters." Considering all that was happening to me, it felt good to know I was trusted in a crisis situation.

Preparing the summary teletype was critical to the investigation. It would also be our link to the outside investigative world. My job was to evaluate and prioritize the avalanche of information, leads, and strategies pouring in. Once that was done, I had to get the approval of every supervisor responsible for each specialized area of the investigation. I would ultimately have to get Kuker's and Hughes's signatures before sending the teletype.

A new summary teletype was prepared each day. It was transmitted to FBI headquarters and all field offices nationwide. From headquarters it would go to State, Defense, the CIA, etc., *and* the White House.

I had a breather later in the day and left a message on Brian's answering machine, canceling our plans for the evening. I said I would try him again by phone as soon as I had the chance.

Media coverage of the bombing was extraordinary. A television set in the command post brought us live TV coverage from the bomb site. Brian would no doubt hear the news and, having been in the military, would be well aware of its significance in terms of the national interest.

That first day ended for those of us in the command post at about midnight. We worked through the weekend and continued working at twelve- to fourteen-hour days, seven days a week. My particular job became even more demanding as the investigation broadened and lengthened. Few agents would want to do what I was doing. Sometimes I felt like a one-man newspaper operation with a daily deadline to meet—and some of the most important readers in the world.

The Rogers investigation dominated my life throughout March and April 1989. Though Brian and I talked on the phone whenever there was an opportunity, I seldom saw him or anybody else during that time.

I was working closely with Hughes and Kuker in the command post, and they never mentioned the administrative inquiry or OPR's investigation of W. J. I thought maybe my work on the Rogers case had caused headquarters to reconsider the entire matter. I was even more optimistic when, in late April, I was asked to be one of the agents in charge of the investigation.

14.

Kuker entered the command post the morning of May 1 and asked me to join him in his office. I closed the door behind us.

"I just received a call from Ray Arras," Kuker said, remaining standing. "He wants you to call him immediately. Apparently they want you to fly back to Washington tomorrow."

"Did they find W. J.?"

Kuker shook his head. "But other things have come up."

"I really wonder if all this is worth it, Tom," I said. I don't know why, but before leaving, I shook Kuker's hand.

I called Arras from an interview room, and he said OPR wanted to talk to me about a nude photograph.

"A nude photograph?" I said sarcastically. "You've got to be kidding."

"We'll talk about it when you get back here. There are some other things we also need to discuss."

Brian said later, "They're just harassing you, Frank. After how hard you've been working the last two months, this is ridiculous! You don't need them; they need you! Why don't you just tell them to go to hell?"

Maybe I was just tired, but Brian seemed more upset than I was.

The two of us had seen very little of each other in a long, long time now. The Rogers investigation and the OPR investigation were taking an emotional toll on me. Brian was busy with school and work and seemed tired of the FBI's dominating our lives. I knew very little of what was going on in his life, and there didn't seem to be enough time to find out. Neither did I have the energy.

I left my house at 6:30 A.M. the following day and arrived in Washington around 5:00 P.M. There wasn't even time to talk to Tom Homann before leaving. Why, I wondered, was there such urgency after months of bureau silence? And was it important enough to take me away from the Rogers case, considered at the time one of the most important in FBI history?

In contrast with the cold weather I had experienced on my last trip to Washington, spring had definitely arrived. It was sunny and warm, and the cherry blossoms were in bloom. I was reminded how much I liked this city.

I had taken my parents to Washington in the summer of 1965. It was one of their few vacations from work in the factory, and I was a twenty-year-old about to enter my junior year of college. My parents both had to drop out of high school to work. While they never made much money, my father would say—more as a blessing than a boast—that we had all we needed: food, clothes, a roof over our head, and good health.

It was the first time any of us had ever been to Washington, and my mother looked like a schoolgirl as we walked up the front steps of the Capitol. "It's so beautiful," she said, her face flushed with emotion. "I've seen pictures of this ever since I was a little girl, but I never thought I would see it in person."

■ ■ ■

Ray Arras and I shook hands in the reception area of OPR at nine the following morning. He said that Sandra Fowler had been transferred to another office and another agent would be taking her place. As we walked to the interview room, I noticed that he didn't seem as friendly as before. I thought perhaps it was because he would be the lead agent now. The lead agent was responsible for the overall interview, and Arras seemed nervous.

We waited in silence a few minutes, and then SA Brad Benson came in. He identified himself as a supervisor in the Security Programs Unit. I had never heard of it before, but then again there were many units at headquarters I didn't know about.

Benson was about my age, taller than I was, and seemed to have a friendly, sincere manner. He advised me that he was taking part in the interview because of bureau concern about my trustworthiness regarding national security. This surprised me. I thought I had satisfied these concerns. I wondered if something new had come up in this regard.

I signed the same forms as before, and the questioning began.

Arras summarized my previous signed statements. He then said the bureau was curious as to why I had never told my parents and family I was gay, how I met other gay people, and what pressures I felt leading a secret life in the bureau.

I did the best I could. I saw how difficult it was trying to explain these matters to heterosexual FBI agents. They didn't understand me and my world.

I said I hadn't told my parents basically because I didn't want to worry them. I told them once again that I met other gay people basically through mutual friends and gay personals. I said I had adjusted to my life as a gay agent, and the main pressure I felt over the years was that the FBI would fire me if it found out.

Arras was called from the room, and Benson and I began talking informally. We had joined the bureau around the same time, and in the course of our conversation he mentioned that he was married with children. In a good-natured way he told me he had been asked in 1974 what he would do when the first gay FBI agent came forward and wanted to keep working for the bureau. He had jokingly replied, "I hope to be retired by then."

We laughed, but then he became more serious. "You're our worst nightmare. You're bright, articulate, and a good agent. The question is whether we can trust you."

"Why not treat me as if I were an applicant and conduct a thorough investigation to resolve that issue?" I said. "Plus, as opposed to an applicant you know very little about, I have almost twenty years of proof that I'm trustworthy."

Arras came into the room at that point, and we resumed the interview.

Benson asked if I had written the letters myself, implying that I might be having a mid-life crisis.

I couldn't help smiling. "No, Brad. I may be a little masochistic, but not that much. Not to go through all this."

Arras wanted to know why I hadn't told Hughes at the outset about the note to my parents, and I said again I hadn't viewed the letter as threatening, only mean. When asked if my homosexuality affected my work, I answered no, even though I wanted to tell them that the OPR sessions were the only things affecting my work.

"We would like the names of your homosexual friends and associates," Benson asked.

I had expected the bureau eventually to ask this question. I knew that the CIA, the Naval Intelligence Service, and other agencies and branches of the military services routinely asked gay people to reveal the names of their homosexual friends. I thought of the McCarthy era and its destructiveness. I thought about what naming names would do to my friends—those not out to family, friends, or employers.

If I didn't answer the question, the bureau could fire me for being uncooperative.

"I will not give you their names without their permission," I said, and perhaps sensing my resolve, they didn't challenge me. I made a note that the bureau did not ask for the names of my heterosexual friends.

The interrogation abruptly shifted to the investigation of W. J.

"We haven't been able to determine who wrote the W. J. letters," Arras said. "However, we did interview two people. One lives in San Diego; the other, in the Midwest."

Arras gave me their names. I recognized one as the name of the person I wrote to at the Del Mar address, but I didn't recognize the second name.

"They said they don't know you," Arras added. "And both denied writing the letters to your parents and the bureau."

Arras said the man in the Midwest had placed his ad in a gay magazine in 1986. He was living in Del Mar at the time and received several responses. "He said one of the people who wrote him sent a nude photograph. It was of a white male, approximately in his forties, from the shoulders to the knees."

This was infuriating. Was I going to have to defend myself against every crazy accusation that came along? "Can I see the photo?" I asked, trying to remain calm.

Arras said the man no longer had it.

"If this person doesn't know me, and the photograph didn't show anyone's face, why are you asking me about this? That description probably matches millions of men—including you, Ray."

Neither Benson nor Arras responded, and I said I wanted the record to show that "I have never had a nude photograph taken of me, nor would I ever send such a photograph to anyone."

Arras and I ate lunch together in the cafeteria afterward. Despite the questioning and the anger of that morning, he reminded me of so many others in the bureau I knew and liked. At one point in our conversation he talked about the class-action suit Latino agents had filed against the bureau. The suit, which charged the FBI with ethnic and religious discrimination, was making headlines across the country. Arras said he had joined the FBI in 1977, and I told him that when I joined in 1969, there had been few Latinos, African-Americans, or other minorities—and no female agents. "A lot of that was due to Hoover's prejudices against minorities."

We talked more, and I added, "Even though there's a lawsuit going on regarding the treatment of Latinos, at least you're allowed to be agents. I'm fighting for my career because I'm part of a minority that is being discriminated against with governmental approval. In the past, Ray, people justified excluding minorities from certain jobs by saying they weren't capable of performing the job. If the bureau won't allow gay people to be agents, how can we prove we can do the job?"

It was time to go back.

"I really think the bureau should judge people as individuals and not by some negative stereotype," I said.

Benson joined us in the interview room.

"The man in the Midwest says he moved from the address quite a while before you told us you wrote him," Arras began.

I said maybe the person had vacated the address, and his mail was being forwarded. I reminded them that a second letter had been returned.

"Did the bureau find out who made the credit inquiry last May?" I asked, and Arras shook his head no.

"They checked with the company, but there wasn't any way of determining who made the inquiry or why it was made. They also had no record of your doing business with them."

"If you tell me more about these two guys or show me photographs of them," I said, "maybe I'll recognize them."

It's not standard procedure to photograph people we interview, but they could have gotten their photographs from driver's license records. No handwriting exemplars were taken from these two individuals. While the bureau checked the note for the fingerprints of one of them, it hadn't checked for the other. I asked about these things and other details of the investigation and began to wonder if the bureau was only going through the motions. Its focus was on me, not these two individuals, and the bureau had resolved precious little in the investigation.

The interview ended early that afternoon, and Arras said the statement would be ready for signing the following morning. I left the building and tried to find a quiet place to be alone with my thoughts. The apparently poor job the bureau had done with the W. J. investigation was dispiriting. I had been counting on the investigation to help resolve many of the bureau's concerns. That we were going back over the same issues we had gone over several times before did, in fact, feel like harassment to me.

I entered a public library and found an isolated spot. I took out my notes. This might be the last statement I would ever sign for the FBI. I wanted to commit something to writing. Everett had been right. There was no end to the bureau's questions.

When I was done writing about an hour later, I called Everett. He was living in San Diego now. I told him about the OPR interview, and he was as disappointed as I was that the bureau had failed to determine the identity of W. J.

"It sounds like they're trying to wear you down so you'll quit," he said. "That they'll continue to harass you like this until you eventually resign."

I told him that these were my feelings, too, and that I had written something for the record. I asked if he would mind listening.

When I finished reading the statement, he whistled. "Good for you. You've come a long way since December," he said. Before hanging up, he asked where I was calling from. I told him I wasn't sure but described the library's location.

"That's the Martin Luther King Public Library. How appropriate."

■ ■ ■

"There's something I would like to add," I said to Arras and Benson the following morning. I handed them what I had written. My statement concluded with the words "I will not resign from the Bureau. If I lose my job because of this issue, I will seriously consider reinstatement through the courts. I believe a person's sexual orientation has nothing to do with their ability to do their job."

I had volunteered to take another polygraph, and Arras asked if I wanted the same polygraph examiner as before. I said I preferred somebody else, and he didn't ask me why. Arras called the polygraph unit, but he was told everyone there was extremely busy. I would have to wait until the following morning. I told Arras I would make arrangements to fly out early the following afternoon, and he said that would be fine because the polygraph wouldn't take long.

I was disappointed at not being able to return home that night but decided to make the best of my stay in Washington. It was still a beautiful day, and after changing clothes at the hotel, I went on a walking tour of the city.

I visited the Lincoln Memorial, then headed toward the Vietnam Memorial. I thought about how my brothers and I had been spared from this tragedy. Tony had been discharged from the Army before the war began, and Lou had been a conscientious objector. Though I was politically opposed to the war, I had passed my physical and would have served if drafted. Later my draft number in the lottery came up very high, and I also received deferments for teaching and then for being an FBI agent. Sometimes, though, I felt I should have volunteered to fight.

Nearing the Vietnam Memorial, I saw the new statue I had heard so much about. It was of three American soldiers, and something in their appearance made it seem as though they were about to turn in the direction of the wall, as if they were going to see the names on the wall for the first time. I was struck by how young the faces were in the statue but then remembered that the average age of those whose names were on the wall was nineteen.

As I neared the wall itself, I could see my reflection in the shiny black granite. Tears formed as I noticed others crying or laying flowers and baseball caps and letters on the grass at its base. I put my hand on the wall and said a prayer for all those who had died, for their families and loved ones, and for the gaping hole it had left in the life of this country.

I walked past the Washington Monument, the Smithsonian buildings, and the Capitol. Ray Arras had suggested I visit Union Station. I hadn't seen the inside of the building since sight-seeing in 1969, and the restoration was beautiful. I toured the shops and exhibits and took the escalator to the roof, which had been made available to sight-seers. Nobody was on the roof but me.

I walked to the southwest corner and marveled at the beauty all around me. I thought about my problems with the bureau and about how much I loved my job. I loved this country, too, and would never betray it or my badge. I looked around and was still alone. I softly began to sing the words to "The Star-Spangled Banner."

15.

I met Arras at headquarters the following morning, and he escorted me to the polygraph unit. A few minutes after we arrived, a man came out of a back office and introduced himself as Bill Teigen. He was about my age and height and a little overweight. I vaguely recalled having met him before.

Arras went back to Teigen's office with him. I browsed through a magazine and waited. I wondered what was taking so long. Almost an hour went by, and I didn't think I was going to be able to make my afternoon flight. I just wanted to go home.

They both came out, and Arras said good-bye. Teigen led me to the same room used by Morgovnik in December. It was about 10:30 A.M. now.

I told Teigen about my one o'clock flight, and we went back to his office. I made reservations for a later time. We returned to the room, and Teigen moved his chair so that he was sitting opposite, and close to, mine, just as Morgovnik had done.

Teigen asked how I felt, and I responded that the room made me a little claustrophobic, but that I would be all right. The room seemed much warmer than it had been in December. I took off my jacket and tie and rolled up my shirt sleeves. Teigen left his jacket on.

I signed the forms again, and then Teigen put them away. Looking at me, he said, "I want you to know I find homosexuality offensive."

I thought it was a strange way to start a supposedly objective test and didn't know how to take it. I waited, aware of the presence of the video camera in the corner of the room near the ceiling. It was pointing squarely at me. I reminded myself to be careful and keep my emotions under control.

Teigen then said he found it hard to believe that my first homosexual experience had occurred in 1974. There had to be "precursors," he argued, and began with questions about my adolescent years. I said I remembered horsing around with another boy as a teenager and being surprised when I climaxed, but that was about it. Teigen bore in at that point, wanting all the details. He didn't believe that what had happened had been accidental or that the other boy had been unaware of what was going on.

I explained to him that I didn't realize I was gay until five years after joining the bureau. "Otherwise," I said, "I would not have applied."

Teigen went back to questions covering my adolescent years. He said that I could have been blackmailed or exploited by the other boy.

I thought this was preposterous. "First of all, we were teenagers, Bill. No one ever tried to blackmail me about it, and a teenager having that kind of experience is not all that uncommon. It doesn't mean you're gay."

He asked how I met the person with whom I had had my first homosexual experience in 1974 and what kind of sex we had engaged in. I answered, wary of him now.

"You would have been killed in 1974 in the [FBI] squad bay in Birmingham, Alabama," Teigen said matter-of-factly. "If you said, 'I just answered an ad in a gay magazine and went and had a guy jerk me off in Los Angeles,' you'd be killed. Literally, I think you'd be killed. I think that would have happened."

I said it might have been true in 1974, but times had changed. I told him I wasn't afraid of something like that happening. "My only fear is getting fired from the bureau for being gay."

It was close to noon, and I wondered when we would start the questions. He didn't appear to be in a hurry. In fact, he couldn't get off that 1974 date.

"I can't imagine the light going on in 1974, and you saying, 'I'm homosexual.'"

I did my best to explain that it wasn't a light—but more of a dimmer switch. "A dimmer switch that's turned down low. There's just a little light, and that's the light of homosexuality. Discovering my homosexuality was an evolutionary process."

He began to argue with me about this point, and I explained that it was common for gay people to become aware of their sexual orientation at different times in their lives. I had friends, I said, who knew they were gay when they were five years old and others who were in their thirties or forties before realizing it. "A few were even married with children," I added, thinking of Everett.

Teigen went back to my adolescence; only this time his language became crude. He talked about "coming" and "jerking off," asking for details of my "ejaculations." He interrupted himself at one point, saying he wasn't being "perverted" talking about such things. "I'm asking you these things so that I can ask the right questions during the polygraph," he said, but I wasn't sure if it was for my benefit or that of the camera.

Teigen wanted to go over my sexual experiences one more time from high school to the present. I glanced at my watch. Prepolygraph interviews were usually brief, and most of that time was spent drawing up questions. He turned his attention to my high school teaching career, and I immediately sensed where he was going. I got up from the chair. I looked at the one-way mirror, then turned to face him. "I have no sexual interest in children, Bill. I have already gone through all this with OPR." I wanted to stop there but couldn't quite do it. "I don't have a problem answering that question or any other question. But Bill—I mean—do I have to go through every page of my life? How many pages of my forty-four-year life on this earth do I have to open up to the bureau? How much of my personal life does the bureau need to know? It just all gets too personal."

He didn't answer, just watched, as Morgovnik had done.

"Where does it end?" I said, angrily. "I can never satisfy all the bureau's concerns about my homosexuality. Fire me or let me do my job! Come on, let's get on with this thing. Put me on the box, and ask me the questions. You know, it gets to a point of torturing me."

I was pacing back and forth, getting more and more angry. "Why do I have to defend myself? I haven't done anything wrong. I didn't commit any crimes. All I am is homosexual. I mean, that's all. And I'm a good agent and I do a good job."

I told him that I had thought about quitting the bureau, that I had thought about finding out who was behind all this and handling it my own way. I stopped pacing. "Carmen Basilio is from my hometown, and he was a boyhood hero of mine. Basilio didn't quit no matter how tough it got in the ring, and I'm not going to quit either. I want you to know that. My father said if you're right, stand up for your rights—and that's what I'm going to do."

I couldn't control the tears that spilled from my eyes. "How do I convince you that it's all right to be homosexual? That I believe it's all right to be homosexual?"

"It'll never happen, Frank," Teigen responded. His voice sounded condescending. He then added that I had probably found some relief in talking with him about this, especially in identifying that my homosexuality started before 1974. He told me it was "healthy" for me to talk about it.

I exploded. "I don't have to explain it to somebody else to get it off my chest! It wasn't on my chest!"

I felt spent and sat down in the chair. Teigen began talking about meeting me in San Diego. I now remembered meeting him in our office but didn't remember much about it. That seemed to upset him.

"You sat forward in your chair, and you sat with your elbows on your knees. You were talking to me almost nose to nose, toes to toes. It was inappropriate behavior."

I shrugged. I didn't know what the hell he was talking about. I told him that another agent and I were about to conduct a very important interview in the Rogers case. "My mind was on that," I said. "Besides, there were four of us in a very small room."

He seemed obsessed with the incident. "I was offended by your behavior because now in hindsight I'm thinking, *That son of a bitch was leaning forward on me and closing in on my body space.*"

I gave him a disbelieving look.

He said I was trying to make him feel uncomfortable because I remembered him from the polygraph office the previous December. I told him I didn't recall seeing him when Morgovnik polygraphed me.

Teigen asked questions about my correspondence with W. J., and I was surprised that he knew so little about it. Having calmed down somewhat, I walked him through its details. He asked the same questions in this regard that others had asked.

It felt as if it were never going to end, as if every time a new person in the bureau came along, I'd have to go all over it again. I got up from the chair. "Why is the bureau unable to determine W. J.'s identity?" I asked. "Don't you think the bureau should find out who the hell this guy is? I mean, doesn't the bureau protect its own? Does it leave its dead out there?"

He responded slowly, as if he were giving a speech. "We're a powerful organization. And the only reason we're successful is because we band together. Our strengths outweigh the weaknesses of the people we're investigating. That's why we, as FBI employees, don't like to know that somebody we're working with is going through bankruptcy. We don't like to know that somebody we're working with has extramarital affairs that are private and secret from their family, that's costing family money. . . . We don't like to know about people being homosexuals. Because once again that's a distraction from our strength.''

I interrupted, telling him his reasoning might be true for some but not all FBI agents. He didn't acknowledge my remark.

"We don't enjoy somebody outside the organization knowing the weaknesses in our organization,'' he was saying. "We are the premier law enforcement agency in the country. We don't have to pull out our guns and shoot 'em in order to get something done. We just say we're the FBI. That's why there aren't a lot of gunfights.''

"We've been very fortunate,'' I said, nodding, but part of me wondered when was the last time this guy had pulled a gun on somebody. I had put my life on the line numerous times, and Teigen was telling *me* about danger?

"But if everybody knows our weaknesses, then we're going to have to go in with our guns out and they're going to have to be blazing. And we're going to have to be the FBI because we've got more firepower.''

I interrupted again. "When you're talking about weaknesses, are you talking about homosexuality?''

"I'm talking about *any* weakness.''

"Do you feel homosexuality is a weakness, Bill? Being that we have homosexual agents?''

"I don't know that we have homosexual agents,'' he said angrily. "I know that we have a homosexual agent.''

Sandra Fowler had told me the first day of questioning that OPR investigated one case per week involving homosexual employees. As a polygraph examiner Teigen would likely have known about this and may even had polygraphed some of these people. But, I thought, maybe gay employees were forced to resign long before this stage.

Teigen returned to questions about my teenage sexual experiences. I listened and told him simply that it's difficult to pinpoint exactly when you are sure you're homosexual.

Teigen began talking about his own personal sexual experiences.

"Were there any guys, Bill?'' I asked, laughing, and Teigen's face seemed to flush with anger. "Bill, I was only kidding.''

"No, you're not kidding. There were no guys!''

Teigen asked if the other boy I was with was homosexual.

"I've seen him since then, and I'm sure he's not gay.''

"What's his name, Frank?''

"We were young kids, Bill. I'm not going to tell you his name."

It was almost one-thirty, and we had been at it for three hours. I told Teigen I was tired and hungry. As we both stood up, I looked him directly in the eyes. "If I have to get up before the office in San Diego and say I'm homosexual, I can do that. I'm not afraid of that. If I've got to go to court and say I'm homosexual and I was an FBI agent, I may—I may do that. I don't know. I'm not trying to threaten the bureau, but somebody has to have the courage to stand up and say, 'Hey, you know, this is wrong. This is wrong. I'm homosexual, and I'm a good agent.' "

I left the building. My shirt was wet with perspiration. I ordered a sandwich and soda at a nearby deli. The air conditioning felt good. All I wanted was to go home.

I returned a half hour later, and Teigen went back over areas he claimed not to understand. We finally began to draw up questions for the polygraph. Then Teigen hooked up the electrodes and strapped me in. He told me to sit absolutely still. As hard as I tried, I couldn't conjure up peaceful images of the canyon, or Rusty, or me.

Teigen asked me the same questions several times, each time changing their order: "Have you ever mailed a photograph of a nude male to anyone?"; "Since you have been an FBI agent, has anyone, with your full knowledge, taken a photograph of you in the nude?"; "Are you purposely concealing the true identity of W. J. from me today?"; and "Have you purposely lied to me when answering any one of my polygraph questions on this test?"

I answered each question no and when we finished, it was about three-thirty. Teigen unstrapped me and took off the wires. He told me to wait in the room while he left to review the charts. As I waited, I wondered if Teigen, or others, were watching me from behind the one-way mirror. I closed my eyes and tried to rest.

Teigen was gone for a long while, but when he returned, he seemed friendlier then before. He started talking about the Rogers investigation and said he had some ideas he would call me about the following week. I thought I had passed the test and this was the reason for his current behavior.

He spread the polygraph charts out on the table. "I've carefully examined your responses to all the questions, and they all are indicative of deception."

He continued talking, about the questions, height lines, and technical aspects of the test, but I couldn't really hear him. My mind was spinning.

I had just told the truth and was told it was a lie! Teigen began to ask more questions, about W. J., my personal life, and my conduct as an agent. Each of my answers led to more questions.

I thought he was going to conduct another polygraph, but he didn't say anything about it. He told me that he had already contacted Ray Arras and that OPR would need to talk to me about the polygraph results and the new information I had provided. I looked at my watch. It was 5:20 P.M., and I had missed my flight.

As we walked toward the door, Teigen stopped and said he hoped I didn't feel degraded by the questioning. I stared at him but said nothing. I wanted to punch the bastard out.

Arras was on the phone with Teigen when I arrived. A female agent had been brought in to act as a witness. Another stranger would know intimate details of my personal life.

Arras said reservations for a 7:20 P.M. flight back to San Diego had been made. He wanted to know, however, if I preferred staying the weekend and finishing the statement on Monday. It was almost six o'clock. I said we could probably finish in time.

Arras asked me a few more questions as he prepared a handwritten statement. He included information I had provided Teigen, and I stated I had not lied on the polygraph. After signing the statement, I hurried from the building. It was raining, and I flagged down a cab. I told the driver to hurry and arrived at the airport ten minutes before the plane's departure.

But the plane was delayed, so I tried to call Brian. He wasn't at home, and I reached Everett. I asked if he would mind contacting Brian to pick me up. Everett asked how things had gone, and I started to tell him about the polygraph but had to cut the story short. The plane was about to begin boarding again.

It was close to midnight before I arrived in San Diego, and the airport was deserted. As I walked down a long hallway, I was glad to see Brian and Everett waiting for me. I was glad they both were there. They were quiet on the way home, and I assumed Everett had told Brian that things had not gone well on the polygraph.

Rusty and Jake, Brian's German shepherd, were excited when we got home, and Rusty kept jumping on me as I tried to get a beer from the refrigerator. Brian and Everett were already sitting in the living room, and I joined them.

''I was disappointed the bureau had not identified W. J., but I thought everything was going pretty well until today,'' I said. I told them about Teigen and the questions I had been asked about my personal life. ''The room was so hot I could hardly breathe. And when it was over, Teigen said I had lied on every question.''

Neither one of them said anything. I took out the signed statement and began reading. I looked up. ''This was the worst day of my life,'' I said, and then started to cry. I got up from my chair and started walking around the room, talking and crying at the same time. I'm not sure what I said or how much time passed before I finally regained my composure. I apologized to Brian and Everett for putting them through all this.

Before leaving, Everett hugged me and said he loved me. ''You need to get some rest.''

It was nearly 2:00 A.M. when I stepped out of the shower. I kept scrubbing, as if the sweat and dirt were inches thick. Brian was in bed, and the light was off.

''Are you still awake?'' I whispered as I lay beside him. He said that he was. Brian was on his side with his back toward me, and I put my arm around him. I moved closer to him. ''I'm glad you're here,'' I whispered.

He didn't respond, and after a while he was asleep. I took my arm away and moved toward my side of the bed.

I didn't think I could handle another day like that one. The thought of suicide crossed my mind—fleetingly, like a swallow passing through the sky. I prayed for this nightmare to end. Sometime before dawn I slept.

16.

I usually looked forward to going to work, but not that Monday morning. I stood in the shower longer than usual. I thought about calling in sick. Instead my brother's words came back to me about going on anyway.

The command post agents greeted me warmly, and I was glad I had decided to go in. The usual joking and other small talk ended when Hughes and Kuker entered the room. I observed them carefully, looking for some sign that they were aware of Friday's polygraph results. But both offered their customary "good morning," sat down, and the meeting began. The first order of business was a review of the previous week's investigation.

Because the investigation was massive, we continued to identify suspects other than Iranian terrorists. We had information on dozens of people and groups that might be responsible. Some lived in San Diego, but others were from other parts of the country or world. While our investigation eliminated some of these suspects, we still weren't sure of others. A long list of suspects meant more work, but there was nothing worse for investigators than having no suspects at all.

Two months had passed since the van bombing, and the investigation remained a major national priority for the bureau. Initially most of San Diego's two hundred employees were involved full-time on the case. Though several people, including me, remained full-time on the case, most of the others now began to assist on a part-time basis. In spite of our efforts, it was extremely frustrating not to have solved the case. We all were apprehensive that the bombing was the beginning of a terrorist campaign directed against American citizens in this country.

I stopped in to see Kuker later that morning and asked if he had heard about Friday's polygraph results. He said no, so I told him a little about what happened. I asked if I could see a photograph of the two individuals he had investigated, and his response caught me completely off guard.

"You wouldn't recognize them, Frank, and they wouldn't recognize you. It's not physically possible that they know each other or that they know you."

I felt uneasy. OPR questioned me about sending a nude photograph to one of the men. Teigen said I was deceptive about knowing W. J. What did Kuker know that made him so sure of what he had told me? Why the continuing questions and judgments of me?

I called Teigen's office the next morning, as he had requested. He greeted me and talked in what seemed like an overly friendly manner, acting as if nothing had happened. He asked that I write down my thoughts about the polygraph so that he could improve his skills.

I called Tom Homann and told him about the week at headquarters. It was the first time I heard anger in his voice. "Had I known they were going to get into all of that, I would have insisted you not take the polygraph."

I told him about Teigen and said I felt like writing him to tell him exactly what I thought.

"That's a bad idea," Homann advised. "Don't have any more to do with him. Nothing at all."

I called the polygraph unit back and left a message that I would not be sending the letter Teigen had requested.

When I got home the following evening after work, I didn't feel hungry. I took Rusty for a walk in the canyon. The San Diego Padres were playing later that night on television, and I planned to spend a quiet, relaxing evening at home watching the game.

It was a beautiful spring evening, and the normally dry creek bed in the canyon had flowing water from a recent rain. But my mind was swirling with thoughts and emotions, and I began to feel dizzy. I called Rusty, walked quickly back to the truck, and hurried home.

I didn't turn on the baseball game and tried to read the paper. I couldn't concentrate, and I couldn't focus on the pages. I couldn't figure out what was happening to me. I was becoming even more nervous and uneasy. I got up from the chair and paced. I was having difficulty breathing, which made me more anxious.

I dialed Brian's number, but he wasn't in. Neither was Everett. I desperately needed to talk with someone I trusted. I took out my address book and flipped through the pages. I decided to call a psychologist friend in San Francisco. He answered on the second ring. We hadn't talked in nearly a year, but it didn't take him long to get to the point. "Are you all right, Frank?"

I hesitated for a moment. "No. No, I'm not."

I struggled to control my emotions and tried to explain what was happening with the bureau, but it became confused and jumbled. He nevertheless listened patiently, and when I was finished, he began to speak in a calm, reassuring manner. I don't remember much of what he said or his advice, but when our conversation ended, I felt more at ease.

I felt better the following day. Then, at our 4:00 P.M. conference in the command post, I found my mind wandering. I was normally upbeat and encouraging at these meetings, but whenever I spoke, it always seemed to be in a negative way. The meeting ended, and I quickly left the room. I got a cup of coffee, went into one of the interview rooms, and locked the door behind me.

For months I had been insisting—to OPR, Hughes, and Kuker—that my personal life never interfered with my work. But that afternoon I had been ineffectual. I didn't know if anyone else noticed, but I was embarrassed by my performance. For the first time I thought seriously about resigning.

Brian and Everett were more aware than others about what I was experiencing, yet Brian had gotten even busier at school and work. I also didn't know if the way I was feeling would frighten him. In the past he had often expressed his admiration for the way I coped with problems. I didn't know if he wanted to see a side of me that was weak, vulnerable, and a little scared.

It had become much easier to talk with Everett about these matters now. Perhaps it was because he was older and more experienced or because I hadn't been romantically involved with him. Everett seemed to offer advice that helped. I called him and asked if we could talk that evening. I suggested we meet for dinner at DiMille's on Adams Avenue in Normal Heights.

The restaurant reminded me of the one in Miami the other agents and I had frequented during the Mitrione investigation. Italian food, red wine, and that particular ambiance always seemed to raise my spirits—perhaps because it reminded me of home.

Everett was waiting outside when I arrived. As usual, DiMille's was crowded and noisy. It was one of the reasons I had chosen the place; our conversation would get lost in the din of other voices.

"It's my treat, Everett," I said as we looked at the menu. "Live it up."

I was trying to make out that I was a big spender, but Everett would have none of it.

"You *should* be treating me," he said with a laugh. "I'm on a fixed income!"

"And I may be without *any* income soon!"

I ordered a small carafe of wine, poured myself a glass, and took a sip as Everett watched. Perhaps because he was a minister, or just a good friend, he already seemed to know the purpose of my call.

"Frank, I've never seen you like you were Friday night. I've thought a lot about you the past few days. Tell me what's happened since Friday."

"Well," I began slowly, "I planned to go in to work over the weekend but didn't. I also couldn't motivate myself to do any of the things I normally enjoy doing on the weekend. I didn't think very much about Teigen," I said, and then shook my head. "This has not been a very good week for me, Everett."

I did most of the talking during dinner. Everett nodded occasionally but asked very few questions. I told him about my difficulty in concentrating, both at work and at home. "It seemed like I couldn't connect with the others, including Brian. Last weekend, for the first time since I've known him, I felt emotionally distant from him. It was almost as if we were strangers. He must have felt the same way because he didn't stay with me Sunday night, and I haven't talked to him since."

As we finished our dinner, I said, "In the last few days I've been feeling depressed. That's unusual for me." I looked around and then leaned forward. "It bothers me that I don't seem to be in control of my emotions, Everett."

The waitress cleared the dishes from the table. I knew Everett would be direct and honest. That was another reason why I had called him. He seemed more gentle than usual, though, when he began to speak.

"For twenty years the FBI has been a family to you, Frank. And you have experienced the joys and sorrows that come from being a member of that family. But last week was different. Last week your family turned on you."

He cleared his throat. I glanced around. A lot of time had passed, and the restaurant had become fairly empty. Everett looked around and lowered his voice. Leaning toward me, he said, "Last week, Frank, you were raped by a member of your family."

I let out a small groan, and Everett paused, perhaps searching for different words.

"It wasn't a physical rape. It was psychological. But because it was psychological doesn't mean it was any less traumatic for you. At first you blocked it out, but now you're dealing with the trauma of what was done to you."

I hadn't thought about Teigen in those terms, and it all started to come back now: the hours answering questions in that small, hot room; Teigen's condescending attitude; his gutter language. I couldn't control the tears that meandered slowly down my face. I turned away, and Everett reached over and gently touched my arm. "Your response doesn't mean you're weak, Frank. It means you're human."

The waitress brought the bill, and I picked it up. Everett wasn't finished. "Teigen didn't act that way on his own. I think the bureau encouraged him to treat you that way so you would resign."

"I expect to be fired at any moment, Everett. This week, for the first time, I've seriously considered resigning."

"You need to get therapy, Frank, just as if you were the victim of a rape. Otherwise it's going to affect your work, and they'll fire you for that. Get some professional help before you make any decisions about resigning."

As we stood up, Everett added, "And at some point, Frank, you will need to forgive Teigen."

The following morning, while working in the command post, I received a phone call from FBI headquarters. The caller identified himself by name. He was a headquarters supervisor and asked to speak to me in private. I had the call transferred to one of the interview rooms.

"I felt so bad about what happened to you on Friday," the caller began. "I felt so bad that I almost called you at your home over the weekend."

I closed my eyes. Thank God somebody else knew what had happened. "I can't tell you how much your words mean to me," I said. "Friday was the worst day of my life."

"It shouldn't have been. There was no reason why you shouldn't have made your early flight."

I told him Teigen's comments about finding homosexuality offensive. "He later said I would have been killed by other FBI agents in the past had they known I was gay."

The headquarters supervisor seemed shocked. "He said that?"

We talked some more, and before hanging up, I thanked him for having the courage to call. I knew he was putting his job on the line.

"I suggest you make a tape recording of what happened that day, Frank. Six months from now you will have forgotten a lot of it." He told me not to give up and wished me luck.

That night I took the phone off the hook and sat down in my living room with a tape recorder. It took me several tries to get through the ordeal with Teigen, but I managed. I felt better afterward and put the tape in a secure place.

■   ■   ■

I decided to see Dr. Andrew Mattison, a psychologist in San Diego. He had been highly recommended by Tom Homann. I knew of his book, *The Male Couple,* which he coauthored with his lifetime partner, Dr. David McWhirter. The book deals with long-term relationships between gay men, and both Mattison and McWhirter were highly respected in the gay community.

On my first visit with Drew Mattison, I explained that I would pay for the visits myself rather than submit claims through my FBI health plan. I didn't know any bureau employees receiving psychiatric care but was concerned that the word might get out I was receiving treatment. The bureau could say I was mentally unstable and therefore no longer competent to continue as an FBI agent.

At various times during the next several weeks I explained my story to Drew. There were some intensely difficult moments, but at long last I began to feel I was better able to manage my emotional life. Talking with Drew was one of the wisest decisions I had ever made. It also may have saved my life.

At work the pressure to solve the Rogers case remained intense throughout June and July. Though international terrorism remained the more publicized motive, a San Diego newspaper somehow learned and publicized information that our investigation was delving into a past extramarital affair of Captain Rogers.

Because of the extraordinary amount of information we had developed, the investigation was subdivided into several parts. Several agents were put in charge of the case, and each one was responsible for a major avenue of investigation. Each was also expected to be fully knowledgeable and up-to-date on his or her specialized area.

My day still consisted of reviewing the new information we were developing. It also included discussions with the agents in charge of specialized areas and the scores of law enforcement and intelligence agencies involved in the case here and abroad. The Naval Intelligence Service was still working closely with us, and several times a week we met to share the latest developments and plan future strategy. At least once a week the entire office was briefed on the progress of the case. The summary teletypes were now weekly instead of daily.

Our sixty- to seventy-hour workweeks were scaled down to fifty and sixty hours. We also began to take off an occasional day and even some long weekends. The investigation was so broad and complex that in the absence of a major break, we began to see it might take months or perhaps years to solve. If we didn't start taking some time away from the case, we could easily burn ourselves out.

No one else in the office gave any indication he or she knew about my situation. Occasionally I asked Hughes and Kuker if they had heard anything from headquarters about my case, and they continued to answer no. Nearly three months had passed since I'd seen Teigen.

17.

July 28 had always been a special day for me. It was my mother's birthday, and she was to be seventy-one. Her health was good, and I was grateful for every day she was still alive. July 28 was also my EOD date—the date I "entered on duty" in the FBI. And 1989 marked my twentieth year of service in the bureau.

I expected there would be the usual all-employees conference to mark the occasion—and perhaps milestones for others. I had never imagined that after twenty years I would be fighting to save my job.

One night, as I sat reading in my living room, the phone rang. I was walking to my office to pick it up when I heard an attempt to retrieve messages from the answering machine using my two-digit code. I called Brian and told him what had happened. "The same thing happened a few weeks ago when you were out of town," he said. "I assumed it was you calling for your messages."

I told him it hadn't been me, and I replaced the answering machine with a more sophisticated one. I didn't notice the attempt again. Given all the time that had elapsed and all the pressures of the Rogers investigation, I had pretty much put W. J. on the back burner. Now I wondered if this had been just a prank or something more serious. I began to feel uneasy again.

It had been months since Brian and I had spent any time together. One weekend we coordinated our schedules and took Jake and Rusty camping with us. We left early Saturday afternoon for the Cleveland National Forest, an hour's drive east of San Diego. We usually camped in an area of the forest thick with pines. It reminded me of the Adirondack Mountains back home. As usual we hiked during the day and cooked outside in the evening. I told the office where I would be and brought my beeper just in case. Being with Brian again seemed like old times.

We returned home the following morning, July 24. I raised the shades on the solarium windows, and suddenly we both noticed large scratches on the outside of every pane of glass. We looked around the house, and none of the other large glass doors or windows was damaged, nor was there any other evidence of vandalism.

I sat down in a living-room chair. Though I had investigated all types of people in my career, this felt different. This time I was dealing with an unknown threat to my life.

Brian knelt beside me. We talked for a few minutes, and then I called Kuker and the police to report what happened. Brian stayed for a while, but then he had to go home. He said he would return later that night. I talked with my neighbors, but there was no other vandalism, nor had they seen anything that looked suspicious. The damage to the solarium was an estimated six thousand dollars.

I called Everett to tell him what happened, and he reacted angrily. "Whoever did this knows you personally. They knew how important the solarium project was for you. This is a personal assault on you. I'm concerned about your personal safety, and the FBI needs to do something immediately!"

Brian returned, and as we talked, I said, "All this is happening to me, and I can't even tell my family."

"I know how close you are to them," he responded gently. "You could really use their support now."

I didn't respond, but I knew he was right.

I met with Hughes and Kuker the following afternoon. I reviewed the previous incidents involving the attempt to retrieve messages from my answering machine and the materials that had been taken from my house. Although I had submitted communications to Kuker documenting these occurrences, Hughes was apparently not aware of them. "I believe the same person or persons is doing all of this," I said, "but I don't know the reason." By the end of the hourlong meeting, it seemed both Hughes and Kuker were convinced of the seriousness of the threat to me. Hughes asked what I wanted the bureau to do.

"I'd like to have information that might better enable me to protect myself. I want to know more about the two individuals you interviewed for OPR. Moreover, I think the bureau ought to interview the two individuals immediately in order to determine their whereabouts this past weekend and their reaction to the questioning. Finally, I'd like the bureau to conduct a surveillance of my house. Agents can stay inside if you want. I could pretend to go camping again and see what happens."

I told them I hadn't mentioned the OPR investigation to the police when asked about possible suspects. "I was concerned about the information becoming public, and I didn't want to embarrass the bureau." I concluded by saying I viewed the damage to my house as a personal assault. "I have no way of knowing what this person is going to do next. Will he kill my dog? Burn my house down? Attack me? I am concerned about my safety and the safety of people I associate with."

Hughes got up from his chair. "We'll check with OPR to see what we can do. I'll let you know as soon as we get an answer."

I called Brian that night and told him about the meeting with Hughes and Kuker. He thought the bureau was dragging its feet.

"If you were straight and all this was happening to you and your family, the bureau would do something about it immediately." He then repeated what he had said several times before. "You always tell me the FBI investigates cases objectively. But look at the way they've treated you because you're gay. What does that say about how they treat gay people when we're victims of crime?"

Brian and I had gone over the same ground many times before. I believed most agents were objective in investigating cases and put their personal feelings aside. I had never seen or heard a specific incident of gay bashing or harassment since I had been in the FBI.

"Hughes and Kuker have not treated me any differently since they found out I was gay," I told Brian now. "They even made me one of the agents in charge of the Rogers investigation."

■ ■ ■

The all-employees conference of July 28 was only four days away, but I had lost interest in saying anything other than "thank you" and sitting down. Much to my surprise, Brian argued against this.

"That day means a lot to you, Frank. The younger agents, like Martin, Joe, and Henry, look up to you. They should hear what you think about your career and the bureau. You can't let what's going on stop you from doing what's important to you."

I woke up earlier than usual the morning of the twenty-eighth. I always seemed to wake up before the alarm clock when I had something important to do. Brian was still asleep beside me. I slipped out of bed and walked to the window. I opened the drapes a crack and could see the Pacific Ocean out in the distance, the light shimmering on its calm light blue waters.

I showered and, as I began shaving, heard the coffee grinder start. It was noisy, and I reminded myself still another time to replace it. I returned to the bedroom. It was six-fifteen, close to when Brian ought to be getting up. I stood for a moment looking at him. I hadn't noticed before how the lines around his eyes had deepened. He had let his brown hair grow a bit, and he no longer looked as if he were in the Navy.

How our lives had changed from the relatively easy time we had before the letters arrived. I should have appreciated those days more and my time with Brian. Though I think we both knew we would never be lifelong partners, neither of us seemed able to say good-bye for good.

I went to the kitchen and poured two cups of coffee. Brian was usually the one to get up first and bring me coffee. He was rubbing his eyes when I returned. "Good morning," I said, in a large, cheerful voice. His "good morning" definitely lacked enthusiasm.

I put his coffee mug down on the nightstand beside him and gave him a kiss. "Today's the big one," I said. It was something my father would say. I asked if he would listen to the remarks I planned to make that day.

"Sure," Brian replied, taking the first sip from his cup.

I finished dressing and, as I ate breakfast, reviewed my notes. Brian came into the living room.

"Ready?" I asked.

He nodded. "Go ahead, but make sure you go slow. You have a tendency to talk fast when you get excited."

I wrote down his advice at the top of the page, and a few times, while I spoke, he motioned for me to slow down. When I finished, he made a few suggestions, and we both agreed it sounded better the second time.

At around eight-fifteen the announcement about the all-employees conference came over the PA system. A podium was set up in front of the room, and soon most of the office's two hundred or so employees were gathered in and around our work area.

My friend Ann Davis and our squad secretary were the first to congratulate me. "Are you going to say something, huh, Frank?" the secretary kidded.

"Have you ever known me *not* to talk when I had a chance?" I answered, laughing.

I leaned against my desk, watching as Hughes approached the podium. He welcomed everyone, saying that it was a special day for some and that he had letters and awards to present. "But first," he said, "I want to introduce an agent some of you might not know." He then talked briefly about Special Agent John Kelso.

John had been a supervisor in San Diego prior to his transfer to headquarters. He, his wife, and his children had recently returned to San Diego for a vacation when tragedy struck. John and his wife were standing on the curb outside the airport when a van accidentally backed up and pinned both of them beneath its wheels. John's medical treatment had consisted of a drug-induced coma; his wife was still in critical condition.

The room grew quiet as John, accompanied by his two sons, walked slowly toward the podium. His gait was evidence of the pain he was in. In words slow and emotion-laden, John recounted how nearly dying had changed him. He said the prayers, cards, flowers, and personal visits by us had given him and his wife the courage to carry on.

Afterward Hughes returned to the podium and said there were three people celebrating twenty-year anniversaries in the bureau that week. One of the agents was out of town on an assignment. The second, a support staff employee, said a few words about her career and then sat down.

Hughes said I was also celebrating my twentieth anniversary and talked briefly about my career. He joked about my good luck in obtaining three of the bureau's most choice assignments: Tampa, San Francisco, and San Diego. He also read a letter from the director of the FBI, William S. Sessions. I listened carefully for any clues it might contain.

Sessions's letter said, in part, "For many years now you have directed your talents and energy toward the best interests of the Bureau, and we are appreciative of your devotion to duty and loyalty to the FBI. Without this positive attitude on the part of you and others like you, the Bureau could not have been so successful and earned such an esteemed position in the eyes of the public. I thank you for your many efforts on our behalf."

Hughes called me to the podium, and as I approached, there was applause. I was surprised by the emotion I felt. Hughes shook my hand and handed me a blue folder containing my twenty-year service award key and letters of congratulations from people in the bureau. It is customary for other agents to send letters on such occasions.

Hughes asked if I wanted to say something, and I nodded yes. I adjusted the microphone, searching for Martin Hernandez, the agent I had been training. I also located John Dolan, my partner on several cases. John had recently retired from the bureau, only to return abruptly.

I thanked Hughes and then turned in the direction of John Kelso.

"John, I want to tell you how happy we are to see you here today. You and your wife are very courageous people, and we admire your courage. It means a lot to us that you're here. We wish you and your family a full and speedy recovery.

"Boss," I then said, turning to Hughes, "thanks for reviewing my previous office assignments." I looked at Martin. "Martin Hernandez asked me just the other day what my first office was, and it had been so long ago I couldn't even remember!"

There was scattered laughter.

"And as far as my having good assignments? Boss, there's an old adage in the bureau that the best agents are assigned to the best offices!" There was more laughter. Hughes was smiling. "And of course, that applies to assignments for SACs and ASACs!"

I paused and then began the main body of the speech. "A lot of people ask me why I joined the bureau, and, well, I grew up in the 1960s. It was an exciting and turbulent time for America. It was also a time of assassinations—the Kennedys, Martin Luther King. It was the Vietnam War, the walk on the moon, and the civil rights movement."

I talked about graduating from college in 1967 and teaching high school history in my hometown. "But all this history was happening around me," I said. "And I wanted to be a part of it, not just talk about it."

The room became very quiet at this point. I looked around me for a moment. "I thought about becoming an FBI agent and was well aware of the bureau's reputation as crime fighters. But what motivated me most was that I saw the bureau as the only law enforcement agency in the country willing and able to protect the civil rights of black Americans."

I described the changes in the bureau I had witnessed in my twenty-year career: the acceptance of women as agents; the improved recruitment of African-Americans, Latinos, and other minorities. As I talked about these things, I noticed Hughes, leaning against a desk, his eyes downward. Did he wonder if I was going to "come out" to the whole office that day? Was I going to use myself as an example of still another minority fighting for its rights?

"The leadership of the bureau has changed a great deal since I joined the FBI," I said. "I met J. Edgar Hoover just three months before he died, and shaking hands with him was like shaking hands with someone from the history books." I commented about Hoover's enormous power and influence, noting that even after his death agents were careful what they said about him. "We knew it was always possible he'd come back!" I smiled, looking over at John Dolan. He was laughing along with the others. "Actually, in the history of the bureau only one person has ever come back. . . . And that was John Dolan!"

I went on to say that I had seen the bureau's responsibilities change during my career as organized crime, narcotics, foreign counterintelligence, and terrorism became major challenges to the country. I said that I felt fortunate to have had an interesting, challenging, and sometimes very exciting career and that I hoped I had made a contribution to my country. "I feel that I have been very privileged to work with some of the best people in the country. I feel fortunate to have you as my friends and colleagues."

I paused, adding that I wanted to remember three agents who had been assigned to our office and been killed in the line of duty. "Bob Porter. Chuck Elmore. And Jerry Dove. We will never forget them and what they sacrificed for our country."

I glanced down at my notes and took a deep breath. The last words would be the hardest. "I am as proud today as I was twenty years ago to tell people I work for the FBI."

There was a moment or two of silence, and I began making my way back to my desk. People patted me on the back or extended their hand. People began to applaud, surprising me.

The conference ended, but others took time to come by and congratulate me. A young agent working with me on the Rogers case said I sounded as though I were giving my retirement speech. I winked at him. "You never know in the bureau."

A Latino agent thanked me for my comments about minorities, and later in the day an older agent, nearing retirement, commented, "I appreciated what you said. I entered the bureau for pretty much the same reasons as you did in the early 1960s. My first office assignment was in the South, but after I talked about my support for civil rights, the other agents ostracized me." A young female agent from another office who had been temporarily assigned to the Rogers case said, "I hope I feel the same way you do about the bureau after twenty years."

That evening, while alone, I opened the blue folder and read through the letters. A bureau supervisor in Atlanta who had been a classmate of mine when I joined, wrote, "You should feel proud of the fine record you have attained in your span of dedicated service and I know you have contributed a great deal toward the accomplishments of the Bureau." A

San Diego supervisor commended me on my ''guidance and counsel'' in the command post during the Rogers investigation, adding: ''Your service in the FBI has been exemplary and, in my opinion, serves as a model for the rest of us.''

A former ASAC, now assigned to FBIHQ, wrote, ''You are a positive asset for the FBI who demonstrated professionalism and enthusiasm in all your efforts.'' SAC Tom Hughes had also written. He complimented me on my work in criminal and foreign counterintelligence and relayed how I had always conducted myself ''in a most dedicated and competent manner.'' John Dolan's note said simply, ''Your sincerity and generosity are truly your hallmark.''

18.

The following Wednesday I got a call to report to Hughes's office. It had been a week and a half since I asked for bureau assistance in regard to what had happened at my house. Hughes, with Kuker looking on, told me that headquarters could not release any information to me because the investigation was part of an administrative inquiry. Hughes told me I could request information through the Freedom of Information Act. Headquarters also had decided not to reopen the investigation to determine who had caused the damage to my house. Hughes told me to contact the appropriate police or sheriff's department if I was concerned about my personal safety or property.

I was stunned. The bureau was turning its back on me. After a moment or two, without commenting, I got up and left his office. I left the building and went to a pay phone down the street. I told Brian what Hughes had said.

There was a pause. "Maybe they don't want you to know who's responsible."

■   ■   ■

The bureau decided to designate the Rogers case a "special" and sent dozens of agents on temporary assignment to assist in the investigation. The agents helped us interview hundreds of individuals and business owners about the gunpowder and other components of the pipe bomb used in the bombing. Hundreds of follow-up interviews of neighbors and others previously contacted by us were also conducted. Our investigations into both personal and terroristic motives were looking more promising, and I was becoming more optimistic about the possibility of our finally solving the case. A promotion I received in September encouraged me. Additionally I was awarded a "Superior" performance rating for the previous year. I felt good about not having allowed the pressure of the OPR investigation to affect the quality of my work.

Brian and I had not been on vacation together since our cross-country trip in 1984. He would be returning to college soon, and I also felt the need to get away from work and my problems with the bureau. We had had such a good time the last time we were away together that I think we both were hoping it could happen again. We planned to go to Yosemite, Kings Canyon, and Sequoia national parks on a weeklong vacation.

I made arrangements with a good friend to house-sit while I was away. He was about my age, divorced, and had taken care of my house during the Mitrione case. He lived nearby with his mother and enjoyed the opportunity to get away. I trusted him implicitly. He was straight and didn't know about my sexual orientation—or what was happening with the bureau. Perhaps I should have told him, but I didn't.

As it turned out, our vacation together turned out to be another great one. Each morning I made coffee and breakfast, and every night Brian cooked dinner over a wood campfire. One day we hiked for miles and spent the entire afternoon completely alone at a beautiful glacial lake in the Sequoias. Though I wasn't crazy about horses, Brian talked me into riding horseback with him along a creek bed near our campsite. We talked and laughed a lot that week, and it was the most relaxing time we had spent with each other in a very long time.

One day after we returned to San Diego, I went to the hallway closet where I kept extra sets of car and post office box keys. I still had the post office box where the original correspondence with W. J. had taken place. But I had also obtained a new post office box for additional privacy.

I drove the short distance from my house to the post office and entered the lobby. At that point I realized the key to the old post office box was missing from the key ring, even though the key to the new post office box was still there. I went back home, searched the house, but couldn't find it. I called Brian. He was silent for a few moments after I finished.

"Do you think it's W. J. again?" he asked.

I told him I wasn't sure. "Not that many people knew I was on vacation," I said, thinking out loud, "but someone could assume I was away because my RV was not parked in the driveway."

"It's the second time we took the RV and someone broke into your house. Either someone is watching your house or it's somebody that knows exactly when you're leaving and coming back."

I knew Brian was thinking about the bureau. When an agent leaves town, he or she has to fill out a form which includes the dates of travel, destination, the mode of transportation, and a contact number where the agent can be reached. Several people in the office knew I was on vacation. I had called the office to check for messages and to talk to agents in the command post. The form detailing my vacation itinerary was kept in a message folder with my name on it in the squad area. Anyone in the office had access to it. I hadn't told Brian, but I had also given the number of my old post office box to the bureau the previous December.

I wondered if mail had been taken from the old box, and to find out, I sent a letter to a friend using the old post office box as an address. I asked if he would write me back at my new box number. When he did, he told me in the letter that he had written me previously at the old post office box. I had never received the letter. Somebody was stealing my mail.

"Call the postal inspector's office and tell them what happened," Everett said when I told him about it later.

But I didn't want to do that. I was afraid the information about my being a gay FBI agent might become public knowledge and the bureau would react to the disclosure by firing me. "I want this issue with the bureau resolved first, Everett."

"Frank, your life is in danger."

"I can take care of myself!" I snapped. "I'm not afraid of this idiot. Whoever is doing this is a coward. He's gutless! Writing to my parents and the bureau and doing things to me when I'm not at home. I wish he *would* try to confront me."

"Calm down, Frank," Everett advised. "You don't know what this person's motive is, and you can't be sure of anything else about him. If he intended to harm your relationship with your parents and get you fired, then he may be frustrated that he has not been successful. Outwardly he has had no effect on your life."

In the week that followed, I changed the locks on the doors to my house. I also talked to a couple of agents in the office about buying a home security system. One of them asked if there was a problem, but I commented generally about the increase in crime in San Diego.

I wrote another memorandum to Kuker. I advised him of the break-in and the missing post office box key and letter. I also changed my normal routine as much as possible and became more careful about my movements.

I told a close friend about the missing key and letter, and he offered to send a letter to my old post office box. The letter would include his telephone number. We hoped whoever had stolen the mail would see the letter and try to contact my friend. If such a meeting took place, I would be there.

A few days later I looked through the glass door of the old post office box and saw my friend's letter. When I checked later in the week, the letter was gone. I wrote still another memorandum to Kuker advising him of this. As was true for my previous memos, I didn't hear back from Kuker—nor did my friend ever receive a call from whoever had stolen his letter.

19.

On Friday, September 29, things were quiet in the command post, so I decided to try to find an individual we wanted to interview. I had spent most of the past five months in the office, and it felt good to get outside—even for a short while. I made the turn onto E Street in Chula Vista and was fairly close to my destination when the office radio dispatcher called my signal number. I responded, and she said to call the SAC's secretary as soon as possible.

I saw a pay phone at a nearby 7-Eleven and pulled into the parking lot. I slipped on my suit jacket to conceal my gun and dialed the office number. A new lead in Atlanta, Georgia, was currently being investigated, and I hoped the call would be about that. But as I waited, I had the sinking feeling it had to do with me.

The SAC secretary said Hughes wanted to see me immediately, and I advised her I'd be back in fifteen to twenty minutes. I took the most direct route back and pulled the bureau car into its proper space in the garage. I nodded to a few people on my squad as I walked to my desk. I took out my notebook, locked my gun in my briefcase, and glanced at pictures of my family in the six-sided cube on my desk. In one of the pictures Brian was sitting with my dad, my brother Tony, and me at my parents' house. We were about to sit down to dinner, and everyone was smiling.

Hughes greeted me with his usual dispassion, and I sat down on the couch opposite his desk. He then called in Kuker. No agents from the Rogers case were present. The meeting was about me.

Kuker entered, nodded in my direction but didn't speak. I assumed they had already discussed whatever was going to happen. Hughes got up and walked to a small room in the rear of his office. When he came back, he was holding some papers. "This is a sad day for the San Diego office," he said. "You are a dynamite investigator." Hughes sat down and looked up at me. "However, I have been directed by Gary Stoops, the bureau's security programs manager, to advise you that you are being placed on administrative leave—with pay—for twenty days. This is to become effective immediately."

I had expected a letter of censure or perhaps a few days' suspension for my initial denial about writing the letter to W. J., but I had never heard of the bureau's disciplining somebody by putting him or her on leave *with* pay.

Hughes handed me a letter. It was from FBI headquarters and dated September 25. The letter began with observations about Top Secret security requirements for FBI agents and the national security. It said the bureau was proposing to revoke my security clearance on the basis of my "past and present conduct and association with unknown individuals in the homosexual community." My behavior, it stated, carried the "potential for coercion" in that it "constitutes exploitable sexual conduct." The letter claimed I was either unwilling or unable to assist the FBI and other law enforcement agencies regarding my "trustworthiness."

Toward the end it accused me of not furnishing the names and identities of those I associated with "in what appears to be a secret homosexual society." The letter said I displayed "a lack of candor during the inquiry and a refusal to cooperate."

I read through the letter a second time. Though it was confusing, there was no mistaking its intent. The bureau planned to revoke my Top Secret security clearance, and without this I could not be an agent.

Hughes asked me to sign and date the bottom of the letter's first page, and I did. I handed it to Kuker, who signed and dated it as a witness. Hughes gave me a copy of the letter, saying, "Of course, we'll maintain the secrecy of all this." After an awkward moment Kuker said, "We'll have to obtain your bureau equipment. And we can probably do that without anybody in the office knowing."

I glanced down at my watch. It was nearly 4:00 P.M. I had the feeling that once I walked out of the FBI office, I would never be coming back.

After what I had just read and heard, it was time for me to speak for myself. I paused for a moment. "Boss, relative to your keeping this a secret," I said, trying to contain my emotions, "I don't care who knows I'm gay. It's not my secret anymore. It's the bureau's secret."

I looked at Kuker, then back again at Hughes. "I want you to know I appreciate your support and kindness throughout all of this." I then mentioned Rosa Parks and the bus boycott in Montgomery, Alabama, and how injustice didn't change until people were willing to stand up against it.

"This is not fair," I said. "I'm going to appeal this. If I don't get my job back, I'll seriously consider taking it to court. I plan on seeing this through to the end." I took a deep breath. "I just hope I have the courage to do it."

I walked to an interview room and closed the door. I called Brian, got his answering machine, and left a message for him to call me at home. I called Everett and told him about the suspension. He asked if I was all right. "I'm sorry, Frank," he said.

I called Tom Homann. He was uncharacteristically quiet as I told him what happened. He said he was sorry about the suspension. "Why don't you come in Monday morning and we'll get started on the appeal?"

I thanked him for his help and half joked about taking this to the Supreme Court.

"I've argued before the Supreme Court in the past," Homann answered.

Because I had been assigned a bureau car since the Rogers case began, I didn't have a ride home. The last thing I wanted was to ride home with someone from the office, with whom I could not share what had just occurred. I did not want to leave in a cab. A friend of mine worked downtown, and he said he'd pick me up.

No one was in the command post, and I sat down in my usual seat, looking up at the charts, photos, and maps covering the walls. A large black-and-white blow-up of the Rogers van engulfed in flames hung on a side wall. When I was discouraged about the lack of progress in the case, I would look at the photograph and remind myself how close Sharon Rogers had come to being killed. I also sometimes wondered about the perpetrators. Did they think we were close to finding out who they were?

A phone rang, and I moved to answer it. It was the unmistakable voice of John Dolan. "Hey, lad," he said, and gave me a brief overview of what he had learned in Atlanta.

When he was done, I said, "Have a safe trip back, John."

"And you have a good weekend, lad," he responded. "See you on Monday."

It was almost 4:30, and I knew I'd better get moving. The normal office workday ended at 5:00 P.M. I looked through my work box, a small, rectangular wooden box that agents use to store their office work in. I took out some personal items and left the box on the table. I picked up a very large accordion folder and headed for the bureau garage.

I took my bulletproof vest, FBI raid jacket, and FBI baseball cap out of the trunk of the car I had been driving and stuffed them into the folder. I put the keys in the ignition, and grabbed my gym bag out of the back seat. About half the squad had returned to the office when I got back upstairs. A couple of agents were sitting in the cluster of desks near mine. One kidded, ''So how are things in the ivory tower?'' He meant the command post. I nodded and smiled.

As inconspicuously as possible I went through the contents of my desk, putting some of the personal items in a second, smaller envelope. I left the photo cube and nameplate on my desk. I unlocked my briefcase and emptied the bullets from both my guns. One of the guns was a small five-shot Smith & Wesson I sometimes carried in an ankle holster. The other was the weapon I had been issued when I first joined the FBI. It was a larger, six-shot Smith & Wesson. I always carried both guns in arrest situations.

I put the bullets in the large envelope but left the guns in the briefcase. I also left my handcuffs and some pens and pencils inside. When I was done, it was after 5:00 P.M. Almost everyone else on the squad had gone home. I took one last look through my desk, picked up my things, and walked over to the attendance register. I recorded the time and signed out. I returned to the command post to make sure I hadn't forgotten anything. Out of our big picture window I saw a boat passing through the harbor heading out to sea. I took one long last look around the room then turned off the lights.

''I've collected my things, Tom,'' I said, setting the envelopes and briefcase on the corner of Kuker's desk.

''Let me get the boss,'' Kuker responded, walking from the room.

Hughes returned with Kuker but didn't say anything. He did seem a little sad as he sat down in a chair on the far side of the room.

Kuker had an inventory sheet listing my bureau property. I remained standing and opened my briefcase. I placed both guns, chambers open, on his desk, and Kuker checked off their serial numbers. I handed him the bullets. After that I gave him the speedloaders, raid jacket, cap, and handcuffs. I showed him the contents of the smaller envelope, my gym bag, and briefcase to assure him I wasn't taking any bureau property home with me.

I took out my wallet and unfastened my badge from the inside flap. I was given the badge my first day in the FBI. I handed it to Kuker, and he checked off the number on the back. I reached into my shirt pocket for the small black leather case that contained my credentials.

"Creds" contain a brief description of an FBI agent's duties and responsibilities and are signed by the attorney general of the United States. When Hoover was alive, he signed them. Creds also contain a color photo of the agent as well as his or her signature.

I opened up the case and looked at them for a moment. When I handed them to Kuker, tears fell from my eyes. I turned away. "I know this hasn't been easy for either of you, and I'm sorry you've had to go through this," I said, wiping my eyes.

Neither answered, and I reached for my gym bag and briefcase. Hughes walked over to me and extended his hand; Kuker did the same.

"I'm going to fight this thing," I said. "I want to come back and solve the Rogers case."

They both wished me luck. Hughes said he hoped I'd be back.

The elevator took me to ground level, and I walked the short distance to the corner of First Avenue and Broadway. I waited for a few minutes before my friend pulled up. I didn't look back as he slowly reentered traffic for the trip home.

part four
"do you still love me?"

20.

After we arrived at my house, my friend asked if he could see the letter. He had graduated from law school, and I was very interested in his opinion.

While he sat at the kitchen table with the letter, I went to the bedroom and changed out of my suit, placing it alongside the other suits in my closet. Except when I was working undercover or on occasional surveillances, I had worn a suit to work every day for the last twenty years. "The three-piecers" some cops called us, referring to agents wearing vests with their suits. I wondered if I would ever wear a suit again as an FBI agent.

I returned to the living room just as my friend was finishing the letter. "It's confusing and not very well written," he commented, shaking his head. "It sounds as though it were written by a committee."

I decided to call Drew Mattison, my therapist. When Drew answered, I told him what had happened. He asked how I was doing, and I told him I was with a friend and doing all right.

"What reason did they give for suspending you?" Drew asked.

I read him Stoops's letter.

"I'm outraged!" Drew responded. He suggested we get together the following week. "And don't hesitate to call me anytime if there's a problem."

I heard Brian's car pull up outside. He must have sensed something was wrong by the tone of my voice on his answering machine. "What happened?" he said as soon as he got in the door.

I told him about the suspension and handed him the letter. He had started reading it when the phone rang. The FBI night clerk said somebody in Atlanta wanted to talk to an agent about the Rogers case. The clerk evidently was unaware of my suspension. I told him to hang on and put my hand over the receiver. "It's someone who wants to talk about the investigation. I'll take it in the office."

Brian took the phone and said angrily, "You should tell them to call someone else."

Somehow, even after what happened, I felt responsible for the case. I returned to the living room about fifteen minutes later, and Brian handed me the letter.

"What a bunch of bullshit," he said. "You're one of their best agents. You're in charge of one of their most important cases and they suspend you?"

I tried to say something, but he interrupted.

"After twenty years on the job all they give you is an hour and a half to get out of the office?" He added bitterly, looking over at my friend, "And I guess we're part of the 'secret homosexual society' they're talking about."

My friend must have realized that Brian and I wanted to be alone. I walked him to the door and thanked him for the ride home. Brian had moved to the kitchen and was leaning back against the counter. He had tears in his eyes, and when I put my arms around him, he started to cry. I held him until he stopped.

"I think they wrote a very stupid letter," he said. "So much of what they said is not true. It really shows their prejudice toward us."

He asked what I planned on doing, and I told him of my meeting with Tom Homann on Monday morning.

"I don't want to discourage you, Frank, but I don't think you're going to change their minds."

"I know, Brian. I guess I knew all along that when I told them I was gay, I would eventually be fired. But I did continue working for almost a year afterward. It's possible they might reconsider after our appeal. Especially if they think I might take them to court."

That night, as Brian lay beside me, I kept going over everything that had happened. What mistakes had I made? What options remained for me? The past year could have been one of the best in my entire life, yet it had turned into the worst. I had always known it was possible the bureau would find out I was gay, but maybe I had become too casual about my private life. Maybe I shouldn't have used the personals.

I had somehow thought that mentioning the possibility of a lawsuit might cause the bureau to back off. Perhaps soon I would have to decide whether or not to do that. It would generate enormous publicity, which I did not want.

I also wondered how it would affect others. Brian seemed devastated by the suspension, and publicity might draw attention to him. I wondered if our relationship would survive all that. And what about the effects on my family?

Maybe it was because of what the FBI had done or because Brian was no longer such a key factor in my life, but I knew I needed to tell my family now. I knew I needed them with me on whatever lay ahead. "*Sangue e sangue,*" my Sicilian grandmother used to tell us. It meant "blood of my blood." Family was a mystical entity, and I hadn't felt a part of it in a long time.

I dozed off for a while but awakened at quarter to four. My first thought was about the bureau: Had yesterday been a bad dream? I felt Brian's arm touch mine, and I turned on the light. He was sound asleep, and the light didn't wake him. I thought about yesterday again. A feeling of grief came over me, as if somebody close had died.

I turned off the light and quietly made my way out of the bedroom. The streetlights in the canyon below my house were flickering brightly. They seemed like candles in the pitch-black darkness. I thought about that last hour at the office. Under the circumstances, I thought I had done well. Yet I also knew that while I initially handled difficult situations well, my feelings and emotions usually caught up with me later.

I had never discussed the issue of homosexuality with my brother Lou, in Rochester, New York, but I had the feeling he would be understanding and sympathetic about it. As a college professor and writer he must have had some contact with gay colleagues and students. His wife, Kathleen, had a master's degree and counseled young people and families. From my limited conversations with her, it was evident she also was sensitive to the subject. I would need their assistance in helping my parents handle all that was about to unfold.

I was anxious to make the call, but it was too early, even for the East Coast. *I should use the time to sort through some of my emotions,* I thought. Telling my family would begin the unraveling process in ways I couldn't imagine. Since my teenage years I had carefully hidden from my family my feelings about other males. The face they had come to know was really a mask. Now they would come to see me in an entirely different way. I wondered how they would take the news.

I got the tape recorder out of my office and brought it into the living room. Making a recording of the Teigen polygraph had been extremely difficult, but it had helped me work through my feelings. Perhaps doing the same thing about the suspension would help. Once again I had to stop the recorder several times because I was overcome with emotion.

Afterward I turned my attention to what I should say to my brother. I dialed his number, and his teenage stepdaughter, Kelly, answered. She said he was still asleep, and I told her I would call back a little later. It was 7:30 A.M. EST, and I wished I had waited awhile longer. I poured another cup of coffee.

Lou was a year older than I was, and as children we were sometimes mistaken for twins. We attended the same public schools and college together, even joining the same fraternity at Colgate University. Though we were together a lot growing up, we began to become more and more estranged in the late 1960s. Vietnam was the chief catalyst. Though we both were opposed to the war, by 1969 I was an FBI agent and my brother saw me as part of the establishment responsible for continuing the war. I was also sworn to uphold the law and opposed the violence and law-breaking some opponents of the war engaged in. Though my brother was opposed to violence, he felt it was sometimes justifiable to break the law in the name of a higher law.

I had grown up trusting the government without question and had often viewed issues in black or white terms. That kind of thinking, and my belief in law and order, probably attracted me to a career in law enforcement while it repelled my brother.

When I came home during the late 1960s, Lou and I and our friends would end up arguing a great deal. We all became angry with one another for what seemed like a very long time. After the war ended, my brother and I gradually regained the friendship we once had.

My experiences as both an FBI agent and gay man had also changed me. I came to see that there were shades of gray in many issues on which intelligent, well-intentioned people might disagree. But just about the time my brother and I were becoming close again, the wall I had been building for years, the wall of my homosexuality, was well above eye level.

I weighed how best to tell my brother as I redialed his number. Kelly answered again and said Lou was up. I asked him if this was a good time to talk.

"Wait, Frank, I'll take this on the third floor." The third floor was where he had a combined office and writing studio. I heard a door close, and a moment or two later he was on the line again. His daughter hung up the downstairs phone.

"Okay, Frank," he said. He was out of breath. I wasn't sure if it was because of the long climb upstairs or because he was nervous.

"I don't know how to tell you this, and maybe the best way is just to come out and say it. As you probably already know or suspected, I'm gay."

He replied in a calm voice that he always thought so but had never been sure.

"I'm not sick, and I really don't have a problem being gay," I continued. "However, the bureau found out I'm gay, and yesterday they suspended me."

I told him about the support I had from friends. He asked how it happened, and I began with the letter to our parents. When I got to the part about Teigen several minutes later, Lou interrupted.

"That bastard," he said, "he took advantage of you wanting to keep your job. I'd like to meet up with him one day."

"Lou, maybe we should have Carmen Basilio pay him a visit," I said kiddingly, and we had our first laugh of the morning.

I concluded with how I had turned over my badge and credentials. This was still difficult for me to get through. Lou said he wished he could be there with me.

"Even when we were kids," he said, "I always felt there was this wall between us. I thought it was me—my moodiness and later my politics." He paused, "You know, when I got up this morning, Kelly said you called and it sounded like you had a cold—or had been crying. I knew what the call was going to be about, as if I had been waiting for it most of my life."

He asked if I was going to tell Mom and Dad, and I told him I was but wasn't sure just when.

"Tony will want to know, too. But I'm sure you've thought of that already."

"I don't look forward to telling Tony," I answered. "Even though he's our older brother, he always seems to take things so much harder than we do. I'll make sure Barbara is around when I tell him."

As our conversation came to an end, Lou said, "Frank, *I* don't want to sound like an older brother, but I want to pass along something I've learned very recently. I think it might help some." There was another pause, as if he were trying to find the right words. "What I've learned is that it's important not to look at what you do in terms of winning or losing. That only gets you into trouble. It's important to do the right thing for the right reason. Everything else will follow. I'm not saying it won't hurt, but it puts you in touch with the deeper rhythm of what is good and right.''

I said I'd try. There was something else I wanted to tell him. "Last year I received the tape of your speech at the Italian-American dinner just after the bureau called me in for questioning the first time. Brian and I both listened to it, and we were crying afterward. I later wrote down the ending and have kept it with me in my notebook. I just wanted to say that having your words with me was like having you with me.''

Lou didn't respond right away. Then he said, "Ever since that dream I've tried to figure out who the younger man was. It seemed important for me to find out. He was very sad, and I wanted to help him. It was you, Frank, wasn't it?''

■ ■ ■

I didn't set the alarm for work that Monday morning, but I awakened around six anyway. I showered and sat down to coffee. It felt strange not getting dressed and gearing up for the Rogers investigation.

At 8:20 A.M. I called the squad secretary to make sure she knew I was on administrative leave. She said that the supervisor had told her but that he didn't know why. "Are you going undercover, Frank?" she asked in a playful voice.

"It's a secret," I answered similarly.

Before I hung up, I told her I would call in periodically to check for messages.

I met with Tom Homann later that morning. He read over Stoops's letter and then commented, wryly, "Secret homosexual society indeed." He butted out his cigarette. " 'Exploitable sexual conduct'? It's such a terrible letter I'm not sure where to begin.''

Homann jotted down a few notes, thinking out loud as he did so. "We need to get all the reports of their interviews and investigation of you, including the polygraph results. I'll send out a request for the immediate release of these documents and also ask for an extension of their deadline. Twenty days is a very short time to prepare a suitable response.'' Homann suggested I draft the appeal letter and he would review it afterward. This might save us time.

As I left the office, I felt a little better. At least I could do something to help myself. I thought about Brian's comment when we were discussing my appeal: "This is the biggest case of your life, Frank. And you're its subject."

That evening I called a friend from the office, Ann Davis. She was aware that I was on administrative leave and asked if anything was wrong. I said I'd prefer to talk to her in person. She lived close by, and as I drove over, I decided to be as straightforward with her as I had been with my brother.

After my arrival we went into a small room off the living room. I closed the door and took a chair near her. "I hope you won't be offended that I have not shared this with you sooner, but I think you'll understand why." I told her I was gay and then explained what had happened with the bureau. She remained silent throughout.

"I'm sorry this happened to you, Frank," she said. She told me she suspected I was gay because of my close friendship with Brian. "When I saw you leaving Kuker's office on Friday, I thought that there was an illness in your family or that something had happened to Brian."

She cleared her throat. "It doesn't make any difference to me, Frank. Please know that, but I am concerned what the bureau is going to do now."

I told her that I planned to appeal the suspension and that I had decided not to disclose any of this to others in the bureau.

"I won't say anything, but let me know if there is anything I can do.

"The office isn't going to be the same without you," she whispered as I hugged her before leaving. Little did I know that a tragedy in her own family would bring us even closer together.

21.

The next morning I called my parents. "Happy Birthday!" I told my father. It was his seventy-fifth—or "seventy-five big ones," as he said.

"Who's older now?" I kidded. "You or George Burns?"

"I'm just a young kid compared to him," he joked back. "I'll tell you something else, Francis: If I knew I was going to live this long, I would have taken better care of myself!"

I could hear Mom pick up the second phone. "Are you coming home?" she asked.

I said that I was working on something important but that I might come home when it was done.

"Is it the Rogers case?" asked my father. "Are you close to solving it?"

"I really can't say," I told him.

We talked for a long while. Though I tried to act the same toward them, I wondered if they sensed something was wrong. They usually asked about Brian and maybe because of the W. J. letter now realized I was gay. I knew I would have to tell them soon and in person.

I sat at the dining-room table most of the week working on my appeal letter. Since I was a member of the FBI Agents Association, I also called the association's legal counsel in New York City. The attorney I spoke with commented, after I explained my situation, "What does your homosexuality have to do with your ability to do your job? . . . New York City cops have more rights than FBI agents. The New York City Police Department would never be allowed to get away with what the bureau is doing."

He offered me advice on the appeal letter, and recommended that I keep it brief. He was reluctant to get involved in the case, however, because I had already obtained counsel. He offered to speak with Homann and to review the letter before it was submitted to the bureau.

Later that day John Dolan called from the office. He didn't greet me in his usual friendly way, and I prepared myself for the worst. Because of his closeness to both Hughes and Kuker, I assumed he knew why I had been put on administrative leave.

John asked how I was doing and if there was anything he could do. I told him I was fine yet anxious to get back to work on the Rogers case. Naturally we didn't talk about it, though I was eager to find out if anything new had happened. When our conversation ended, he said, "Take care of yourself, lad."

John's call made me realize, on a personal level, how much I missed my job.

Before giving my appeal letter to Tom Homann, I had Brian, Everett, and Lou review it. They agreed it sounded strong yet respectful. I addressed every issue raised by Stoops and challenged his conclusions. I emphasized my twenty-year unblemished record and said I was proud of my reputation for honesty, dedication, and loyalty to the bureau and the country. I conveyed my strong desire to continue working for the FBI.

Once that was done, I began preparations to visit my parents. I confided to Everett that I was concerned that telling them I was gay might be too much for them, considering their ages.

"You're not giving them enough credit for all the years they've lived and the hardships they've overcome in their lives," Everett said in his usual direct way. "They're a lot stronger than you think. They love you, and their love for you will allow them to understand and accept you."

Despite Everett's advice, I was already beginning to have second thoughts about telling them on this trip home. There would be so many questions, and I would have to talk a lot about my personal life. They would be concerned about the rest of the family's finding out—and how others in Canastota would react. They would want to be prepared to answer questions from other people, especially those who opposed homosexuality. They would have to deal with the religious indoctrination from the religious right that had become so much a part of their lives since retirement. I would also have to insist that they not discuss it with anyone else. Contrary to what Homann thought, I still believed that publicity would kill any chance I had of keeping my job.

I arrived at Hancock Airport in Syracuse late Friday afternoon. My parents no longer were able to drive the twenty miles or so to the airport, so John Patane, one of my best friends from high school, usually picked me up. As John and I talked on the way back to Canastota, I realized I would be telling him, too, one day.

My father must have been watching for the car because he was standing inside the kitchen door, ready to open it. We shook hands, and I kissed him on the cheek. My mother was standing at the stove, cooking pasta e fagiole, and I walked over to her. We kissed and then hugged each other for a while without speaking.

As I walked to the back bedroom with my bags, I glanced at the wedding picture of my parents that had always hung on the living-room wall. I stopped. The picture had been there for years, but I never really looked at it before. Dad, handsome with his curly hair and broad shoulders, looked like Tyrone Power from the movies. He was twenty-five years old. My mother, four years younger, weighed less than a hundred pounds and looked elegant in her white silk dress. But it was her eyes that caught my attention now. She seemed to be looking out into the world with a youthful innocence and an abiding faith that everything would turn out all right.

I was grateful for having my parents with me so long, but it pained me to think of them no longer here, of my not being able to step into this world again of familiar objects, and smells, and sounds coming from the kitchen.

My father had a glass of homemade wine already poured when I returned to the kitchen. John sat with us awhile before leaving. After the long trip home and the cool October air the wine tasted good. My mother placed the large bowl of pasta e fagiole on the table, and the three of us held hands while she said grace. It was good to be home again.

As usual my parents and I talked a lot Friday night and that Saturday morning. They were always so interested in my life, and as we talked, I grew more confident that I would be able to tell them.

On Saturday afternoon my mother and I attended the wedding of one of my cousins. My father was having problems with his eye and was unable to go with us. My mother and father seldom went anywhere without each other anymore, and at the wedding I could tell she missed and was worried about him. Many of my relatives asked how work was going at the FBI.

As I drove my mother home from the wedding, I thought about Drew Mattison's advice: that I speak to my parents in positive terms about my homosexuality and address their concerns. As we neared home, I told my mother there was something I wanted to talk to her and my father about on Monday morning.

She turned toward me with a worried look on her face. "Are you all right?"

I told her I was fine, but she continued looking at me.

"It's just something I want to share with both of you," I said. "Don't worry. It's nothing bad. I'm just concerned how Dad might take it. He might need your support."

I knew I would be asking her to choose between the son she loved and what the television preachers had told her to believe about God and the Bible. I knew that two concerns would predominate for my father.

He was both an Italian-American and a hardworking "man's man," and I wasn't sure how disclosure of my homosexuality would affect him. He was also profoundly respectful of the Buttino name, and I did not know if he would think I was bringing dishonor to it.

I called Lou in Rochester to tell him I was going to tell our parents. I knew he'd be worried.

"Do you want me to be there?" he asked.

"No, I think it would be better for me to talk to them alone."

"Okay," he said. "Kathleen, Maggie, and I will come home next weekend. We'll have a chance to talk, and after you leave, I can take care of any further questions they might have. Maybe there are some things they'll feel more comfortable asking me about."

"I've already prepared them a little for it. I'm hoping they'll handle it better if their focus is on each other."

My mother cooked rigatoni with meatballs and sausage for the Sunday noontime meal. It was a dinner I had probably eaten hundreds of times at that very table. While she cooked the pasta, my father and I took our wine out onto the breezeway.

My father did most of the talking, and I could see how much he missed my brothers and me. He talked about the garden and reminded me to take some peppers back to San Diego. I waited before telling him there was something I wanted to talk to him and Mom about the following morning.

"Is it about your job?" he asked.

"That's part of it."

"You're going to leave the bureau and come back to live with us?" he said, smiling.

I shook my head. "No, it's about a lot of things. We'll talk about it tomorrow. In the meantime, I don't want you to worry about it."

Dad knew I could be stubborn at times, and perhaps that was why he didn't press me further at that point.

"I wanted to prepare you a little today. I'm not sure how Mom's going to react, and I need you to support her."

We sat in silence until my mother called us in to eat. She thanked God for all the blessings bestowed upon our family, giving special thanks for my being home.

I told her, as we began eating, that she made the best sauce in the world.

She laughed. "I had a good teacher."

My father had taught her how to cook.

"Often the student becomes better than the teacher," I said, and we all laughed.

My father mentioned that the sauce was made with fresh tomatoes from the garden. "This week we'll cook you some sausage and peppers," he said.

As we ate, they took turns talking about the family and Canastota, but I started to have a hard time concentrating. Perhaps it was the second glass of wine or simply the good feeling of being with them, but I knew this was the time to tell them I was gay. I moved my chair back and tried to relax as their conversation died.

I began to speak, then hesitated. They both looked over at me. I wanted my words to come out smoothly and cause no hurt or hardening in their hearts. I felt like making the sign of the cross.

"Mom, Dad," I began again, "there's something I want to tell you. I was going to wait until tomorrow, but I think this is as good a time as any."

My mother was sitting opposite me across the table, my father to my right. They started to look a little nervous.

"I've waited a long time to tell you something, probably too long, but I have come home for a special reason."

I paused, and both of them looked down. They did not look up again until I was done.

"As you probably have suspected for a long time, I'm gay. I want you to know that I'm not sick and I don't have AIDS."

Neither showed any reaction, and I began my story. I told them that although I had gone out with women, after a time I realized that I had stronger feelings for men than for women. I talked about my relationship with Brian and explained that while I felt comfortable about my homosexuality, the problem was the bureau. I tried to simplify and downplay what came next: the letter W. J. sent to the bureau, the FBI's subsequent questioning. I left out the break-ins, the stealing of my mail, the damage to the solarium, as well as the Teigen polygraph.

Another tough part was coming up. I could still picture them when I told them the news that I had been accepted into the FBI. My mother had gotten on the telephone to tell her friends. My father had taken his time, slowly going from house to house of family and friends. I think being accepted into the FBI was proof to them that as Italians and Italian-Americans we had finally arrived in America.

"A couple of weeks ago the bureau suspended me from my job. I was put on administrative leave with pay, and they are deciding whether I can continue working for them. There is a real possibility I may be fired."

Their heads remained bowed, and I decided to go right through to the end.

"I've hired an attorney, and I'm appealing their decision. I want to go back to work, but at this point it's hard to tell what they're going to do."

I glanced at the clock hanging on the wall over the kitchen table. Nearly an hour had gone by since I first began. I looked at my parents, and their heads were still down. It pained me to think of the sadness I had brought them. I got up from my chair and walked over to them. Standing between them, I asked my father if he still loved me.

He glanced up at me quickly, I guess to read the expression on my face. He also reached up, with his large hand, put it behind my neck, and slowly pulled me near him. "I love you even more," he whispered.

I felt tears coming into my eyes. I looked at my mother. "How about you, Mom?"

There were tears in her eyes, too. "I'll always love you, Francis," she said, and began to cry.

22.

In the week that followed, I shared many things with my mother and father. Everett had been right: They *were* stronger than I had expected. They were also full of questions.

Their primary concern had to do with AIDS, and I took my time explaining to them how the disease is transmitted. I assured them I was healthy and had not engaged in high-risk sexual behavior. I pointed out that in most of the world the HIV virus was predominantly a heterosexual disease. "It's a virus," I said, "and not God's punishment for being homosexual."

My mother wanted to know how I "became" gay. She said it as though she had done something wrong to make me this way.

"You were the same parents to Tony and Lou that you were to me," I said. "You're not to blame, and neither is it something wrong. I was born gay, just like my brothers were born heterosexual. The only choice I had was to be true to my feelings once I understood those feelings."

One morning my mother said, "It makes me sad to think that when you get old, you'll be alone."

I said that I understood her concerns but that gays and lesbians had long-term relationships, too. Neither of my parents understood the term "lesbian," so I explained it to them. I reminded them that nearly half of all heterosexual marriages ended in divorce.

At one point my father asked, "How come you never told us before?"

"Growing up, I thought I was heterosexual," I answered, "and it took me a long time to realize I wasn't. I was in my thirties before I knew for sure I was gay, and at that point I was in the bureau. If I told you, I knew it would worry you even more."

One night my mother went to bed early, and my father and I watched a movie. He commented about a pretty actress, and I agreed but added, "I like guys who are good-looking and have good builds."

Dad didn't react much, saying simply, his eyes still on the TV, how he could understand that.

I almost had to pinch myself. I couldn't believe that after all these years I was having this kind of conversation with my father!

The following morning, as the three of us sat in the living room drinking coffee, my father asked if I was still a Catholic.

I said I believed in God but no longer considered myself a Catholic in part because of the church's antigay stance.

My mother was listening carefully, and I turned to her. "It bothers me to hear Pat Robertson, Jerry Falwell, and the others on television condemn me and other gay people."

"The Bible says it's wrong. That it's the work of Satan," my mother said.

"I don't believe that, Mom. Besides, the Bible says we're not supposed to judge others. Those people condemning me don't know even know me or the kind of life I lead. Don't you think they should examine their own lives before they start pointing the finger at others?"

I had raised my voice for the first time in all our discussions and tried to regain my composure. "When Jesus was on this earth, He welcomed everyone into the kingdom of God. He spoke of love and tolerance for all people—no matter who they were or what their station in life."

"Do you believe there will be a day of judgment?" she asked.

"I believe we all were created by God. That means God created homosexuals, too. I don't believe God made a mistake in making me. And I believe when I die, I'll be judged for the life I lived and how I treated others, not whether or not I was gay."

By the end of the week my parents seemed more upset about the bureau's suspending me than my being gay!

"It isn't fair after all the hard work and sacrifices you made for them during your career," my father told me. "Why don't you just quit and do something else?"

I told him that I couldn't do that now, that I had to see it through. "You wouldn't expect Carmen Basilio to quit when things were going badly for him, would you?"

"Then you fight them on this," he said. "Your mother and I are behind you all the way."

Lou, Kathleen, and their infant daughter, Maggie, arrived Friday evening. The next morning they read Stoops's letter and my response. Along with Mom and Dad, we drove to nearby Chittenango Falls Park for a walk. My parents watched Maggie, while Lou, Kathleen, and I went off by ourselves. Lou seemed especially anxious to know how things had gone at home.

I described it all to them and then told them, for the first time, about the break-ins at my house, the attempts to retrieve messages, the theft of mail, and the damage done to the solarium. I said I hadn't told Mom and Dad about these things or about Teigen. "I don't want to worry them any more than they already do," I said.

Maybe the emotion of the week had finally caught up with me, or it was just plain hard talking face-to-face rather than on the phone. I began to feel very troubled. "Who is this guy, Lou, and why is he doing this to me?" I said, turning to him.

Lou and Kathleen slipped their arms around me.

"You've got some guy stalking you and the bureau doesn't even help you?" Lou said angrily. "They give you a hard time and even take your gun away?"

Kathleen squeezed my arm. "Fran, I am worried about your safety. Whoever is doing this is crazy, and there's no way of knowing what he might do next."

■　■　■

Monday morning my parents and I sat in the living room, waiting for my friend John Patane to take me to airport. I thanked them for being so understanding. I said I was probably more fortunate than some gay people who knew they were gay when they were very young and were picked on by others.

"I remember you used to tell us about being called names because you were Italian. But when you went home, your parents supported you. Most gay kids can't tell their parents they're gay because they're afraid of being disowned. They have to go through it all by themselves. So many gay teenagers commit suicide, and their parents never know why."

■　■　■

Brian was waiting as I passed through United's passenger exit. I had talked with him during the week, and he knew that I had told my parents I was gay.

"It was an incredible experience," I said on the drive to my house. "It's a great feeling not to have to lie to them anymore. And I've never felt closer to them."

Brian was subdued. "Did they ask about me?" he asked.

I looked over at him. "I told them about our relationship."

I sensed he was uncomfortable about what I had done because he remained unusually quiet the rest of the evening.

■　■　■

I called my attorney Tom Homann to see if there were any new developments. He said that Stoops had granted us an extension with respect to the appeal but that he still hadn't received any of the documents we had requested from the FBI.

I felt it best to use my time and energy constructively. I continued to run and to work out at the gym. I also started to repaint the interior of my house. The damaged windows of the solarium were replaced.

During the week I received several calls from people in the office asking me how I was doing. One afternoon, while I was painting, one of my closest friends in the bureau stopped by.

"There are a lot of rumors going around the office about you," he said as we sat at the kitchen counter. "But yours has got to be the best-kept secret in the bureau."

More than three weeks had passed since my suspension.

He asked if I wanted to hear what was being said.

"Sure," I answered. "This should be interesting."

Several rumors had to do with the Rogers case: that I had leaked information to the media or done something wrong in the investigation. Some thought I was having legal problems with my rental properties, and a few wondered if I had misappropriated government money or misused bureau vehicles or stolen equipment. But my agent friend told me most people discounted these possibilities because they felt me to be honest.

"Plus I have a lot of money anyway," I said, and we both laughed.

One agent thought I had messed up an undercover assignment along the line, and another insisted I was just going "deep" undercover.

He hesitated, and I wasn't sure why. "One rumor has to do with your involvement in the Big Brother program."

I knew what he meant, and I bristled. "Just between the two of us," I said, "none of the rumors are true. I really wish I could discuss it with you. Someday I'll be able to, but not just now."

He got up to leave, and I thanked him for stopping by. I walked him out to his car, and we shook hands. Some of what he said still bothered me. "Whenever you hear any of the rumors again," I said, "you might want to ask people to think about this: If I had been involved in criminal conduct of any kind, would the bureau have put me on administrative leave *with* pay?''

Later in the week my brother Tony and his wife, Barbara, came over. I had called them a few days earlier. I opened a bottle of wine and poured each of us a glass. We sat in the living room and chatted about their daughter, Chrissy. I could see they were anxious about why I had called them and began my story. Neither Tony nor Barbara seemed shocked or disturbed when I told them I was gay. They knew Brian fairly well and said they had pretty much assumed I was gay. They added that it never made any difference to them.

We talked about my health and how I had realized I was gay, and then I told them about my problem with the bureau. I went through the events associated with the W. J. letters and the bureau's investigation of me. The part about the Teigen polygraph was always difficult, and it took me awhile to get through it. Tony and Barbara became visibly upset at that point but didn't comment. I told them about the damage to the solarium and the other things that had happened at my house.

"I told Lou a few weeks ago, and I went home last week to tell Mom and Dad. They all seemed to handle it pretty well. I didn't tell Mom and Dad what happened at my house or about the polygraph." I said I hoped they were not offended because they were the last in our immediate family to know. I told them I had wanted to discuss it with them in person.

Tony stood up. He was angry. "I'd like to get my hands on that SOB Teigen," he said.

I told him Lou said the same thing, and we laughed.

Tony excused himself to go to the bathroom, and Barbara began to cry. I knelt beside her, putting my arm around her.

"It bothers me that all this has happened to you," she said, wiping her eyes. "But what bothers me most is that you had to go through it without us. Without your family. I wish you had told us so we could have helped."

Tony returned at that point and overheard her. Tears formed in his eyes. "I don't know what I can do to help," he said, "but if there's anything, anything at all, brother, just let me know."

■ ■ ■

The harassment at my house stopped after the suspension. Perhaps the new security system I installed helped, or maybe it was because I was home more. Then again, maybe W. J. was content because he had accomplished what he had set out to do.

Six weeks had passed, and I was still on administrative leave with pay. I continued getting phone calls from the office, and people were as curious as ever. There seemed to be more questions about my health in this round of calls. I suspected some of the callers thought I had AIDS.

I was invited to a going-away luncheon for a married couple at the office, both of whom were being transferred. I debated for a long time whether I should attend. I still felt very much a part of the bureau, but I thought attending would be too awkward. At the last minute I decided to go.

Upon arriving, I was immediately put at ease. Most people greeted me warmly, and though no one asked what was going on, everyone wished me well. The good feeling from the luncheon ended, however, when the others walked back to work and I went back home.

I received a call one evening from a retired FBI agent whom I hadn't seen in a while. He invited me to join him and two other agents for coffee the following morning. The three men had retired from the bureau in the early 1980s and were working part-time for another government agency. The three of us had worked organized crime cases together and remained good friends. When I was working, we usually got together every three or four months for breakfast or a Padres game.

We met at the usual Denny's restaurant. We talked and joked about the bureau, sports, and just about everything else, as we had always done.

I assumed they knew I was on administrative leave, but I didn't bring it up. As time slipped by, one of them told me they all knew. He glanced at the others, then back at me. "Did they pull your creds?"

Taking away an agent's credentials was unusual and considered serious. It was a major step toward being fired.

I hesitated for a moment. I had not disclosed this information to anyone associated with the bureau.

"Yes, they have," I said, and an uncomfortable silence followed.

"But I want you to know I haven't engaged in any criminal conduct. I'm not in any serious trouble, and I haven't embarrassed the bureau."

I knew the remark was pretty vague, but since the matter was still under review by the bureau, they would understand why I wouldn't want to talk about it.

"It's really a personal matter," I added. "It's a matter of principle, and I've decided not to cave in to the bureau on it."

We left the restaurant and walked to the parking lot. We shook hands, and one of the former agents lingered behind. "Frank," he said, "I don't know what's going on, and it's none of my business, but I've always respected you. Do what you think is right for you. You've always been a good friend, and none of this will change our friendship. Call me if you need any help."

23.

Richard Tanner called me the afternoon of November 11, 1989. Richard and I had become friends because of his long-term relationship with my friend K. D.

Kiertisin Dharmsathaphorn was of Chinese heritage and had grown up in Thailand. He graduated from Bangkok's medical school and emigrated to the United States after receiving a fellowship in gastroenterology from Yale University. He was a physician, a professor at the University of California at San Diego, and an internationally renowned researcher. K. D. was in his late thirties, and we had met through mutual friends in the early 1980s, when he first arrived in San Diego. He was a quiet, extremely polite man—and the most intelligent human being I had ever known. I loved listening to his insights on almost any subject.

K. D. and I often jogged together. He and Richard, and Brian and I, had also socialized together. K. D. often invited us, along with others, to his home for the splendid Thai dishes he would prepare. I reciprocated with baked lasagna, rigatoni, or some other Italian dish. I would kid K. D. that there was never an invitation for Italian food he ever turned down.

K. D. and I were usually the ones who called each other to arrange our get-togethers, so it was unusual for Richard to be calling me.

Richard said I would probably want to know that K. D. was not feeling good. I was surprised and asked how long he'd been sick.

"For about two weeks."

K. D. was an extremely healthy person, and a bad feeling came over me.

"You know he tested HIV positive, don't you, Frank?"

I leaned against the kitchen counter, trying to catch my breath. Richard quickly apologized for telling me in such an abrupt manner. He had assumed K. D. had already told me. "He's just not been himself," Richard added.

I asked if there was anything I could do.

"I'm sure he would enjoy talking to you. He thinks a lot of you and enjoys your company."

I called K. D. later that same afternoon. For the first time I detected a certain sadness in his voice. As usual he was concerned about my situation with the FBI and said he would like to see me when he was feeling better.

I told him I thought he should take it easy and rest. "I'm sounding like the doctor now," I said, and he laughed in that high-pitched way he had.

Brian came over that evening, and I told him I had received some bad news about K. D. He immediately sensed what it was. He became visibly upset.

"We keep hearing more and more about how fast this disease is spreading. It's not fair that anyone should come down with this disease, especially someone like K. D., who is so bright and doing so much to help others."

I shook my head, fighting back my own tears. "K. D. is such a good person and has always been such a good friend. I'm going to do whatever I can to help him."

AIDS became an even more integral part of my life that month. My worst fears for Tom Homann were confirmed when a gay friend told me that Tom had AIDS.

■　■　■

The media were carrying stories almost daily now on the emerging world-wide AIDS epidemic. President Reagan had been in office for nearly seven years before even saying the word "AIDS" out loud. Some suspected this was because the majority of its early victims were gay men.

Local gay newspapers carried stories about volunteer organizations in the gay community being formed to deal with the crisis. I wanted to become involved but knew if I did, I ran the risk of my situation becoming publicly known. I decided not to get involved until the situation was resolved. As a result, I was isolated from both the gay community and the FBI.

In that same month of November SAC Tom Hughes called and said he had some documents for me. My brother Tony and I were working together on some home repairs, and we met Hughes near the Federal Building downtown. Hughes handed me an envelope, and we talked briefly about his impending transfer to the Boston division. We wished each other luck.

I opened the envelope in the truck and read the letter from Gary Stoops first. Homann had written Stoops requesting documents pertaining to the FBI's investigation of me. Stoops wrote that he was denying my request except for the enclosures. I looked, and they were my own statements, thirty-five pages of them. I swore. "The bureau is saying I wouldn't cooperate," I told my brother, "and then they send my own testimony back to me!"

There was a second letter in the envelope, from the Freedom of Information section of the bureau. The letter spelled out the reasons why my request for documents was denied. It advised me that I could appeal the decision to an assistant attorney general at the Department of Justice.

I called Tom Homann, and he said he had received copies of the same letters. He said he would write an appeal letter to the assistant attorney general and contact me when it was done. We both thought it curious that Stoops did not mention my response to his letter of suspension.

By the end of November I was becoming frustrated by the lack of progress in my case and decided to write a personal letter to FBI Director William Sessions. I wanted to make sure he was aware of my case as well as emphasize my desire to continue working for the FBI. In the letter I requested that Sessions personally review my case before a final decision was made. I asked to meet with him personally to discuss the bureau's policy regarding homosexuality, my sexual orientation, and my record as an FBI agent.

Since becoming director, Sessions often publicly talked about his commitment to recruit and hire minorities for FBI employment. He wanted the bureau to reflect more accurately the minorities it served. I also thought that as a former federal judge he might be sensitive to discrimination issues.

I wrote to the newly appointed head of the FBI's Equal Employment Opportunity Office. I asked for FBI official policy in regard to homosexual applicants and agents. Dr. Soskis, the psychiatrist on retainer with the bureau, didn't know, and the FBI's own manuals didn't mention homosexuality at all. Yet the explicit reason for my being investigated was "alleged homosexual activities."

■　■　■

I mailed drafts of these letters to Tom Homann. He suggested that we also write Stoops and request that he not make a final decision about revoking my top secret security clearance until the Department of Justice had had a chance to rule on my appeal for documents. Homann said he would get back to me after he had reviewed the letters. He sounded tired.

The month of December began, and I remained on administrative leave with pay. I still called the squad's secretary on a regular basis for messages, and she continued to ask me when I was coming back. I had always kidded her that she reminded me of Peg Bundy on *Married with Children.* So, when she said she missed me this time, I couldn't resist, "But I see you every Sunday night at nine!"

In addition to calls from people at the office, I received a call from a retired agent with whom I had worked organized crime cases. When he retired, I had told him he was the best agent I ever worked with. He was of Italian descent, and now I immediately recognized his distinctive Brooklyn accent.

"I just heard you're on administrative leave," he said, loudly.

"Administrative leave *with* pay," I responded.

"How long has it been?"

"Two months."

He said he never heard of anybody being on administrative leave that long. "I don't know what's going on, and it's none of my business anyway," he said, his voice getting increasingly louder, "but I know what kind of a guy you are. Whatever it is, it's a bum rap!"

"That means a lot coming from you," I said.

"If you ever need anyone to testify on your behalf," he told me, his voice booming again, "you just call me, pal!"

A few days later I called the legal counsel of the FBI Agents Association and brought him up-to-date on my situation. I discussed the possibility of filing a lawsuit against the bureau at some point. I asked if the association would assist me.

"We are a fledgling organization," the attorney said. "Perhaps some of the agents in the larger offices might be liberal enough to support you, but a number of our members throughout the country would not want their membership fees spent defending a gay agent."

I thanked him for his honesty and for his help in the past. He asked me to keep him informed about the case and said he hoped other agents would benefit from what I was doing.

On December 4 Tom Homann asked me to come down to his office to sign the letters to Sessions, Stoops, and the Equal Employment Opportunity office. He looked considerably thinner and less energetic than when I had last seen him. As I signed the letters, he apologized for not having written the letter of appeal to the assistant attorney general yet. He suggested I write the letter myself. I was anxious that it go out, but it was clear why he hadn't finished it.

Homann called me a few days later and asked that I come down to see him. When I arrived, he was sitting on a couch in his outer office, staring out the window. He was smoking, and though it had been only a short while since I last saw him, he looked even more drawn than before. I did not ask him how he was doing. I greeted him instead with a smile and a hello.

"You know, Tom, it's been exactly a year since I called you from Washington."

"And I remember wanting to jump on a plane and fly to Washington that night," he answered, looking over. He managed a smile.

We both remained silent for a moment. He looked out the window again and said in a very matter-of-fact voice that he was shutting down his law practice. "I think you have a great case, and I would love to continue working on it, but I just don't have the energy anymore to do it justice."

He had never asked for money for his services. Though I sent him a check a couple of times, I was never certain if the amount was appropriate. Before I left that day, I asked him to send me a final bill. He waved me off, saying he'd get around to it someday.

There was an awkward silence when we shook hands good-bye. Though I was anxious about the possibility of losing my job, he was facing the certainty of death. I could see the sadness in his eyes and tried not to show my own sad feelings as I thanked him for all his help. He said he would work with me in finding an attorney to take his place. Then he just kind of smiled and wished me luck.

■　■　■

Brian told me he was going to go snow skiing with a gay friend during his Christmas break from school. I had never met his friend, though Brian occasionally mentioned him. Brian asked me to join them, but I decided to stay put in case the bureau reached its decision. Brian said he would be back early enough to help me prepare for our annual New Year's Eve party.

I spent Christmas Day with my brother Tony and his family. We called Canastota in the afternoon, and Lou and his family were there with our parents. The following week I invited Tony and his family to my New Year's Eve party. For the first time they met most of my gay friends. Brian returned at the last minute from his ski trip, and I was angry he hadn't returned earlier, as promised. But maybe I was angry because I could see he was becoming more independent of me. I had encouraged this, of course, but I didn't like it when it began to happen. He did not stay the night.

■　■　■

I sent a card to Tom Homann and enclosed a check. I again thanked him for his help and told him that his courage and lifelong work on behalf of gays and lesbians had given me the courage to fight for my job.

On New Year's Day I walked alone on Pacific Beach. I was normally optimistic about beginnings. I reached the jetty in Mission Beach and turned around to head back. The wind was picking up.

Some good had come from the previous year, but it had come on the heels of anger and disappointment. The two worlds I had kept apart for so long were now interweaving and in some places colliding. These were uncharted waters, and the ocean seemed uncharacteristically wind-tossed and uneasy that day.

24.

"Richard Gayer wrote the book on gay people and security clearances," Tom Homann said. "He fought the government for his own security clearance in the 1970s, and he's been fighting the government ever since. I've had occasion to call him in the past, and he's the best in the country for this kind of case."

I wanted the best attorney possible, and I also knew my case required special legal expertise. The problem was that Richard Gayer lived in San Francisco, five hundred miles away. Despite this, I decided to seek his counsel. I briefly explained my situation and advised him that my current attorney was ill and could no longer represent me. I emphasized that my goal was to keep my job and that I wasn't seeking any publicity. "I like the people I work with, and they probably would not have a problem working with me."

Gayer answered right away, "That may be true, but they aren't the people who will be making the decisions in your case. Have you ever met Stoops?"

"No," I answered, surprised by his directness.

"I've dealt with people in government for years. You need to realize you're dealing with bigots who fear and hate gay people. They don't know you personally, nor do they want to know you. Your exemplary record means nothing to them. You're just another gay person they're going to get rid of."

I didn't respond.

"Given the current legal and political climate in this country and the FBI's history of antigay discrimination," he continued, "I think your chances of keeping your job are not very good. But that doesn't mean you shouldn't try." He asked me to send him copies of any relevant documents I had and said that he would get back to me when he had a chance to look them over.

Before the conversation ended, I told Gayer I wasn't sure what I wanted to do if the bureau in fact fired me. "A lawsuit is a possibility," I said, "but I believe there are other ways of changing FBI policies."

"Standing up on a soapbox after you've been fired is not going to do you a lot of good," he shot back. "Nobody's going to pay a lot of attention to you. You will, however, get the media's attention, and consequently the FBI's attention, by filing a lawsuit." He paused briefly, then added, "But it appears we have a long way to go before you will have to make that decision."

In early January I received a response to the letter I sent to the bureau's equal employment opportunity officer. He detailed the kinds of discrimination prohibited by Title VII of the Civil Rights Act of 1964, stating: "Title VII's prohibition on sex discrimination applies only to alleged discriminatory actions based on gender and does not prohibit actions which may be based on sexual preference." The civil rights laws I had been responsible for enforcing did not apply to me.

Around then I received a letter from the Department of Justice's Office of Information and Privacy. I was told that the office had "a substantial backlog of pending appeals received prior" to mine. I would have to wait for my request to be processed, and there was no assurance I would receive my personnel file and other documents related to my case. Nearly four months had passed since my suspension, and I was frustrated that so little progress had been made.

I still hadn't received a response to my letter to Director Sessions and suggested to Homann and Gayer that I contact Congressman Don Edwards. Edwards was a former FBI agent and the current chairperson of the House of Representatives Subcommittee on Civil and Constitutional Rights, which had oversight responsibility for FBI operations. Homann and Gayer told me to go ahead, but neither of them expected the FBI to be greatly influenced one way or another by a member of Congress.

I called Edwards's office in San Jose, identifying myself as an FBI agent who wanted to speak confidentially with the congressman about an important matter concerning the bureau. His secretary set up a telephone appointment, and Edwards and I talked the following afternoon.

I told him my name and that I was an FBI agent assigned to the San Diego Division. I then asked that he not publicly disclose what I was about to tell him.

"I assure you it will be kept confidential," he responded.

I explained my situation, and Edwards sounded more sympathetic

than I had expected. He said he had discussed this issue in the past with
the bureau. He thought the FBI was "out of step" with other law enforcement agencies that had openly gay officers and asked how he could
help me.

I told him about my letter to Director Sessions, and he said he would
"take it up with Bill" at their next breakfast meeting. For the first time
I felt encouraged that something positive might happen in my case.

Joe Johnson had replaced Tom Hughes as the SAC in San Diego, and
I called him at the office to introduce myself. Johnson said he was aware
of my situation but did not know any of the details. I told him I'd be
glad to meet with him and discuss it.

At the beginning of February I called Edwards's office in Washington.
Edward's legal counsel said that the congressman had spoken with
Director Sessions about my situation but that he didn't know the outcome.
He promised to get back to me as soon as he found out.

On the morning of February 8, SAC Johnson called and asked to
meet with me that afternoon. We agreed on a restaurant in Mission
Valley, and Johnson gave me a physical description of himself. He didn't
ask for mine, and I assumed he had seen the office photograph of me.

I wasn't able to reach either Homann or Gayer before the meeting,
and I couldn't tell from Johnson's voice whether the news was going to
be good or bad. As I drove to the restaurant, I tried to remain optimistic.
But emotionally I prepared myself for the worst.

I was standing in the waiting area of the restaurant when Johnson
arrived. He seemed a little older than I was, about the same height and
weight, and had dark brown hair. He was dressed in a dark blue pin-
striped suit. I purposely wore a blazer and tie. It was important to me
that I not lose my identity as an FBI agent and that Johnson see me this
way. As we shook hands, I noticed he was carrying a manila envelope.

The waitress showed us to a booth, and we sat opposite each other.
"Frank," he said, "I understand you have an excellent reputation in the
office. Everyone speaks very highly of you."

The waitress took our order, and then, without speaking, he opened
the manila envelope and took out its contents. "I was asked to give these
to you. Please take a look at them, and if you have any questions, I'll
try to find the answers for you."

He handed me two letters. Both were dated January 31, 1990. I read
the one-page letter from John E. Otto, the FBI associate deputy director
first. My eye was drawn to the line "By now you have been notified of

the decision of the Security Programs Manager to revoke your security clearance.''

The words hit me like a punch in the face. I was really going to be fired! I could feel my anger mount, and I looked at Johnson. He was staring at me without expression. Otto's letter went on to say that my request to meet with the director had been denied.

I read the second letter, which was from Gary Stoops, the bureau's security programs manager. Stoops stated that he was revoking my security clearance for the reason cited in his September letter of suspension, but there was one new distinction. He said his decision had nothing to do with my ''sexual orientation.'' It was, instead, based upon his belief that I was ''not truthful in answering questions posed during the inquiry.''

Stoops gave me twenty days to appeal the decision to D. Jerry Rubino, the security officer for the Justice Department. The letter said that if I didn't file an appeal, the matter would be referred to the FBI's assistant director, Administrative Services Division, ''for appropriate administrative action to determine your suitability for continued employment with the FBI.''

I reread both letters. Stoops had originally accused me of being part of a ''secret homosexual society'' and engaging in ''exploitable sexual conduct.'' Now he was claiming my homosexuality had nothing to do with his decision!

The past year and a half had been a sham! The bureau had taken its time to give the appearance it was being rational and fair. But it had really intended to fire me the first day I told it I was gay. What I said, how many questions I answered, or how many polygraphs I took had never really mattered. The bottom line was that I was gay and the bureau was not going to allow any gay people to work for it.

I put the letters down and looked at Johnson. He would probably report my reaction back to the people at headquarters, and I knew exactly what I wanted them to hear.

''This is ridiculous,'' I said. ''After J. Edgar Hoover and Clyde Tolson the bureau is firing *me* because I'm gay?''

I was convinced that Hoover and Tolson were gay lovers. I had not mentioned it during the investigation, however, because it was neither my business nor anyone else's. But the hypocrisy had finally gotten to me.

Johnson did not react.

''You know as well as I do that there are agents in the bureau who are lazy and incompetent, agents who have done very little worthwhile work in their entire careers. And the bureau is going to fire *me*?''

The more I spoke, the angrier I became. "There are agents in this office who have serious alcohol and financial problems and agents who cheat on their wives. But the bureau looks the other way because they're heterosexual. I don't have any of those problems. All I am is gay."

I wasn't finished. "And look at Miller [the FBI agent convicted of espionage], a bumbling, incompetent agent for twenty years, but he was heterosexual. The bureau never fired him, and he ended up betraying the country. I never compromised the bureau or the country—nor has *any* homosexual for that matter."

The waitress brought our coffee, and I sat looking at the letters. When she left, Johnson asked me to sign a form promising I would not reveal classified information to anyone outside the bureau.

I was insulted. "I've never done that in the bureau and would never do it outside the bureau."

I took out my pen, signed the form, and handed it back to Johnson. My anger began to subside. I knew I hadn't been fair to Johnson. He was just the messenger.

I apologized. "I really care about my job, and I'm going to appeal the bureau's decision."

Neither of us spoke for a few moments. "If I get fired, Joe, people in the bureau will always wonder what I did to have my Top Secret security clearance revoked." It was time to leave. "The bureau has given me a black eye by revoking my clearance, but if this thing ever goes public, the bureau is going to end up with two black eyes. Not from me. But from its own conduct in all this."

After returning home, I called Homann, Gayer, and my family, to tell them of the bureau's decision. I later reached Brian, and he seemed less sympathetic than the others. He couldn't understand why I was so upset. I was angered by his attitude, telling him that barring a miracle, I was going to be fired. He responded that I should have been expecting it.

I called Everett after hanging up and told him about the meeting with Johnson. Of Brian's response, Everett said, "You're two very different personalities, Frank. You can't expect him to react the same way you do. Perhaps this is just becoming too much for him, and he's apprehensive about the future."

"So am I, Everett," I shot back. "But what am I supposed to do—roll over and quit?"

"You know how I feel about what you should do," he responded in a gentle voice. "But only you can make that decision."

■ ■ ■

I met with Drew Mattison and tried to come to terms with my feelings of anger and betrayal. We talked about the effect my suspension and potential termination was having on my relationship with Brian. He and I saw each other even less now, and we seldom spent the night together.

■ ■ ■

Gayer agreed to represent me, but because of the demands of his other work, he requested an extension of the appeal deadline. In his letter to the Justice Department, he also suggested the FBI reconsider its decision "before the Bureau shoots itself in the foot by terminating [your] employment and creating a Gay rights test case the Bureau is likely to regret."

In February we received a copy of a letter Congressman Edwards had sent to Director Sessions. Edwards posed a number of questions with regard to FBI policies toward gays and lesbians. He pointed out that homosexuals were being accepted by other police departments without problems, "and the country as a whole has moved toward acceptance of homosexuals." Edwards said he was "concerned that the FBI is out of step."

As Gayer and I worked on the letter of appeal, I began to think about taking a cross-country trip back to Canastota in my RV. I had spent months in San Diego waiting for a decision and needed to get away and think about the future. The appeal was my last hope for keeping my job, and if that failed, I would have to decide fairly quickly about filing a lawsuit. It would be a decision that would change not only my life but also the lives of my family and close friends.

As an FBI agent and a closeted gay man I had lived a very private personal life. A highly publicized lawsuit would mean the loss of that privacy. My sexuality, my private life, and my professional life would be opened for examination and judgment. Additionally, the bureau would likely attempt to discredit me and make me appear unfit to be an FBI agent.

Gayer thought we would receive a response from Rubino in about a month and recommended that I take no longer than that for my trip. I talked to Brian about going with me, but he said he couldn't be away that long from college and his job. We hadn't been away together for a long time, and our last cross-country trip together had made us closer than we had ever been.

25.

Rusty and I left in my RV on March 27, 1990, the day the appeal letter was finished. Lou suggested I make tape recordings of my experiences along the way. I also began making separate tapes of what I had learned about my ordeal during the past two years. Perhaps being away from San Diego would help me find the perspective I desperately needed.

I purposely drove through Arkansas on the way to Canastota because I wanted to see Central High School in Little Rock. The first major confrontation over implementation of the Supreme Court's 1954 decision outlawing racial segregation in public schools had occurred there in September 1957.

The front entrance of the large stone building brought back images from television of the angry mob shouting, ''Go home, niggers!'' But federal troops, bayonets pointed to deter opposition, allowed blacks to enter the school. Even today I was in awe of the courage of those black children and their parents.

When I arrived in Canastota, I talked at length with my parents about the likelihood of my being fired. I told them I hadn't decided whether to challenge the bureau in court. I knew that they would be concerned about the reactions of relatives and neighbors and that a lawsuit would probably bring a lot of publicity. ''If I file a suit, I'll explain my reasons to the family and neighbors.''

I was surprised when my father told me he would take care of that for me. My parents said they would support me whatever decision I made.

I was also concerned with how a lawsuit might affect my brother Lou at his job. He was a professor at St. John Fisher College, in Rochester, New York, a small liberal arts school with a Roman Catholic tradition. Lou said he thought the president, Dr. William Pickett, and the vice-president and academic dean at the time, Dr. Thomas McFadden, would be supportive and not retreat from controversy. He was right. When my brother met with each of them privately, their support was unequivocal and has remained so.

Before my problem with the bureau, I had talked to Lou about the possibility of collaborating on a book once I retired. Now he raised the idea with renewed intensity and a different purpose. "People need to know what's been happening to you, Frank," he said. "And they're never going to find out from newspaper accounts. The FBI should not be allowed to get away with what they've done."

On the way back to California I stopped in Phoenix, Arizona, and called the parents of a man with whom I had once been very close. Todd's parents had stayed at my house in San Diego, but I had not seen them or Todd in nearly ten years.

Todd's mother answered the phone, and I introduced myself. She said she remembered me and asked how I was doing. When I returned the question, her voice suddenly changed. "The last few weeks have been very sad for us," she said. "You know we lost Todd."

"I'm so sorry. No. I didn't know." I wondered if his death had been caused by AIDS.

"He was very sick for a long time and finally came home so we could take care of him. It was very sad."

Todd was a recovering alcoholic, and we had become good friends. But his substance abuse became too severe, and I severed our friendship. For a long time afterward I had missed him.

"We would like to see you, Frank," she said.

Under the circumstances it would be difficult, but I accepted.

Todd's father was waiting when I arrived, and I hugged them both. They were about as old as my parents, and I was struck by how much they had aged since I'd last seen them. We talked for a while, and then I got around to telling them about my problem with the bureau. I was surprised by the vigor they showed in encouraging me to stand up to the FBI.

They talked about Todd's life since he had returned home and how terribly he had suffered in the past few months from AIDS. "We never thought any of our children would die before us," his mother said, starting to cry. "He was only thirty-nine years old, Frank."

She took out an album they had prepared of Todd's funeral service, which included letters and cards from family and friends. As I looked through it, she got up and left the room. When she returned, she was carrying a framed color photograph of Todd taken when he was still healthy. He looked the same as I remembered—handsome, with a mischievous smile. I held the picture for a while, and Todd's eyes seemed to be looking directly into mine.

■   ■   ■

I phoned Gayer after returning to San Diego, and he said he still hadn't heard from the Department of Justice about my appeal. I called Edwards's office and was told Director Sessions had not responded to the congressman's letter yet. I called the legal counsel for the FBI Agents Association that week to find out how an agent actually got fired. I was told the SAC might call me into the office or I could be notified by mail.

Phone calls from people at the office now seemed to indicate that they knew about my being gay. Then a call came confirming my suspicions. It was from an agent with whom I had worked closely for a number of years. Gruff and outspoken, he had often made derogatory comments about gay people in my presence both on and off the job. He had called before, offering his support, but this time the tone of his voice was different.

"Frank . . . " he began, and then hesitated. He always talked loudly, and I had to hold the receiver a slight distance away. "I've heard some terrible rumors about you. We've worked together for a long time, and I never detected that in you."

I didn't respond. "It's honestly caused me to change my attitude toward the subject. I want you to know I'll be a character witness for you if you think it will help. You'd be surprised at all the support you have from people in the office."

I told him his words meant a lot to me.

"You know, with the way the bureau treats its employees, your efforts will probably help us all."

Charles Gorder, an assistant United States attorney in San Diego, also called that week. Charles and I had worked several major cases together, including the Rogers investigation. Charles was hardworking, extremely competent, and considered one of the best prosecutors in his office. We were friends and occasionally had lunch or saw a Padres game together.

He talked briefly and in general terms about the lack of progress on the Rogers case and said the investigation could surely use my help. I assumed he knew what was going on with me, but neither of us talked about it. Before hanging up, however, he offered to be a character witness if I needed him.

Toward the end of April I decided to call Gary Hall. Gary had grown up in Canastota and was in Lou's high school graduating class. Gary and Lou had been best friends, and when he converted to Roman Catholicism, he had asked my parents to be his godparents.

Gary had spent a lot of time at our house in those days and been like a member of the family. We all played sports together, and Gary was a star athlete in football and baseball. He was also an expert in karate. Later, after college and a stint in the Marine Corps, Gary graduated from George Washington Law School. He became an assistant United States attorney in Washington, D.C., and later transferred first to Los Angeles and then to San Francisco. After several years Gary had left the United States attorney's office and was now in private practice in Oakland, California. He and I had kept in touch, and I occasionally saw him when I went to San Francisco.

When I called Gary that Sunday morning in April, he immediately sensed something was wrong. "How *are* you?" he asked.

For the first time I told him I was gay and about my problems with the bureau.

"Do you have an attorney?"

I told him about Gayer and our appeal to the Department of Justice. I said I was expecting to be fired soon and was seriously considering filing a lawsuit.

"I'm sorry about what's happening to you, but I am glad you shared it with me. I only wish you had talked to me about this sooner. You know I've always respected the FBI agents I worked with, but I've represented several agents who sued the bureau. I've known firsthand how the FBI treats its people, and it's not good, Frank!"

Before our conversation ended, Gary offered his assistance. "You're facing an uphill battle. The bureau has enormous resources, and it will use them."

May became the eighth month of my suspension, and there was still no response from the Department of Justice. Brian seemed to become uneasy whenever I talked about the possibility of filing a lawsuit. During the month he and I talked about spending time together, but we didn't see much of each other. When we were together, we sometimes argued over the most trivial things. One time he criticized my driving, and I started swearing angrily at him. I wish now I had seen Drew Mattison or Everett more during that period. Maybe Brian and I could have salvaged whatever was left of our friendship at least.

One afternoon I stopped by Brian's apartment unannounced. I met the guy he had gone skiing with at Christmas. I didn't stay long, and when I left, I was both sad and hurt. I recognized I was jealous even though I had been the one who encouraged him to see others.

I had been running and working out on a regular basis, but in May my back started bothering me. I seldom had any physical problems and tried to ignore the pain. Eventually, though, it became so severe I made an appointment with an orthopedic physician. The doctor prescribed some mild muscle relaxants and back exercises. The pain eased a little, but I was no longer able to run. Friends suggested the ailment might be stress-related and encouraged me to relax more. Running, however, was my way of relaxing.

Toward the end of May I found myself waiting around the house every day until the mail arrived. I was anxious and irritable, and the pain continued with ever-increasing intensity. I spent most of my days alone and felt more isolated than ever from the outside world.

On the afternoon of May 29 the long-awaited letter from the Department of Justice arrived. I sat still for a few moments before opening it.

The seven-page letter was from D. Jerry Rubino, the Department of Justice security officer. It began with a review of my case and then focused on the main issues involved. It was soon apparent Rubino believed I was both a liar and a threat to national security. Like Stoops, he claimed his decision had nothing to do with my sexual orientation.

"Based on all of the above considerations, as well as careful review of the investigative records and appeal," Rubino concluded, "I am simply unable to conclude that continued access to classified information is clearly consistent with the national security. I am, therefore, denying your appeal and upholding the FBI's revocation of your security clearance."

Many of the facts on which Rubino based his decision were simply not true. This angered me. He had relied on polygraph results to support his charges. I thought about Gayer's comment when I had first talked with him. He had said that one of the most important decisions in my life would be made by people who didn't know me or care about my record.

It was time for me to make a decision. I could resign and avoid the stigma of being fired from the FBI. I had enough money to support myself until I found another job, and I could probably find a position where my being gay didn't matter. It would avoid my beginning a long, costly, and highly publicized lawsuit.

I sat in my chair for a long while. I thought about all I had gone through since the bureau learned I was gay. I hadn't been very courageous at the beginning of all this. So many times I wanted to just walk away from the conflict and go on with my life.

The courage of Carmen Basilio in the ring came to mind, and the courage of the black children in Little Rock. The sacrifices of Harvey Milk and Leonard Matlovich reminded me of the countless gays and lesbians fighting for justice.

From the beginning Everett had recognized my reluctance to take a stand against the bureau. And he had continually encouraged me to fight for myself, knowing that in the process the struggle would contribute to obtaining justice. Could I live with myself if I turned away and took the easy way out? I had spent most of my life denying who I was—but never again.

I picked up the phone and called Gayer. He recognized my voice.

"I take it you've received some news."

"Yes, I have." I told him about Rubino's decision.

"Have you decided what you want to do?"

"I want to file the lawsuit."

There was silence on the other end, and when Gayer spoke again, I could hear the excitement in his voice. "We'll need to move very quickly," he advised me, "before they fire you. I should have the papers ready by next week. Why don't you come up at the beginning of the week and we'll file on Friday, June eighth?"

I told him about Gary Hall and his offer of assistance.

"By all means. We'll need him," Gayer replied. "He can help guide us through the minefield we'll be walking through."

part five

other doors open

26.

I called my family, Gary Hall, Tom Homann, Brian, and other close friends to tell them of my decision. I asked everyone to keep the information confidential. I was concerned that if the bureau found out my plans, it would fire me before I had a chance even to file the suit. It would be the first time in the eighty-two year history of the bureau that one of its agents charged it with discrimination based upon sexual orientation.

It was pretty heady stuff, but I suspected that once this became public, some people would no doubt view me as a disgruntled employee seeking notoriety or even money; others, as a sexual deviant who should never have been hired in the first place. But many in the gay and lesbian community, and civil rights proponents, probably would look upon my lawsuit as a major challenge to the government.

Since I had first considered filing a lawsuit, I had thought I should pay my own legal expenses. I believed pro bono representation should be reserved for those who could least afford an attorney. By paying my own way, I could also maintain control.

I put Gayer in touch with Gary Hall, and I talked with both several times before going to San Francisco. My back was a little better, so I decided to drive. I arrived on Wednesday evening, June 6, at the home of my two longtime friends Roger and Phil. We had remained good friends since I first met them in the Los Angeles area in the mid-1970s. I rented a room from them, so I would have a place to stay for the remainder of my lawsuit. It would also satisfy the legal requirement for residency. Without it the government might challenge my filing the lawsuit in San Francisco. Gayer and I both believed that San Francisco's reputation of tolerance toward gays and lesbians was strategically important to my case.

The following morning I drove down to Fisherman's Wharf. It was warm, and I had a clear view of the Golden Gate Bridge in the distance. I had breakfast and then walked for a while along the shore-line. My life had changed enormously since I had first visited San Francisco in 1972. No doubt my life was about to change in ways I could not imagine.

I drove to Gayer's home, which doubled as his office, near the Castro area. I found a parking space and walked up the steps of the two-story residence. I was expecting a larger, more imposing person, on the basis of the sound of his voice and his attitude. Gayer looked about fifty, five feet eleven inches, and weighed about 150 pounds. He wore glasses and had a brush cut and neatly trimmed mustache. He reminded me more of a college professor than someone who battled the U.S. government.

He led me to his office and then left to answer the phone. I sat at a table which I assumed also served as his dining-room table. The room was clean and orderly, but it was difficult to see where Gayer's residential life ended and his office began. The walls of the room were lined with books and music tapes. As an agent I had visited a lot of law offices, and perhaps I was fortunate this one wasn't fancy. Gayer was charging me at a rate far less than standard fees. Gayer told me later he did this so that gay rights cases would not be abandoned.

Gary Hall arrived, and I introduced him to Gayer. Gary apologized for being late, and I took the opportunity to kid him about being a rich and famous attorney.

The three of us sat down and looked over the papers Gayer had pre-pared in order to file a preliminary injunction. Its purpose was to obtain a temporary restraining order to prevent the FBI from firing me until the facts in the case had been reviewed. We would file a ''John Doe'' lawsuit. I was concerned that if I used my real name, the FBI would be able to argue that because my identity was known, I could no longer be effective as an agent. It might use this as a reason not to hire me back.

We made some minor changes, and Gary commented about the ex-cellent quality of Gayer's work. Gary turned to me and asked if I was sure I wanted to go through with this. ''The FBI is not going to be frightened because you're suing them. You're in for a long difficult fight, and the government has a lot of resources.''

I told him I had thought through my decision and I was angry at how unfairly the bureau treated me.

Gary shook his head. ''Your mistake was thinking the bureau was going to treat you fairly.'' He had another appointment and got up to leave. ''Do you see now why a lot of people don't like the FBI, Frank?''

I didn't comment. It seemed that no matter how angry I was at the bureau, criticism of it from "outsiders" was still difficult to hear.

■ ■ ■

At ten the following morning, June 8, I met Gayer in front of the Federal Building. We took the elevator to the office of the clerk for the federal district court. Another person was filing papers ahead of us, and I sat down. My back had started to bother me again.

A reporter for the San Francisco *Examiner* spotted Gayer and asked if he had anything important. Gayer suggested he review the legal filings later in the day. The reporter looked at me with curiosity, but Gayer didn't introduce us.

The clerk called Gayer's name, and he handed her the original and several copies of the document she had prepared. She assigned a number to the case and stamped the date and location of the filing on each package of documents. Federal Judge Eugene F. Lynch was assigned my case, and Gayer winced. "Bad news," he whispered to me.

As we walked to the U.S. attorney's office in the same building, Gayer said, "There are several other judges we could have gotten who would have been much more sympathetic than Judge Lynch."

Lynch was a Reagan appointee who often sided with the government. He was currently hearing a lawsuit brought by Julie Dubbs, who worked for a private company under contract to the CIA. Dubbs had been denied a security clearance when the CIA learned she was a lesbian. Gayer was representing her before Judge Lynch.

We left copies of the filings at the U.S. attorney's office, and Gayer and I had lunch on Castro Street. It was striking how different we were in terms of personality, appearance, and background. But both of us were gay and understood how it felt to be discriminated against by our employer—the government.

Originally from Philadelphia, Gayer had spent most of his nearly twenty years as an attorney fighting the government on gay civil rights issues. Gayer could be very intense and direct, and getting to know him personally, I suspected, was not going to be easy. I did remark about his name in this regard. "How appropriate," I said.

■ ■ ■

When I returned to Roger and Phil's house, Gayer called to say he had been contacted by radio and newspaper reporters, as well as by the AP and UPI. They all were asking for my name and wanted to interview me. Gayer explained why I didn't want my identity known and did the interviews himself.

It was strange to hear myself talked about on the radio. In a San Francisco *Examiner* story about the case the following morning, an FBI spokesman was quoted as saying the bureau would not discuss the case. He also refused to comment on whether or not the bureau viewed homosexuality adversely. He did say, however, that homosexual behavior was "a significant factor" in the hiring and retention of bureau employees. The statement did not make sense to me.

I arrived back in San Diego late that same afternoon. As I turned onto my street, I wondered if the media would be waiting for me. In many respects, San Diego was like a small town, and it was possible the media had learned of my identity—either on their own or because the bureau had leaked it to them.

Only Brian's car was in front of my house, and when I entered he told me the phone had been ringing all day. "But before you answer the calls, I want you to sit down." A few moments later he returned carrying a copy of the San Diego *Tribune*.

"Congratulations, Frank," he said smiling, holding it up, "you made the front page!" The headline said, FBI AGENT SUES TO HALT FIRING. It surprised me that Brian didn't seem at all upset by the publicity.

The article in the *Tribune* was lengthy and well written. The FBI spokesperson this time stated: "Our concern is sexual conduct, not sexual preference. Individual sexual orientation, whether homosexual or heterosexual, may involve conduct relevant or adversely affecting employment with the FBI."

Go ahead, I thought. The more public comments the bureau made about homosexual or heterosexual conduct, the more I felt they would help my case. A key point in my lawsuit was that my homosexual conduct did not affect my ability to do my job. My performance ratings of "excellent" and "superior" would support that argument. Moreover, if it hadn't been for an anonymous letter about my personal life, the bureau would never have known about my homosexuality at all. I remembered a few weeks before an agent's saying, "When the bureau starts looking into the sexual conduct of its employees, it's opening up a can of worms."

The *Tribune* article also mentioned that the FBI was exempt from the civil service procedures that guarantee a government employee the right to an impartial hearing before possible termination. The article contained enough personal information to enable an enterprising reporter to identify me.

While Brian made dinner, I went through the messages on my answering machine. My brother Tony, Charles Gorder, Ann Davis, and several others had called, all voicing their support. It was obvious at least to these people that I was the agent referred to in the newspapers. It would just be a matter of time now before others would find out. I started returning calls, and at the end of the one with Gorder, he joked that he would still go to Padres games with me.

"I can always wear a bag over my head, Charles."

"The way the Padres are playing"—he laughed—"you might not be the only one wearing a bag!"

An old friend who had recently lost his longtime companion to AIDS said the newspaper article had brought tears to his eyes. "There's so much discrimination out there against us," he said, "but what you're doing is going to help change that."

I saved the call to my brother Tony for last. "I'm your brother, Fran," he told me, "and if you need me anytime, day or night, just call me."

I sensed there was something more he wanted to say. After a moment or two he added, "Sometimes when I hang up the phone after talking with you, I can't help but cry. I told Barbara I'm worried that something is going to happen to you."

"I've bought a gun, Tony, and I'm being careful. But it's the love and support from you and so many others that's helping me do this."

Brian and I brought our meals into the den and turned on the local news. There was a short segment about my case, followed by coverage of San Diego's annual Gay Pride Parade and Festival.

"Good timing, Frank," Brian said with a grin.

The phone started ringing early on Monday morning. One call was from a Naval Investigative Service agent who had worked with me on the Rogers investigation. "I just want you to know my wife and I support you and we admire your courage," said the NIS agent. "You're the best FBI agent I've ever worked with, and I would trust you with my life."

A veteran FBI agent who had worked foreign counterintelligence cases most of his career called to offer his support. He also said he was willing to testify on my behalf regarding the blackmail issue. "I've had a lot of experience with hostile intelligence agents, and they seldom use blackmail against homosexuals," he commented.

Gayer called late that afternoon. "I don't know how long we're going to be able to protect your identity. I just received a call from a San Diego newspaper reporter who wanted to know if John Doe was really Frank Buttino."

I told Gayer the word was already out at the office, but he should try to hold off the press as long as possible.

At about 6:00 P.M. two veteran agents from the office pulled into the driveway. Each, like me, had about twenty years of service in the FBI. One brought a bottle of wine as a gift. I thanked him, saying I would like to save it to celebrate my return to work.

They said that most of the agents in the office supported me but that a few were upset by the negative publicity about the bureau. I told them briefly what had happened and how I had tried to keep my job without resorting to a lawsuit. Afterward both agreed the bureau left me no choice.

Before they left, one of the agents, who was very religious, asked if he could say a prayer. We bowed our heads, and he asked God to bless us all, especially me, in this time of trouble and pain. He said that God did not give a person a cross too heavy to bear and he hoped it was in God's plan that my example would bring about change in the FBI.

■ ■ ■

I wondered if the mother of my "little brother" in the Big Brother program saw the story in the newspaper and realized that I was the agent being talked about. I called her and made arrangements for lunch. When I arrived, I noticed a worried look on her face. Whenever we had talked in the past two years, her son was usually present.

I asked if she had seen the newspaper article over the weekend about the FBI agent suing the bureau, and she answered no. As we walked toward Horton Plaza together, I told her I was gay. She did not comment, and I continued my story.

She turned to me afterward and said, "What does your homosexuality have to do with your job? It's your private life and shouldn't be anybody else's business."

She told me that when I called, she thought I was getting transferred or was too busy to continue being a big brother to her son. "You've had such a positive affect on Andy," she said. "He's matured a lot these last two years being with you. His attitude and personality have changed so much for the better because of your influence."

We sat down to lunch and talked at length about my situation and the potential effect on her son if my name became known. I felt it necessary to tell her about the rumor in the FBI office that my problem stemmed from my involvement in the Big Brother program.

She thanked me but said it was not something she would ever worry about. If that was still all right with me, she wanted me to continue my relationship with her son. We thought it best if I told Andy what was happening.

The following day I had lunch with a veteran agent I knew well.

"We were talking in the office about how difficult it must have been for you all those years working in the bureau," he said, "knowing you could have been fired at any moment if they found out you were gay." He apologized for the derogatory comments he had made in the past about gay people.

"Most of the time I just ignored the comments," I replied. "But during the past few years comments people made about gay people and AIDS really hurt. A few times I responded angrily."

He said that my case was the main topic of conversation in the office and that a number of people were upset that Hughes and Kuker had never called an all-employees conference to explain what was happening. "You've got a lot of support in the office," he said, "and people want to know how they can help you."

I told him that letters to the judge on my behalf might help, and he said he would pass that information along. "You know as well as I do that some people might be afraid to write those letters," he added.

We kidded each other the remainder of lunch. He asked if I wanted to hear some of the humor in the office about me. I nodded, and he leaned closer across the table.

"Two agents pass each other, and one stops, looks at the other, and asks, 'Are you John Doe?' The other agent responds, 'No! I saw you making eye contact with me!' "

We were about to leave when he said, his voice serious now, "I like you as a person, Frank, but I have got to be honest. I don't approve of your life-style."

I smiled and in as nice a way as I could told him, "I don't need or want your approval of how I live my life."

He tried to talk softly, something impossible for him. "And if you ever make a pass at me, Frank," he said, quite seriously, "I'll knock you on your ass!"

"Don't worry," I answered, still with a smile, "I'm only interested in younger, good-looking guys who are in shape!"

■ ■ ■

On Saturday I drove my "little brother," Andy, to the Sunset Cliffs area of Point Loma. A winding road along the southwestern end of the cliffs offered a spectacular view of the ocean, and Andy and I walked for a while. We sat down at a quiet place facing the sea.

Andy was only fourteen but bright and sensitive, and he had talked about becoming a psychologist. I told him that I had something very important to tell him and that it had to do with me. When I finished my story, I said, "You and I are friends, and I wanted to share this with you. I value our friendship, and I don't want what is happening to get in the way of that."

He looked up at me, and his eyes were red. "This isn't fair, Frank. You're a great agent. And I'm behind you all the way."

■ ■ ■

The pain in my back worsened, and I tried a Pacific Beach chiropractor whose specialty was treating sports injuries. I began to see him on a regular basis, and he recommended specific exercises and a strict diet.

Meanwhile, Gayer had received a call from Frank Kameny, the gay activist in Washington, D.C. Though Kameny was not an attorney, he had been asked to represent an FBI file clerk whose security clearance was recently revoked when the bureau found out he was gay. The clerk was appealing the decision to D. Jerry Rubino, and Gayer provided Kameny with information about my case. I had named Rubino in my lawsuit. Gayer and I were curious about whether Rubino would go along with the bureau's decision and risk a second FBI employee's suing him and the government.

■ ■ ■

Despite the exercises, treatment, and diet, the pain in my back worsened and now moved into one of my legs. I had difficulty walking and had to spend more and more time lying down at home.

Midmorning on June 20 there was a knock at the door. Rusty started barking, and I slowly moved to answer it.

When I opened the door, I was surprised to see SAC Johnson and ASAC Tom Kuker standing outside. Neither had been to my house before, and Johnson asked if they could come in.

I was wearing a T-shirt and sweat pants and hadn't showered or shaved yet that morning. I told them to wait a moment. I cleared the coffee table of legal documents from my case and put Rusty outside. I let both men in, and we sat down in the living room.

Johnson had a notebook with him and without any preliminary remarks opened it and began reading from a document inside. My stomach tightened as I sensed what was coming.

"As of the close of business today," Johnson read, "you will be dropped from the rolls of the FBI."

The three of us sat in silence for a moment. Johnson then advised me that I had thirty days to appeal the decision to the director of the FBI. He handed me a card outlining the procedure for receiving state unemployment benefits. Twenty years of service as an FBI agent, and this was what I received? I tossed the card on the coffee table.

"I would have appreciated your calling me instead of coming over unannounced," I said angrily.

Johnson said he thought it would have been too impersonal to handle it on the phone.

"I would have come down to the office or met you at a restaurant," I responded. "It would have been better than firing me in my own living room."

A few moments passed, and Kuker broke the silence. "We can make arrangements for you to obtain the things in your desk."

I didn't respond.

Both men got up and walked to the door. None of us said good-bye. In a few short hours I would no longer be a special agent.

■　■　■

The hearing before Judge Lynch was only nine days away, and I had thought the bureau would not fire me before then. By not waiting for the court hearing, the bureau was demonstrating how it dealt with employees who dared challenge it. But by firing me, the bureau had now lost its control over my life.

I called Gayer, and he launched into an angry analysis. "It shows that the FBI will do whatever they want, irrespective of our court action. If you were still working for the bureau when you appeared before the judge, it would be easier for him to let you stay on the payroll until he made a decision. Now it's unlikely Judge Lynch will reinstate you to your job."

I told Gayer we had thirty days to appeal to the director, and he laughed scornfully. ''There must be something magical about twenty- and thirty-day appeals in the government. It's been four months since Edwards wrote to the director, and they haven't even responded to Congress yet.''

I called the payroll office at FBI headquarters to inquire about my health benefits and pension. The woman who answered said that she hadn't been notified of my termination yet. She informed me that I would now have to pay a greater share of my health insurance costs. She said that I could withdraw the money I had contributed to my retirement fund but would no longer qualify for a pension.

The woman was curious about why I was leaving the bureau, so I told her.

''Doesn't the bureau realize these are the 1990s?'' she commented, and wished me luck.

The loss of my salary, health insurance, and pension package was in excess of one million dollars.

That evening I called my family and close friends to tell them I had been fired.

My father was particularly upset. ''After you risked your life all of those years? And all your undercover work, and Miami, and all the rest and they fire you? The hell with them!''

My mother was on the second phone and remained silent throughout our conversation. I asked my father if she was all right and he told me she was crying.

27.

"The name of your lawsuit has been changed to *Frank Buttino versus the FBI*," Gayer said, by phone from San Francisco. "The government's motion to the court demanded that you use your true name instead of John Doe. They argued that the public has a right to know your identity."

"They've got a lot of nerve making that argument when they won't even give me my own personnel file," I responded bitterly.

Gayer and I anticipated the move, though I didn't want to believe the bureau would actually do it. Its intent, Gayer thought, was to intimidate. It figured I would drop the lawsuit rather than use my name, that I would be embarrassed by being identified publicly as a homosexual.

I had talked to Gayer before how disclosure of my identity might jeopardize the secrecy of my previous undercover assignments.

"The FBI does not seem to share your concerns about their operations being disclosed," he countered. "And what about *your* safety should your name become known? Is that of concern to the FBI?"

Not revealing my name could harm our case in a more fundamental way: The government could claim I was still susceptible to blackmail because I wasn't completely open about my homosexuality.

We acceded to the government's request. We made certain, however, that it agreed to the following condition: "Were plaintiff to prevail in this action, the disclosure of his true identity in this lawsuit would not be an impediment to his returning to work for the FBI."

There was another matter of some urgency to Gayer. "I'm getting more and more requests from the media to interview you. They're not going to be satisfied talking to me much longer. At some point you will have to talk to them directly."

Throughout my career I had been conditioned to view the media as the bureau's adversary. The FBI severely punished agents who talked to the media without permission. On the surface it seemed logical: Talking to the media might jeopardize the confidentiality of bureau operations and identify FBI agents. Yet it also served to stifle any public knowledge of internal bureau problems. Without public scrutiny the FBI could and did resist the social and intellectual changes affecting the country—to the detriment of the bureau, bureau employees, and the country itself.

But publicity was also the bureau's Achilles' heel. FBI obsession with control seemed to put headquarters in a panic whenever anything negative about the agency was reported. The bureau had moved quickly to redress the grievances of African-American and Latino agents who had publicly complained about discrimination within it.

Headquarters would be incensed by my public challenge, but publicity might help my lawsuit as much as the courts. I would have to overcome not only long-standing prejudice against gays and lesbians within the bureau but also the draconian way the FBI treated employees who challenged it.

I called relatives and friends to prepare them for the fact that my name would soon be released. Little did I realize how fast the wire services carried the story nationwide. In a matter of hours I was "out" to the whole country.

The following morning I began to receive phone calls from people in Canastota. Emily Bertolero, a longtime friend in her seventies, left the message "I just want you to know it doesn't make any difference. And I still love you."

I got back to Gayer and told him I wasn't ready to talk to the media yet. If and when I did, I said I wouldn't want my face or picture used. "People might think I'm just trying to make a name for myself and would lose sight of the fact that I want my job back."

Gayer insisted I not close the door on the subject, and I agreed. I also told him it bothered me that the bureau was saying I repeatedly lied. "They're using that and not my sexual orientation as the reason for firing me."

Gayer responded bluntly, "You're naïve to think that the government won't lie to the court. I've seen them do it before in other cases I have handled."

Other stories about my case appeared throughout the week. In one account Gayer described how the bureau sent agents to my house to fire me. "He [Buttino] didn't think they'd be that cruel, but he said he's not going to back down. It makes him all the more steadfast to fight this."

But in this and other accounts the FBI continued with its claim that

I repeatedly lied. If it said this often enough, people would believe the bureau. It was time for me to defend myself and my reputation. I called Gayer and told him I was ready to talk to the media. I was about to break the FBI code of silence.

■ ■ ■

Because of these developments, I had been talking with K. D. only by phone. He was deeply disappointed at having to relinquish his teaching, and medical work research. When I invited him to lunch, he asked if I would mind driving. Evidently he was losing his eyesight as well.

I picked K. D. up at his home, and we drove to his favorite Vietnamese restaurant on Convoy Street in Kearny Mesa. Though he had once been a marathon runner, he now looked emaciated and walked like a very old man. I tried to conceal the sadness I felt seeing his condition.

K. D. ordered his favorite soup but ate only a few spoonfuls. I tried to cheer him and even got him to laugh a few times. Toward the end of our meal, though, he became uncustomarily sad.

"I feel very weak," he explained, slowly, his voice above a whisper. "It seems I have very few pleasures left in my life. I no longer have my work and no longer even have the pleasures of food or a good night's sleep."

He paused. I tried to find his eyes behind his thick glasses. His voice sounded hoarse when he spoke again, as if his few words of that afternoon were already too much for him.

"But I am lucky to have good friends like you," he added. "I am also fortunate to have Richard, who loves me and cares for me."

I walked K. D. to the door of his home afterward and gently embraced him. I told him I'd be back soon. As I drove away, a terrible sadness came over me. I was watching life emptying from my friend. My problems with the bureau and my lawsuit had preoccupied me for the past two years. I needed to keep it in perspective. Even if my lawsuit were unsuccessful, my life would still go on. I faced possible disappointment, not certain death.

■ ■ ■

The judge was to decide our preliminary injunction motion on June 29 in San Francisco. A press conference was to follow. It was my first, and I thought about it a great deal. I worked, by phone, with my brother Lou on a brief opening statement. We tried to anticipate what might be asked and how best to answer. Lou encouraged me to focus on a few basic points and not get bogged down in details. My loyalty to the bureau must have shown, as I hedged one of my comments. My brother said to be straightforward with my answers. "You don't have to protect them. You need to get your side of the story heard."

I decided to fly to San Francisco, not to drive, because my back and leg were bothering me. The day before the hearing I met again with Gayer and Gary Hall. Gayer gave me copies of the letters of support sent to Judge Lynch by current and former bureau employees, neighbors, and friends. Reading them would be like listening to my own eulogy.

Reporters swarmed around us as we approached the courtroom. A reporter from San Diego remarked how I looked more like somebody on *Hill Street Blues* than an FBI agent.

"Haven't I seen you in a gay bar in San Diego?" I said with a grin, and he and the others laughed.

I started answering questions but then stopped as the court proceedings began. Judge Lynch, gray-haired and about sixty, entered from the back, and we all stood up. The hearing was brief: A technical question gave rise to the judge's ordering both Tracy Merritt, the Department of Justice attorney, and Gayer, to file papers supporting their respective claims. He said he would make a decision regarding temporary reinstatement by July 20 and would decide the overall case within three to four months.

Trailed by reporters, Gayer and I made our way to the twentieth-floor press office. I reminded myself to be careful about my responses. I also had the feeling I would be doing this again, and I'd better get used to it.

Gayer and I sat at a long table opposite the reporters. They were obviously anxious to get started with the interview, so I handed them my text rather than read from it. As I did, I stated it was time for the FBI to be honest about its attitude and record in regard to gay and lesbian employees. I emphasized my desire to return to work and continue serving the country. "I want the bureau to understand that sexual orientation has no bearing on an individual's ability to work for the FBI."

A series of questions focused on the origins and development of my problems with the bureau. Afterward one reporter asked why I would want to go back to work for the bureau at all.

"There is a difference between FBI employees in the field and the bureaucrats at headquarters," I answered. "I have the deepest respect and admiration for the people I work with. They're dedicated, and their work makes this a better country. Many of them have also been supportive of me.''

Another reporter asked if I knew of other gay employees in the FBI. I told them about the FBI clerk and that the bureau's own investigators admitted to there being others. ''I'm hoping my lawsuit will benefit them.''

I was prepared for the questions of blackmail and national security. ''The FBI's first concern when they found out I was gay was that I was a spy. It was insulting. The idea of homosexual blackmail is a myth perpetuated by the CIA and FBI to justify discriminating against gay people. No gay American citizen ever committed espionage in response to gay-related coercion or blackmail. However, this is not the case for heterosexual employees in the FBI and CIA.''

Sitting in the hard chair was starting to aggravate the pain in my leg. I tried to ignore it, focusing instead on the questions. The press conference lasted about an hour.

■　■　■

When I returned to San Diego and was turning down my street, a neighbor stopped me. ''We heard about your case, and my family thinks it's unfair,'' the man said. ''We hope you win.''

Rusty kept on greeting me as I tried to check the answering machine and mail. One letter officially fired me and seemed anticlimactic. Another had ''Commanding Officer, Tactical Training Group Pacific'' as a return address, and I opened it. ''Dear Frank,'' the letter began:

> *Just a note to let you know that you have Sharon and my support as you tilt at the bureaucratic windmills.*
>
> *We considered you one of the few bright spots among the multitude of people who have worked our case. You are a professional, please know we are thinking of you.*
>
> *With regards,*
> W. C. ROGERS, III
> *Captain,*
> *U.S. Navy*

■　■　■

Brian came by on the weekend. He stayed awhile and talked, but something felt wrong. It seemed as though his mind were on other things.

Because of the pain in my leg, I didn't have the energy to pursue it. We had talked of late about remaining best friends, and I wondered if this had changed.

The pain grew still worse. In fact, it frightened Brian so much he wanted to take me to the emergency room. Instead I saw the chiropractor the following morning, and he referred me to an orthopedic surgeon. A friend drove me to the surgeon's office. The surgeon suspected I might have a ruptured disk, recommended a CT scan, and prescribed pain-killers. Though the pain-killers helped, they made me extremely drowsy, and I slept a great deal during the next several days.

The following Monday I had to report to the State Unemployment Office in person to sign up for unemployment benefits. I didn't take my usual allotment of pain-killers that morning because I had to drive. The reception area was packed, so I took a number. I couldn't stand or sit, the pain was so severe. I lay down on the floor next to a wall. I hadn't shaved, and a state employee must have mistaken me for a homeless person and asked me to leave the building. I showed her my number. She looked at it, shook her head, and walked away.

My life certainly has changed dramatically, I thought, and then started to laugh. The same state employee was watching me. She must have thought I was deranged—and this made me laugh even more.

■　■　■

I spent the remainder of the month lying on my back—sleeping, reading, or watching television. People from the office and others phoned, and a close friend or two occasionally stopped by. But I had become more and more of a recluse. Shaving, washing dishes, and even grocery shopping were difficult and sometimes impossible to do.

Brian neither called nor stopped by anymore. I left a few messages, but he didn't call back. As bad as my problems with the bureau were, the physical pain was a hundred times greater. It was the worst period of time in my life, and I didn't know when it would end.

When Brian finally called, I took my anger out on him. "You're supposed to be my best friend and you don't even call?"

He stopped by that night, and I couldn't even get up to greet him. We said hello but didn't embrace. I waited for him to speak first. I was expecting an apology.

"You know I'm not very good at talking about personal things," he began. "We probably should have had this conversation a long time ago."

He talked about how our relationship had changed during the past two years. "Especially with all the problems with the bureau," he said.

I shifted a little on the couch to ease the pain but continued to stare straight ahead.

"That guy you met a couple of months ago wanted to have a relationship with me, but I couldn't because of my feelings toward you. He's seeing somebody else now."

There was a long pause. I sensed he was gathering up his courage. "I want to have a relationship with somebody else," he said finally. "Somebody closer to my age."

I was usually energetic and physically fit, so this hurt more than it might have otherwise.

Brian said his employer had asked him how I was handling all the publicity surrounding my lawsuit. "I was embarrassed, Frank, and felt uncomfortable about going into work the rest of the week." He said he was also concerned about his parents' finding out he was gay because of the publicity.

I still hadn't spoken.

"Heterosexuals have to live in only a heterosexual society," Brian continued, "but gay people have to live in both a heterosexual and a homosexual society. Some people are better at living in both worlds than others."

He talked a little more, but I didn't really hear much afterward. He got up to leave, and I followed him to the door. He waited until I caught up with him. He turned around at that point and was crying. "I love you," he said.

"I love you, too."

We hugged each other. My tears came as I closed the door.

It would be easy to blame W. J., the bureau, or something else for the end of our relationship. No doubt we had been under a lot of stress during the past two years. Perhaps it had only accelerated the inevitable. It wasn't that we didn't love each other, but we had grown apart. And no matter how much we tried, the distance between us now seemed insurmountable.

All I could do was lie there, thinking about it all: the past and the present and the pain that breathed along with me.

28.

A new round of phone calls from the office began. These fell into two main categories. First there were those who related rumors that there was more to my firing than just being gay. The implication was that criminal activity perhaps unprovable in court was involved. One retired agent told people they were going to regret writing letters on my behalf.

A second interpretation was succinctly put by a veteran agent who said, "Frank, many of us believe you were caught between the old Hoover people who are in positions of leadership at headquarters and the new bureau. Unfortunately Sessions listened to the Hoover people, and you lost."

There was one interesting twist to my public acknowledgment I was gay. A number of people confided they had friends, relatives, or loved ones who were also gay. A former FBI employee still in law enforcement said, "My brother is gay, and I love him very much."

■ ■ ■

My brothers and I had planned a fiftieth wedding anniversary party for our parents at Lewis Point, a resort area on the shores of Oneida Lake. Its date, August 5, was set before news of my case broke in the papers. Lou seemed particularly anxious. He thought perhaps our parents would want to cancel the event, but they assured us otherwise. Lou was also concerned about my facing the entire family at one time. There are some fiercely independent and vocal individuals among them. My brother described family gatherings as "a convention of anarchists."

But these and other concerns were of little consequence to me. I just wondered if I would be able to make the journey at all. Sitting on a plane for seven or eight hours in pain was going to be excruciating, and the doctor continued to advise against it.

■ ■ ■

The July 20 date for Judge Lynch's ruling about the preliminary injunction passed without a decision. Gayer called four days later. "Judge Lynch denied our request. He didn't think you would suffer irreparable damages if he did not reinstate you immediately."

The ruling was not entirely unexpected, so instead of making us discouraged, we redoubled our efforts to try to obtain files of the FBI investigation of W. J. and my own personnel file. Without this, it would be my word against the FBI's. The judge, we feared, in all probability would rule in the bureau's favor. Perhaps the FBI was intentionally withholding the information to obtain this exact result.

Gayer and I sent out court-sanctioned notices to "depose" D. Jerry Rubino (who bore ultimate official responsibility for my firing) and FBI Director William Sessions. Depositions are statements taken under oath that can be used in court in place of the spoken testimony of witnesses. Gayer described the taking of a deposition as a "civilized fistfight."

■ ■ ■

A week before my parents' anniversary party I received my first cortisone shot. "I don't care if I ever run again," I told the doctor. "I just want to be able to live without this pain."

If the cortisone wasn't effective, back surgery was a possibility. The first shot didn't help, and I returned to the doctor's office for a second injection. The pain slowly diminished, and I decided to make the trip to Canastota. It was my first trip home since the publicity about me, and I wondered what I would face. All these "firsts" were in many ways exhilarating *and* exhausting. It was hard starting life over.

■ ■ ■

More than two hundred family members and friends came to honor our parents. Fortunately, we had rented a pavilion, for it rained the entire day. The band played Italian favorites, and people danced and ate throughout the afternoon.

Carmen Basilio and his wife, Josie, surprised us by coming. In shaking hands with Carmen, I told him he was lucky I had a bad back or we might be sparring with each other.

"I fought a guy like you once," he said. "And the guy scared me."

"Oh, he was that tough?"

Carmen grinned. "No. I hit him once and thought I killed him!"

Midway through the party my brothers and I got onstage to thank everybody for coming. Each of us spoke of our love for our parents. At the end of the event our parents danced to one last song. It was "My Way," and as they danced, my brothers and I, holding hands, formed a circle around them. The rest made an even larger circle around us.

Later that evening, in thinking about the party, I recognized that no one had said anything about my being gay or acted any differently toward me.

■ ■ ■

I called K. D. the night I got back to San Diego, and he answered on the second ring. "You must be doing better," I kidded. "You got to the phone pretty fast."

"The phone's on the bed next to my side," he said weakly.

I hesitated but then, bouncing back, said, "I just got back to San Diego and wanted to see how you were doing."

"Where did you go?"

I had told him about the party many times before. I explained it to him again, and though we hadn't talked long, he was plainly tired. I told him I'd be by the following day.

"Thank you for calling," K. D. said, in his usual polite way.

I sat for a long while after hanging up. K. D.'s memory had been extraordinary, but I feared the dementia that afflicts many AIDS patients was beginning.

I called Gayer the next morning. "Welcome back," he said. "I wish I had good news to report, but I don't. The Department of Justice is filing a protective order with the court preventing us from taking depositions from Rubino and Sessions. They're also moving for a summary judgment decision on September twenty-one."

I had a good understanding of federal criminal proceedings but not civil suits. "What does all this mean?"

"The government is saying that Rubino and Sessions shouldn't have to answer any questions because of their positions," Gayer answered, speaking in his quick, staccato style, "that they don't have to answer for their actions."

"That sounds really fair. They fire me and they don't have to explain why?"

Gayer was already on to the next topic. "By moving for a summary judgment, they're arguing that there are no important facts in dispute. And if the judge rules in their favor, you lose.''

I was taking notes as fast as I could, and Gayer continued, ''Of course, we'll oppose both motions, but I think we should also amend our original complaint and expand the litigation into a class-action suit.'' Gayer explained that a class-action suit would challenge the bureau's antigay policies and that if we won, all gay FBI employees would be protected. ''And if the bureau doesn't stop its practices after such a ruling, the judge could then hold it in contempt of court.''

We talked about the pros and cons of such action, and I told him to proceed.

I wanted to know whether or not we could appeal the judge's decision if he ruled against us for the present time.

''We could,'' answered Gayer, ''but the case might take a year or two to be heard. If we lost on that level, we could also take our appeal to the Supreme Court.''

''By the time I get my job back, I'll be too old to go back to work!''

Gayer said Sessions had not yet responded to Congressman Edwards's letter.

''It's only been five months,'' I said sarcastically.

''I wouldn't expect much help from anyone in Congress on this issue. There's a lot of hot air from politicians about gay rights, but usually that's all it is.''

I hung up the phone. *This is a farce,* I thought. *The bureau fires me because I'm gay and then denies this to the press and court. It refuses to furnish me the evidence it's using against me and won't even let me question the individuals responsible for my firing. Now the bureau wants the judge to throw the case out without a trial.*

■ ■ ■

The visitors' parking lot was full when I arrived at K. D.'s, and I eventually found a space on the busy street in front of the complex. It was a typically sunny San Diego afternoon, and as I walked across the road, I noticed a group of college students leaving a nearby residence. They were laughing and having a good time in one another's company. Little did they know that a short distance from them a small, wonderfully gifted man lay dying from a grotesque, mysterious virus. It had been nearly two weeks since I had last seen K. D., and as I walked up the steps to his house, I felt myself preparing for the worst.

Richard greeted me with a gentle smile. From his low voice I assumed K. D. was sleeping. Richard offered me some tea, and we remained standing in the kitchen while he reheated the pot. He looked tired.

"How's he doing?" I asked.

Richard walked to K. D.'s bedroom, looked in, and then closed the door. Returning, he said, "At times he seems to be doing okay, but other times he's in a lot of pain. The medicine he takes often makes him nauseated, and he has diarrhea, but that is pretty common among people with AIDS."

"How are *you* doing?" I asked.

"I'm all right. We have a nurse who comes over during the day to help and to administer medication, but we're working on having twenty-four-hour nursing care in the near future." Richard paused and looked away. I wanted for him to continue. "K. D. doesn't want to be admitted to the hospital. He's afraid once he goes in, he'll never come home again."

What an enormous responsibility for a twenty-eight-year-old, I thought. I asked Richard what I could do to help.

"Dharm doesn't have many close friends, but he thinks very highly of you. I think just your coming to visit helps a lot."

As we continued our conversation, Richard got up periodically to check on K. D. "He's awake now," he said at one point, and we both went into the room.

"Dharm," Richard whispered, "you've got a visitor."

My eyes slowly began to adjust to the darkness of the room. K. D. lay very still on the bed. Though it was warm out, he was wearing a sweat shirt. A blanket was over him. K. D.'s once-handsome face was gaunt, and the sweat shirt made his head look very small. He looked like a small child and an old man.

I've got to be strong, I told myself.

"How are you, my friend?" I said, softly. I put my hand on K. D.'s cheek.

"It is good to see you, Frank," he answered in a very gentle voice. He didn't open his eyes.

I bent over and kissed his forehead.

■   ■   ■

When I talked to my therapist, Drew Mattison, the next time, I told him about K. D.'s deteriorating health. "It seems all of a sudden my friends, people my age or younger, are dying. K. D. was so physically fit, and his mind was always so sharp. I try not to get depressed, but it is sad to watch him die. I wonder sometimes if I'm going to be able to handle all this, Drew.''

I talked later about Brian. ''It's strange. We were each other's best friend and had been so intimate about everything in our lives, and now we're like strangers. It's like our past together never happened.''

Drew put down his pad and looked up at the ceiling for a few minutes the way he always did. He then leaned slightly toward me and spoke in his usual calm, measured way. ''Frank, you have a number of major changes occurring in your life. You are watching one of your best friends die, the primary relationship in your life has ended, and your career, at least for the time being, has come to an end. You've also become a public figure, and that means you've lost the anonymity and privacy you've enjoyed most of your life.''

I knew he was only saying back to me what I had said to him, but it still caused me to catch my breath. He was my mirror, and my reflection appeared weary. Not sad or bitter, but more like disappointed.

''I would encourage you to maintain your close relationships with your family and friends,'' Drew continued. ''Your friendships and involvement with your FBI colleagues will continue to diminish, and it's important for you to make new friends. I would encourage you to become active in the gay community. There is a tremendous need for people like you to become involved.''

As I left Drew's office that day, I knew that if I took his advice, I would be taking another first step. I was ''out'' to all my friends, the FBI, and even America, but for twenty years had participated in very little outside the bureau. I had followed gay issues and knew who the gay leaders were in San Diego and to some extent beyond. Though Drew was probably right, that involvement would provide me with a measure of a support lacking in my life, it also felt awkward, like a first step not only toward something but away from something. Away from the bureau.

For now, for a short while longer anyway, I would put these questions aside. K. D. was a priority for me.

29.

I began visiting K. D. almost on a daily basis now, and one afternoon, when I called to say I was coming by, he started to cry. I had never heard him cry before, and he sounded like a young boy. "The nurses have told me that I can't go outside today," he said.

People with AIDS often have severe bouts of depression. I told him that it was probably only temporary and that he'd be able to go out again soon.

"Have a good trip," he said.

"I'm not going anywhere, K. D., except to see you."

"What about your trip for your parents' party?"

I explained to him it had already occurred even though it was difficult to get the words out.

K. D. was receiving twenty-four-hour nursing care, so it was possible for Richard to leave from time to time for short periods. There was a lot about K. D.'s situation I didn't understand, and one evening I invited Richard for a walk. I also thought he might need somebody to talk to.

We went to La Jolla Cove. La Jolla means "the jewel" in Spanish and is in the northern part of San Diego. The town is known for its beautiful beaches, houses, and architecture, and a sidewalk borders the grassy park along the top of its coves. Below, huge rocks and small sandy beaches dot the coastline.

We arrived about an hour before sunset. Neither of us spoke for a while. It felt awkward, considering all the time we had spent together these past several weeks.

"I want you to know how much I admire how you're caring for K. D.," I said finally.

Richard kept his eyes straight ahead. "I love him, and I know he would do the same for me if I were sick."

There was another pause.

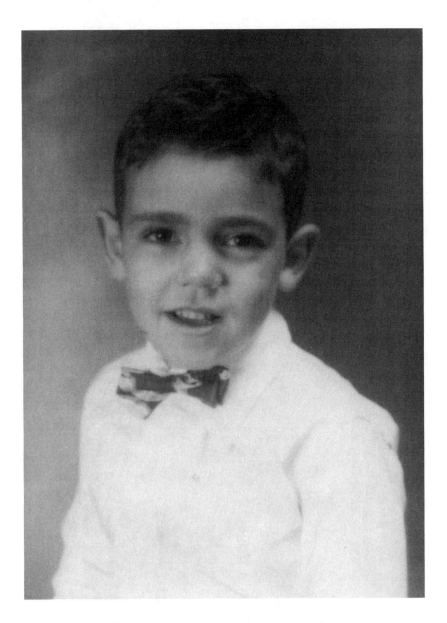

Kindergarten, age six, 1951. My mother had a
fondness for bow ties in those days.

At a family wedding.
The first time I ever danced with a girl.

My brothers, Lou (LEFT) and Tony (CENTER), and
me. We lived close to St. Agatha's Catholic Church
and served mass frequently.

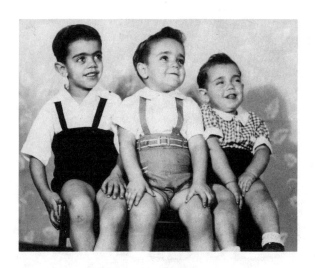

Tony (LEFT) at five years old, Lou (CENTER) at two years nine months, and me at one year nine months. Notice Lou trying to crowd me off the bench!

Tony (CENTER) was a defensive back, Lou (LEFT) the quarterback, and I was a backup quarterback at the time. We think it's the only time in Canastota football history where three brothers played at the same time.

High school yearbook photo, 1963

With my parents after receiving the Most Improved Wrestler award my first year out for the sport

Our parents' fiftieth wedding anniversary party, August 1990. "Coming out" to more than two hundred family members and friends!

*Dr. Franklin Kameny (*LEFT*), me, and my attorney Richard Gayer before the May 1991 deposition of FBI official Gary Stoops in Washington, D.C. Moments later Dr. Kameny exploded at the government's attorney.*

*Close friends Everett Waldo (*LEFT*) and Richard Tanner (*RIGHT*) with Mike Wallace and me after the taping of the* 60 Minutes *segment at my house, April 1992*

ANTHONY LOEW

"How long have you known he was HIV positive?"

"Since July of last year. Dharm started feeling fatigued that spring, and in June he started showing the first symptoms of the disease. At that point he decided to get tested."

Richard must have sensed what I was thinking. "I get tested every six months, and the results continue to be negative."

Because it was late summer, the pathway was crowded with people, many of whom appeared to be tourists. We moved southward, to a less crowded section of the shoreline.

"Dharm had done extensive reading about AIDS and knew a lot about the disease when his test results came back. He knew what to expect from the illness," Richard said. "And from his work in gastroenterology he also had seen the reality of people with terminal illnesses. Dharm decided to become the patient instead of the doctor. He had a lot of confidence in Dr. Hartmeyer and was willing to try any new treatments that could help him."

Tentatively I said, "I'm curious how Dharm handled the result of the test."

"He was not overly distraught. Death does not seem to scare him. He sees life as a journey to another place."

As we continued talking, I realized we were sometimes talking about him in the past tense.

"He was concerned about losing his job and his health benefits," Richard continued. "He had also seen people with terminal illnesses abandoned by their loved ones. I think he was concerned about losing his colleagues and his friends. Although his family is in Thailand, he was also concerned about the pain his family would experience because of his illness."

"That sounds like him," I said. "Always thinking of others."

We stopped and watched the surf breaking on the rocks below.

"Of course, he was concerned how this would affect our relationship, Frank. So we spent a lot of time talking about the disease and our relationship. We love each other, and we both agreed that someone with AIDS can still have a loving relationship with someone who does not have the illness. Early on we decided to try to live as normal a life as possible, to continue to have dinner with our friends and enjoy our quiet times at home together."

We headed back. The sun had set without our realizing it.

"I think one of the most difficult things for him has been leaving his work. Before he left, he spent months working on research grants to ensure that his research would continue after he left the lab.''

Richard then said, almost matter-of-factly, that he was making plans for Dharm's funeral, and he wondered if I would speak at the service.

■ ■ ■

New court filings showed that the FBI chose to believe one of the individuals it had interviewed in its investigation rather than me, one of its own agents. The person I had written to at the Del Mar address had told the bureau he placed his ad in 1986, *not* 1988, as I claimed. The FBI concluded that he had vacated his Del Mar address before I said I wrote to him and that I therefore was lying.

"Mail can be forwarded for quite a while," I told Gayer. I said I was going to look into it.

"Go ahead," Gayer replied. "It might help clarify that point, but it's all pornographic trivia. What difference does it make if or when you wrote to another gay person? It has absolutely nothing to do with how you did your work.''

I scheduled a meeting with the publisher and the editor of the magazine in which the ad appeared. They found the particular issue, and we located the ad I was looking for. The date of the magazine was 1988, just as I had said.

Then the publisher explained that there had been *two* magazines—an older one, which was discontinued, and a successor, in which the ad appeared. He said they had placed ads from the old magazine in the new one. I asked the publisher and the editor if the FBI had been by to question them, and they answered no.

■ ■ ■

The pain in my back and leg was diminishing. I began walking more and going to the gym for limited workouts. I also started painting the outside of my house. At the start I could paint for only a couple of hours a day, but I continued to get stronger and gradually was able to work longer.

Drew Mattison invited me to attend a gay and lesbian fund-raiser for Dianne Feinstein, the former mayor of San Francisco who was now running for governor against Pete Wilson. FBI agents are prevented by the Hatch Act from participating in political activities, so the event would be a first for me.

I recognized many in attendance as leaders in the gay and lesbian com-

munity. Most seemed to know one another, and some glanced at me, probably wondering who I was. Tom Homann arrived. He was pale and thin but
still had that engaging smile and sharp wit. Drew arrived a little later, and
he introduced me to his life partner, Dr. David McWhirter. I extended my
hand, but David hugged me instead. "I'm so happy to meet you," he said.
"I want you to know how much I admire what you're doing."

He and Drew introduced me to several other people, including Dianne
Feinstein. We spoke briefly about my case, and she wished me luck. The
word regarding my identity must have spread because several people
came up to introduce themselves. One was an older man with a mischievous grin.

"Who are *you?*" he asked.

"Who are *you?*" I responded with a laugh.

"Herb King."

"Oh, you're the guy who writes the letters to the newspapers!" I
said. "Well, I'm the guy who got fired from the FBI for being gay."

Herb was aware of my case and said he would like to talk with me
about it soon. We made plans to meet later that week.

I shook hands with Chris Kehoe, a former editor of a gay San Diego
newspaper who now worked for a city council member. I told her how I
admired her work in the gay and lesbian community.

"I've admired your work for a long time," I said, "and I'm glad I
finally have an opportunity to meet you."

One person asked, "How long have you lived in San Diego?"

"Seventeen years," I answered.

"We've never seen you before."

"Well, when you're an FBI agent, you don't go to gay bars or gay
functions. But I know most of you," I said with a grin. "I've been
reading the gay newspapers for a long time and recognize most of your
names and faces."

Later that evening I walked along the Shelter Island shoreline with
an attorney for the state superior court who was also active in the gay
community. "We've lost so many of our leaders because of AIDS," he
said. "So far forty-three of my friends have died, and so many people I
know are sick. I'm tired of seeing people die of this disease, and I'm so
tired of going to funerals."

The parking lot was nearly empty when we returned. He mentioned
some upcoming events he hoped I would attend. "I hope you'll become
involved in the community," he told me before we parted.

My leg was beginning to bother me again as I got behind the wheel of my car. It was the longest time I had been on my feet in months. Regardless, there had been something exhilarating and transforming about the evening. It was my first gay function as an openly gay man. My grandmother used to tell us that when one door closed, the Lord always opened up another. That night I felt the other door being opened.

■ ■ ■

The good feeling from that night quickly evaporated. D. Jerry Rubino, the Department of Justice's security officer, submitted a declaration to the court supporting the government's request to have my case dismissed. Rubino claimed I was subject "to coercion or pressure to act contrary to the best interests of the national security, was not truthful in answering questions posed during the FBI's inquiry, and failed to cooperate fully during the administrative investigation."

He also asserted it was impossible for him "to predict with the requisite degree of assurance" that my "continued access to classified information was clearly consistent with the national security." He said, "Mr. Buttino's homosexuality, homosexual activities or homosexual associates were not the basis for my decision regarding the revocation of his security clearance."

I tossed the letter to the floor. The government couldn't attack my record, and it certainly wasn't going to admit that it discriminated against gay people, so it would keep insisting I was a liar.

I called Gayer. John D. Cramer of the Los Angeles *Times* had called Gayer several times asking to interview me. I had been postponing it but now told Gayer to call Cramer back and tell him I was ready to speak with him.

(In August a story about Special Agent Donald Rochon, who was suing the bureau on charges of racial discrimination, made national headlines. Rochon claimed that other agents had made racially motivated death threats against him. African-American agents reportedly complained about racism in the bureau. Director Sessions responded by appointing John Glover, the FBI's highest-ranking African-American agent, to look into the matter.)

■ ■ ■

Later in the month I drove to Los Angeles to hear Mitch Grobeson speak at a Unitarian church. Grobeson had been a sergeant in the Los Angeles

Police Department, but his career had ended after the department learned he was gay. Grobeson was harassed by other officers, and their failure to provide backup on an arrest caused him to resign. Later he filed a lawsuit against the LAPD, charging antigay discrimination.

Grobeson was very effective as a speaker and also fielded questions well. I waited until most of the people left before introducing myself. He said he had been following my case, and we talked for a while about our respective situations. We agreed to stay in touch.

I also met Morris Kight, a man I had read about for years. He was in his seventies, distinguished-looking with pure white hair. Kight had spent most of his life fighting for gay rights and was revered by many in the gay and lesbian community.

As in my meeting Hoover some twenty years before, shaking hands with Kight was like shaking hands with somebody from the history books. Kight had fought virtually alone, when few believed gay men and lesbians were entitled to any rights at all. Unlike Hoover, Kight was an authentic hero.

Kight mentioned the relationship between Hoover and Clyde Tolson. "You have to remember that Hoover and Tolson grew up at a time when people who were homosexual hated themselves for being gay."

I nodded, and he continued, "You have a very difficult, uphill fight. I admire your courage."

I took his hand again. "Mr. Kight," I said, "you paved the way for people like Mitch and me. Thank you for all your efforts on our behalf."

30.

Judge Lynch advised us he would make a decision regarding the government's motion for summary judgment on October 3. When I called to tell my brother Lou, he said he'd like to be in the courtroom with me.

Gayer and I thought we should call the bureau supervisor who had called me subsequent to the Teigen polygraph. We hoped he might provide us with further information.

I made sure when I called that he could speak confidentially. He remembered me but was unaware that I had been fired or filed a lawsuit. He said he had been concerned about me at the time because another FBI agent, after similar questioning, had committed suicide. Despite this, he now gave me the impression he didn't want to be involved further. That was understandable. If the bureau found out, he would likely be disciplined.

At the end of August I met with John Cramer at the San Diego office of the Los Angeles *Times*. Gayer was on a speakerphone and could respond to any legal questions. Cramer agreed in advance not to use my picture or have any photographs taken. The interview lasted for almost two hours. After years of interviewing people I felt strange to be on the other end of a long, one-on-one encounter.

Cramer's article appeared the following morning. It was a long piece, and he had focused on my idealism in joining the FBI, my unblemished record, and the government's actions when I told the bureau I was gay. Cramer, as expected, raised the question about homosexual blackmail.

I said the government was "building on the myth that gays are open to blackmail, that we are weak and are easily coerced." I was quoted as saying my record in the FBI and my lawsuit against the bureau proved this assumption untrue. " . . . I won't be intimidated, and I won't back down."

Cramer asked about my becoming a martyr for gay rights, but I told him that I was an "ordinary man" who was "going to see this thing through. . . . It's a matter of principle. And I hope it will make it easier for others down the road."

Phone calls from friends followed, and all in all it had been a good day. But then that same afternoon a car pulled into the driveway. I recognized the driver at once as a retired FBI agent who was truly an old-timer. He had joined the bureau in the early 1950s. I didn't know him well, but he had a reputation for being tough and outspoken. I wondered if he was going to give me a hard time.

"I saw the article in the paper this morning," he said, walking toward me, obviously very angry. "And I think it's bullshit! I thought the bureau stopped that nonsense a long time ago."

I was too shocked to say anything.

"My best friend in the world is gay. I've known him for years, and he's one of the best people I've ever known."

We talked about my case for a few minutes, and just as abruptly as he had come, he turned to leave. "You fight them on this thing," he said, slamming the door of his car. "Don't let them get away with it."

I was contacted by another journalist, and we chatted about my case for a while. He then began to talk about the Rogers case. He asked me a specific question about the investigation and promised to protect my identity.

"You want me to be a Deep Throat?" I responded with a laugh, referring to the anonymous source in the Watergate scandal. I explained in a nice but firm way that I would never reveal confidential information about an FBI investigation to anyone.

I made my usual visit to K. D.'s home that night. At first he didn't recognize me. I bent over and kissed him on the forehead. "How's the king of Siam today?" I said softly.

K. D. had recently shown me a photograph of him shaking hands with the king of Thailand, taken on the day he graduated from medical school. I kidded him that with all his nurses and friends and the way he was propped up in the bed, he was being treated just like a king.

K. D. usually laughed when I told him this, but he didn't that night. As usual, though, he asked how I was.

"There was a great article in the L.A. *Times* about my lawsuit," I said.

"What lawsuit?" he asked with a quizzical look.

I patiently explained how I had been fired by the FBI when it had learned I was gay and that I'd filed a lawsuit to get my job back.

"Oh," he said, looking confused.

"Would you like me to read the article to you?"

He nodded his head slowly up and down. "Please," he said softly, and closed his eyes.

I lay down gently next to him. When I finished reading the article, K. D. began to cry. I placed his hand in mine. "What's wrong?" I asked, and he said, "I don't know why they're doing this to you. You're such a superb person."

K. D. had always been very reserved and formal around people, but the disease had changed him. He had become more emotional, and perhaps reading the article to him had been a mistake. But I wanted him to remain a part of my life as long as possible.

"I don't want you to be upset about this," I said. "I can handle the FBI. I just want you to get better."

K. D. seemed to be in more pain than usual that night, and I asked him if there was anything I could do to help. He asked if I would mind rubbing his forehead.

He had resisted morphine because he knew its negative effects. But now a permanent intravenous tube inserted into his chest provided him with morphine on a continual basis.

K. D. directed me to the area on his forehead where he said it hurt the most.

"Let me know if I'm rubbing too hard."

"Okay," he answered back.

The room was quiet. I began to hum "Amazing Grace," and after a while K. D. drifted off to sleep. It was my mother's favorite song.

It was past midnight when I arrived home. I lay on the bed, saddened and drained. This new day, I realized, was Brian's birthday.

■   ■   ■

I gradually increased the distances I could walk. It felt good being able to socialize a little again.

Herb King and I went out to dinner as planned. He had seemed to know everyone at the Dianne Feinstein fund raiser, and I looked forward to getting to know him. I found him bright, fascinating, and a man heavily involved in many gay organizations. Herb was in his early seventies and had a quick wit and infectious smile. While we were eating I kidded him that he looked a lot like Mel Blanc.

"And you look like Tom Selleck." He smiled.

"I'm much younger and better-looking than Selleck."

"But Selleck is employed," he said with a laugh.

Herb was a graduate of MIT and had served in the Second World War. He had moved to San Diego from the East Coast in the late 1960s and was a retired chemical engineer. He lived with a lifetime partner of thirty-five years.

Herb talked about the gay community and AIDS and that he was currently a "buddy" to two men with AIDS. The "buddy program," sponsored by the AIDS Foundation of San Diego, provided support for people with HIV/AIDS who needed a friend, help with medical paper work, rides to the doctor or hospital, or someone just to call and talk with.

"It angers me that the Reagan administration ignored the problem for such a long time while so many people continued to die," Herb said, his smile and laughter now gone.

We were silent for a while before he added, "It's such a dreadful disease, and it pains me to see so many young people dying. There's so much to do. I'm trying to do what these young men will not be able to do in their short lives."

■　■　■

My brother Lou sent me a book he had written that was just published. *For the Love of Teddi* is the story of twelve-year-old Teddi Mervis, who died of a brain tumor. Her courage inspired the founding of one of the largest organizations in the world that deals with all aspects of childhood cancer. Lou thought the book might enable me to cope with K. D.'s eventual death. On the title page he wrote, "To my brother—A Reluctant Hero."

One passage in the book had particular meaning for me:

No matter how much they loved and cared about Teddi, still, in each person who came and waited, there was the fear that Teddi would die when they were in the room. . . . Afterward, they would talk about being . . . alone with Teddi and looking up, anxiously, when she gasped for air. They would stare steadily and long to see some trace of movement in the white sheet draped over Ted-

di's body. Who would be the one, they wondered, that would be in the room when Death, like a cool breeze, would come—rustling papers, making the curtains tremble, taking Teddi's life away? Who would be the one to see this child breathe for one last time?

I now stayed with K. D. longer each day. I wanted to be with him when he died, as I would want people with me at my own death. My grandmother said she wanted people with her when she died so that Jesus would see how much she was loved. I remembered my cousin Carmen kissing his mother to take her last breath.

■   ■   ■

"It's strange," I said to Richard late one night, "but if I hadn't gotten fired, I wouldn't be able to spend so much time with K. D." Being with K. D. seemed to be unlocking a spiritual side to me I never knew was there.

■   ■   ■

On Sunday afternoon, September 9, 1990, I attended an American Civil Liberties Union party honoring Tom Homann for his longtime commitment to civil rights. Walking to the party at a private residence in La Jolla, I saw hand-printed signs sticking in the ground accusing the ACLU of promoting homosexuality.

San Diego police officers were in front of the residence. I saw Herb King, and he said that people had been picketing earlier and that some had taken photographs of arriving guests. I was still avoiding having my photograph taken and wasn't sure how I would have reacted if one of those people had tried to take my picture.

I spotted Tom Homann in a crowd of people. He was happy to see me and introduced me to his parents and several people in the legal profession. "Frank's going to be a famous person some day." He chuckled and told them about my case. I'd heard he had been in the hospital the week before, and he looked very weak. The twinkle in his eyes remained, however.

Herb King introduced me to several individuals active in the gay community. Herb was known for his flashy clothes, and at one point I kidded him with the line "You young guys can get away with wearing those clothes."

"And you look just like an FBI agent," he said of my jacket and tie.

Later, on a stage set up on the lawn, several people spoke of Tom Homann's accomplishments. He was then presented with a beautiful replica of the Statue of Liberty.

Tom responded to some of the good-natured kidding he had received with charm and wit. He talked briefly about his legal experiences and with that became somewhat emotional. He also seemed to have trouble breathing. "I'm going to fight this damn disease," he said. "And I'm going to continue fighting to insure that the majority in this country doesn't impose its will on its minorities!" He was almost out of breath. "And I'll keep on doing it, even if they have to wheel me into the courtroom."

■ ■ ■

Herb King served as my social tour guide and mentor during my first several months of public involvement in the gay community. Herb invited me to a number of functions and introduced me to both gay and nongay leaders of San Diego. Herb thought it important I meet these people, and he wanted them to see the diversity within the gay and lesbian community.

I learned that Herb had personally known both Leonard Matlovich and Dr. Tom Waddell. Matlovich, discharged from the Air Force when it learned of his homosexuality, had fought for ten years before winning his legal battle to receive an honorable discharge. On his tombstone in the Congressional Cemetery in Washington, D.C., is the inscription "When I was in the military they gave me a medal for killing two men and a discharge for loving one."

Dr. Tom Waddell had competed in the decathlon at the Olympic Games and was the founder of the Gay Games. He subsequently died of AIDS. His life is profiled in the award-winning documentary *Common Threads*.

I was curious about the character of both men and what had motivated them to take such courageous stands. Herb said that they were ordinary people and that ordinary people can make a difference if they are committed to bringing out the best in themselves and others.

■ ■ ■

I had always loved history, but in growing up, I was never told that some of the people I was learning about—such as Michelangelo, Tennessee

Williams, Walt Whitman, Gertrude Stein—were homosexual. When young people like myself first discover their homosexuality, they usually feel alone and disconnected without gay and lesbian role models and heroes. What we learn early on about homosexuality is negative and degrading, and so we need to know the truth about historical figures.

I now add Matlovich and Waddell to Michelangelo and the others.

31.

As the months passed, I began to see clearly why people are reluctant to sue the government. Compared with the individual, the government has enormous resources it can use, without hesitation, to frustrate and devastate financially those who challenge it. The taxpayers were paying for all that the government was doing in my case, but that didn't seem to matter to Washington's bureaucrats.

Between 1980 and 1990, 16,919 military personnel were discharged because of homosexuality at an *annual* cost of twenty-five million to thirty million dollars, according to the Government Accounting Office. I wondered how much money the FBI had spent in its long history getting rid of gays and lesbians. I wondered, too, if I should have resigned when all this began. Not only were the costs mounting, but I also wanted to get on with my life.

In September 1990 a letter arrived from the deputy director of the FBI stating that my appeal to Director Sessions had been denied. Concurrently, after a seven-month delay, Sessions responded to Congressman Edwards's letter concerning the FBI's position with respect to gays and lesbians. Edwards sent me a copy of the director's response.

Sessions said *extramarital* heterosexual conduct by an FBI agent or applicant "is not exploitable heterosexual conduct per se." Yet in my case the bureau automatically assumed that homosexual conduct was exploitable. Moreover, Sessions seemed intellectually unbothered by the recent revelation that Richard W. Miller, the first FBI agent in history to commit espionage, had had *extramarital* sexual relations with a female Soviet KGB agent!

Congressman Edwards had asked Sessions if there were any openly gay agents in the FBI, and the director responded, "I am unaware of any."

Gays and lesbians constitute at least 10 percent of the overall population. The FBI had more than ten thousand agents, and the fact that there were no openly gay agents should prove prima facie that the bureau discriminates. Sessions's statement was comparable to the FBI's saying that it does not discriminate against African-Americans when no African-Americans could be found in the FBI.

(In fact, this occurred under Hoover. Newly appointed Attorney General Robert Kennedy noticed the glaring lack of African-American agents and questioned Hoover about it. "How many?" Kennedy asked, insisting on facts and figures. The director told him there were *four* in the entire bureau. Hoover didn't explain that these four were his African-American chauffeur and three other African-American service people who were specially designated as agents!)

Sessions closed his letter to Edwards with the statement " . . . the issue of homosexual conduct by employees of the FBI raises serious policy considerations. Preservation of the national security and public trust and confidence are areas where I cannot compromise."

I tried to make sense out of the letter while talking to Gayer. "You can't make something reasonable out of something that's unreasonable," Gayer explained. "The FBI can't get you on anything else, so they're hoping that the courts will defer to them in the area of national security— an area traditionally the preserve of the executive branch."

Gayer prepared a press release citing Session's comments, and considerable press coverage followed—especially in regard to the director's comment that he was unaware of any openly gay agents. Then John Martin of *ABC World News Tonight* contacted Gayer about an interview. I agreed, upon the condition my face wouldn't be shown.

The confirmation hearings of Supreme Court nominee David Souter were on television, and I watched with particular interest. Souter had never been married, yet no senator asked about this—or his private sexual life.

■   ■   ■

I continued to rub K. D.'s forehead on my visits with him and told him things that might cheer him up. But he usually stared straight ahead now and seldom showed any reaction. I wondered if he knew who I was or that I was even there. One evening Richard confirmed my suspicion that K. D. was nearly blind.

K. D.'s once-strong legs curled under him whenever we moved him, and he also required diapers. One night, even though it was very warm and K. D. was bundled up, his teeth began to chatter uncontrollably and his whole body shook. "Hold me," he whispered.

Richard and I lay down on opposite sides of him and wrapped our arms around him. Severe cramps erupted across his legs, and the night nurse looked on as we massaged his legs gently through the blanket. There was little else to do except hold him and tell him how much we loved him.

It was nearly midnight and my house was dark when I pulled into the driveway. I wished someone were waiting for me.

■   ■   ■

Richard was a member of the Lesbian and Gay Archives of San Diego and invited me to attend one of the group's meetings. The Archives was formed in 1987 to promote the recovery, preservation, and understanding of lesbian and gay history. One of the members explained that gays and lesbians grow up isolated from others who share a similar experience, and many remain unaware of the contributions gays and lesbians have made to science, education, government, the arts, and other fields. Members of the group told me that they were following my case, which they included in their collection.

I was feeling more and more a part of the gay and lesbian community I had only read about for years. I was discovering so much about our history I did not know. I was also learning more about myself and becoming prouder of being part of a minority that had contributed so much to people everywhere.

■   ■   ■

At the beginning of October, and for the first time, I was interviewed by a local San Diego television station. Though I did all right, I knew I could have been a little more relaxed and talked more slowly. Digital effects obscured my face.

That evening, while reading Randy Shilts's biography of gay supervisor Harvey Milk, *The Mayor of Castro Street,* I came to the chapter describing how Milk and San Francisco Mayor George Moscone had been killed. According to Shilts, assassin Dan White shot Moscone twice in the chest and then fired two more bullets at close range into the mayor's head. White then raced down the hallway to Milk's office, loading his gun with hollow-point bullets as he went. This type of bullet explodes upon impact, ripping a hole in the victim two to three times the size of the bullet itself. Perhaps White wanted Milk's death to be even more excruciating and certain.

Milk was seated behind his desk and tried to get up when White came in. White fired five shots into Milk. The coroner later said that the final bullet ripped through Milk's head, tearing open his brain. I remembered the reaction of an FBI agent in the office at the time. "So what?" he said. "They were just a couple of fags."

Hate crimes were on the rise in America, and skinheads and other homophobic extremists were escalating their violent attacks against us. I was becoming more well known and knew eventually my face would be shown. It was possible that someday I could also be the target of someone like Dan White.

The notoriety of my case was affecting my social life in diverse ways. Some people were drawn to me because of the case while others kept me at a distance or drifted away.

■   ■   ■

Lou came to San Diego the first week in October, and we flew to San Francisco together for the court hearing. The government was fighting my demands for my personnel file and information regarding its investigation of me. More important, the judge was to rule on whether to dismiss my case. If he dismissed it, we would appeal. However, a dismissal would severely hurt our chances of ultimate success.

Judge Lynch was on vacation, and the hearing was held before United States Magistrate Wayne Brazil. Brazil listened to oral arguments from Gayer and Justice Department attorney Tracy Merritt. At one point Brazil seemed to scold Merritt for not affording me the same right to evidence I had given criminals as an FBI agent. "The government can't have its cake and eat it, too, in this matter," he commented. Brazil thought Judge Lynch ought to decide about our request for files, but he postponed indefinitely the government's request to have the case dismissed.

He also ordered the government to produce a declaration from Director Sessions "describing truthfully his involvement, if any, with the decisions which resulted in the loss of Plaintiff's security clearance." The order shocked those of us in the courtroom and immediately grabbed national attention. My faith in the justice system deepened a little more that afternoon.

■   ■   ■

Lou and I returned to San Diego. I was anxious to see K. D., and we drove over together that night. K. D. did not respond to us and continued to stare straight ahead. It was the worst I had ever seen him, and we didn't stay long. He was obviously very close to death.

I talked with John Martin of ABC News for the first time, and he requested that my face be shown during the interview. Gayer, Lou, and I had discussed the issue at some length. I decided that concealing my face gave the impression I was not openly gay or had something to hide. Martin was pleased to hear I would appear on camera.

One night Lou said he sometimes got the creeps at night thinking about all the things that had happened to me and my house. "A car goes by, and I find myself noticing," he said.

"A big guy like you shouldn't be scared," I kidded.

"Yeah, but you've got the gun."

"Lou," I said, more seriously now, "this guy has cost me my job and in part my relationship with Brian. I have a lot of good memories in this house of Mom and Dad and friends, and I'm not going to allow him to take that away, too."

I talked to Everett and Drew about Lou's stay. I had gotten angry with him when he inquired into my private life. Before my homosexuality became known, no one asked those kinds of questions. Now my private life seemed fair game for everyone.

"I'm not sure I can handle all this, Everett. My life wasn't exactly easy in the past, but it sure was a lot simpler."

■ ■ ■

The day Lou left I drove over to see K. D. Richard was out on a brief errand, and the nurse greeted me at the door.

"How is he?" I asked.

She shook her head. "Not very good."

We walked in silence to K. D.'s room.

His eyes were closed, and he was having great difficulty breathing. His body no longer could process nutrients, and the intravenous tube had been disconnected.

I sat in a chair next to K. D.'s bed and held his hand as the nurse sat in a nearby chair. K. D. appeared to stop breathing a few times, and each time the nurse and I looked at him and then each other. Occasionally she got up to touch his forehead, but his eyes remained closed, and he did not respond.

I thought about the day K. D. and I met and all the parties, quiet dinners, and wonderful conversations we had shared since then. During ten years of friendship there had never been a cross word between us. I do not pray often. I hope a lot, and maybe that is the same thing. But that night I prayed for God to take him.

I didn't want to leave K. D.'s side, but I had made a commitment to attend the surprise birthday party for a close friend. I waited until Richard returned and gave him the telephone number where I could be reached. I said I'd come by after the party if I didn't hear from him before that. I kissed K. D. on the forehead and told him that I loved him.

The phone rang at the party at about 8:45 P.M. The host called me into the kitchen, and I immediately recognized the nurse's voice. She said that Richard had asked her to call, that K. D. was dying.

I hurried back to his home, but when the nurse opened the door, there were tears in her eyes. "Dr. Dharm passed away a few minutes ago," she said.

I took a deep breath. "Was it peaceful?"

"Yes."

"How's Richard?"

"He's in with Dr. Dharm now."

Richard had his arm around K. D. and was crying when I entered the bedroom. He looked up but didn't say anything. I left the two of them alone and went back into the living room. I closed my eyes and said the Our Father and Hail Mary over and over again, as I had when I thought my mother was dying.

After a while the nurse and I went into K. D.'s bedroom. Richard got up, and I hugged him. Then the three of us lifted K. D. from the hospital bed and placed him in his own bed. I made several phone calls for Richard before returning to the room. The nurse was sitting in a chair at the foot of the bed, and I sat beside K. D. Richard was lying on the other side, next to K. D.

"Would the two of you like a glass of wine?" I asked, and they nodded. I went to the kitchen and brought back three glasses. I sat in the chair again and put one of my hands on K. D.'s.

"I'd like to toast K. D. and his life," I said, and the three of us raised our glasses. "He was a wonderful, bright, and caring man, and I was honored to be his friend. I doubt I will ever know a more remarkable human being."

The nurse spoke next, raising her glass. She said she had come to like and respect Dr. Dharm in the short time she had known him. She looked at Richard and me. "And I want the two of you to know how special I think you are for the love and care you showed for him." She paused, fighting back the tears. "I will never forget all of you."

Richard raised his glass. He started to say how much he loved Dharm but then began to cry. After regaining his composure, he said, "I want you to know how much I appreciate what both of you did for him. You made the last few months peaceful and loving ones for him, and I know he appreciated it."

We gently brought our glasses together. "To Dharm," we said, and drank to him.

I walked the nurse to her car and thanked her for her kindness to my friends. She did not speak, but we hugged each other for the first time. As I watched her drive away, I thought how extremely difficult her job must be, entering lives and then so often seeing those lives end.

■　■　■

I remember reading an Emily Dickinson poem in which she speaks of the bustle in a house the morning after death. K. D.'s home had been transformed into a minihospital, and the next morning I was making phone calls and arranged for the medical equipment to be picked up. One of K. D.'s friends came by, and when I told him K. D. had died, he was shaken. He was also a doctor and from Thailand, and offered to call K. D.'s family. Richard and I spent the rest of the day making preparations for K. D.'s graveside ceremony and burial.

■　■　■

The next day was National Coming Out Day, and I stopped by the San Diego Lesbian and Gay Men's Center to listen as several people walked onto the outdoor stage to tell of their coming out experiences. A lesbian public school administrator came out publicly for the first time. She quoted Horace Mann: "Be ashamed to die until you have won some victory for humanity."

A mother and a father spoke of their love for their two gay sons and about an organization they belonged to called Parents and Friends of Lesbians and Gays (P-FLAG). My friend Herb King emceed the program and mentioned my case as an example of continuing discrimination against gays and lesbians.

Beyond those who gathered directly in front of the stage were others, some of them teenagers. Most were standing alone. They were close enough to hear yet far enough away to avoid being identified gay or lesbian.

I admired the courage of the people who came out publicly that evening. I had one foot out of the closet, but something was still preventing me from coming out completely. Perhaps it was because I had been so anonymous as an FBI agent and so closeted as a gay man. Or perhaps I still feared that if I were completely out, my old life would be gone forever.

■ ■ ■

The sun was unusually bright and hot the following morning. Fortunately K. D.'s plot was partially beneath a tree. Richard asked me to welcome everyone on behalf of K. D.'s family and himself. Several of K. D.'s close friends and colleagues spoke movingly about their relationship with him. The doctor from Thailand and I read from the Twenty-third Psalm, alternating in Thai and English. I then spoke of my friendship with K. D. and the differences in our backgrounds and personalities. "K. D. was a doctor and researcher from Thailand who was quiet, reserved, and polite. I, on the other hand, am Italian, from New York, and an FBI agent who is neither reserved nor shy."

I knew K. D. would get a smile out of that.

And because there were several people from the medical field at the ceremony, I said that K. D.'s spirit would continue to exist in the world as long as they continued to care for the sick and the dying.

■ ■ ■

A few days later news stories reported that Chris Petti was going on trial in San Diego for his role in a money-laundering scheme. The case also involved a well-known California political figure, Richard Silverman. Petti, a highly visible figure in organized crime, was like Sandini: He had little regard for anyone but himself.

Charles Gorder was the assistant United States attorney in charge of the prosecution, and I had also worked with several of the FBI agents who led the investigation. In the early 1980s I had been the case agent in our successful prosecution of Petti for bookmaking. Charles and several bureau employees came over and talked with me about my lawsuit.

Outside the courtroom I also talked with a support staff employee.

She and I had worked together in the command post in the Rogers investigation and had been longtime friends.

"Now you know why I never came to any of your house parties," I said, smiling. "I think people might have been a little shocked had I brought a male date."

"It wouldn't have bothered me at all, Frank," she responded.

I told her that it had been difficult concealing what was going on from her and the others in the command post. "We were working some long hours together. It would have helped to be able to share it."

"Well, you did a fantastic job of hiding it," she said. "None of us had any idea."

A few days later I returned to the courtroom for the verdict and was pleased when the judge found Petti guilty. Government prosecutors and law enforcement officers seldom show any reaction when a verdict is announced, unlike scenes in the movies, but I knew how hard they had worked and the satisfaction they felt.

I congratulated Gorder and another assistant United States attorney who assisted in the prosecution. I then shook hands and congratulated some of the FBI employees and local law enforcement officers who had also been involved in the case. "You started it," one of the FBI case agents said, "and we finished it."

The FBI had very talented and dedicated people who performed a very difficult job. Some had even given their lives in the line of duty. I hoped my presence in the courtroom would demonstrate that I still considered myself a law enforcement officer.

And being there reminded me once more how much I missed being an agent.

■　■　■

ABC reporter John Martin had asked for the names of a few agents who would speak on camera on my behalf. I got in touch with a retired agent who had offered to testify for me before learning I was gay. He told me that he would be out of town on the scheduled date but that he wouldn't be much help anyway. He didn't think homosexuals ought to be working for the FBI.

"I think people should look beyond the stereotypes and judge people as individuals," I said before our conversation ended. Afterward I wondered if he would feel the same way if one of his children were gay.

The following week John Martin and two camera people arrived at my house. "Ignore the camera," Martin advised. "Just look at this as a conversation between the two of us."

Good advice, I thought, but he had just finished telling me that millions would be watching when the segment aired!

The questions were fair, but I hadn't anticipated all of them. Martin asked, for example, what I would say to the director of the FBI if he were watching the interview.

I thought for a moment and then commented: "The director of the FBI has stated on numerous occasions that he wants the bureau to accurately reflect the minorities which comprise this country. There are at least twenty-five million people in this country who are gay and lesbian, and it is time we are represented in the FBI."

At the end of the interview John asked if there was anything I'd like to add. It was a question I'd hoped he would ask.

The past few weeks had been difficult for me, I said, because a good friend had died of AIDS. "He was a doctor and a researcher, and his death put my situation with the FBI in perspective. It's sad to me that the FBI and federal government has spent hundreds of thousands of dollars to get rid of me—and millions of dollars to get rid of other gays and lesbians in the military—when all this time, money, and energy could be used to deal with the important problems facing this country."

John Martin later interviewed former Assistant United States Attorney Bob Rose and retired FBI Agent Gary Laturno. Both attested to my record and reputation in the FBI. After interviewing Gayer, Martin called to tell me he was having trouble scheduling an interview with Director Sessions. Without that interview, Martin said, the segment might not air at all.

32.

San Diego Police Officer John Graham came out publicly in October—the first police officer in Southern California to do so. He was thirty-one years old, a ten-year veteran and, according to the newspapers, had an excellent record and reputation.

I contacted John to congratulate him on his courageous act. He said, "Most of the people I work with talk about their spouses, boyfriends, or girlfriends and their personal lives. I got tired of concealing mine."

I asked how his colleagues were reacting.

"Chief Burgreen and most of the people I work with have been very supportive, and so far everything has been positive."

I could appreciate the pressure he was experiencing from all the media attention. I told him it certainly was an exciting time to be gay. "If I had known it was going to be this exciting, I would have come out a long time ago!"

"And you probably would have been fired a long time ago," he responded, and we both laughed.

I told John about the counseling I was receiving and that I was also making audiotapes to keep track of what was happening. "Besides being therapeutic," I said, "it may be of help to others one day."

John said he and a few others were thinking of forming a support group for gay and lesbian law enforcement officers. He invited me to join them, and a few days later five of us met for the first time at John's residence. We agreed the support group should be discreet and professional. Its purpose was to provide a confidential environment for discussing important issues. We decided to screen new members carefully.

After the meeting we all went to Bourbon Street, a local gay bar. It was Halloween night, and the bar and patio were crowded with gay people, some of whom were dressed in unusual costumes.

Life was certainly strange. Exactly two years before Hughes and Kuker had called me in for questioning about the W. J. letter. Now I was openly gay, in a gay bar, with openly gay police officers, after forming a gay and lesbian law enforcement support group!

If such a discreet, professional support group had been in existence when I was first confronted about my homosexuality, perhaps I would have handled the situation differently. In any case, my experience, and that of others in the group, would be there for others—maybe even for another FBI agent one day.

■ ■ ■

It seemed that others were reluctant to link gay rights with the ongoing struggle of other minorities for their full civil rights. For this reason, I was particularly pleased when a Newhouse News Service article appeared in the San Diego *Tribune* titled ''Racial and Bias Problems Seen Still Festering Throughout the FBI.'' Reporter Kathryn Kahler had interviewed me by phone, and her story opened with the statement that virtually every other federal law enforcement agency had a better minority hiring record than the FBI.

Congressman Don Edwards was quoted in the article: ''The FBI is still run by a club of predominantly white males, a crowd that is not as enlightened as I would like them to be.'' The article also quoted a former FBI agent who had represented Latino agents in their class-action suit against the bureau. He thought Director Sessions had been sensitized and seemed sincere in wanting to end discrimination in the bureau but added that ''the FBI is not run by Sessions. It is run by career FBI agents. I cannot perform a cranial lobotomy to change their biases and prejudices.''

At the end of October Director Sessions's court-ordered declaration arrived. In it Sessions claimed he wasn't responsible for the decision to fire me. He also claimed he had never talked with Congressman Edwards about my case even though Edwards's letter to him clearly stated otherwise.

In November Gayer and I attended a hearing before Judge Lynch. The judge said he didn't realize he was supposed to rule on the release of government files to me. He also postponed until March 15, 1991, a decision on whether to dismiss our case. Judge Lynch denied our request to expand the lawsuit to a class-action suit unless we came up with the names of other gay and lesbian FBI employees and applicants who had been discriminated against. But without the FBI's files in relation to these matters, identifying other gays and lesbians in the FBI would be extremely difficult.

Gayer was exceedingly discouraged. "If we don't get the files, the judge will probably take the government's word and rule against you."

■ ■ ■

An FBI luncheon had been planned for a longtime friend and agent who was being transferred. The agent called me at home to find out if I was going.

"I hadn't planned on it," I told him. "I didn't want you to feel uncomfortable with my being there or to make the occasion any less enjoyable for you."

"Listen, guy," he responded, "none of that other stuff makes any difference to me. We've been friends for a long time, and I want you to come."

I appreciated the call and decided to attend. I arranged to meet Ann Davis beforehand in the parking lot so we could go in together. As I walked with her to the restaurant door, I asked, half-kiddingly, "Are you sure you want to be associated with me?"

"Never mind," she said, patting my hand. "You're my friend, and I'm proud to be with you."

More than a hundred people were in attendance, and upon entering the crowded restaurant, we were immediately greeted by several FBI employees. Many of the women hugged me, and several of the men shook my hand. Throughout the luncheon a number of people came by to say hello and offer their support. Some were agents who in the past had made antigay comments. But there were also others, including good friends, who avoided even looking at me.

After the luncheon I stayed and talked with several people who had seen my interview the previous morning on *Inside San Diego,* a local television program. They said people in the office gathered around television sets when the program came on.

"You answered the Hoover question very well," one agent said.

I had been asked whether or not I thought J. Edgar Hoover was gay. I wanted to answer that I believed he was gay and that countless others like me were living with his antigay hatred, but instead I said that "Mr. Hoover's personal life was a matter of personal privacy, and the main point of my lawsuit was that my personal life had nothing to do with my professional life."

"You didn't take any cheap shots at the bureau," said another agent.

"My fight is not with the people here. My fight is with headquarters."

Before leaving, a Latino agent approached. "We had to go through what you're experiencing," he said. "I guess it's your turn now."

■ ■ ■

John Martin's ABC News segment aired in November. My case was described as still another in a series of lawsuits being brought against the FBI by its own minorities. Director Sessions refused to be directly interviewed but was quoted as saying, "Homosexuality is a factor in whether an agent can properly carry out his or her role as an FBI agent."

The remark was puzzling and insulting. Hadn't I properly carried out my role as an FBI agent? Sessions had never investigated cases or risked his life in the line of duty.

A few days later the San Diego *Tribune* carried a major story about my case. For the first time a large color photograph of me was used. That, coupled with my being on camera in the ABC news story, meant that there was no turning back now. I was definitely out of the closet for good.

Along with these developments was the increasing danger that something could happen to my house or to me. I wondered when I returned home late at night what I might find waiting for me. I was more careful now than when I had been an agent. Whenever I left my house, I felt myself preparing for a possible confrontation.

I wondered if W. J. had seen any of the news stories. I wanted to conduct my own investigation into who he was, but Gayer advised against it. I still believed that someday I would find out who he was and his motivation. I knew the possibility existed that W. J. was somebody in the FBI.

■ ■ ■

Since Judge Lynch advised us that he would reconsider our request for a class-action suit if we identified other gay and lesbian FBI employees and applicants, I had pursued the only alternative available to me. I began to contact individual gay and lesbian publications throughout the country. I called and sent letters to nearly a hundred such publications advising them of my case, and several in turn interviewed me. Their published articles requested that former or current gay and lesbian FBI applicants and employees contact attorney Richard Gayer.

After the ABC News story I was interviewed by *Newsweek*. Gayer and I also were contacted by a producer from *Larry King Live*. Scheduling conflicts prevented participation on the program.

■ ■ ■

I attended a large farewell party in late November for Charles Gorder, who was being transferred to a U.S. attorney's office in another city. Several of us roasted Charles, while making our admiration for him clear. When he spoke, he recognized by name the excellent agents he had worked with over the years. I was surprised when he said my name and even more moved when he added: "Frank Buttino is now undergoing the torture of the damned. . . . And this is one case I hope we lose."

■ ■ ■

At the beginning of December I took Rusty down to the canyon and went for a mile run for the first time since my back problems began. It was difficult, but I was grateful. For a long while I had lived with the apprehension I might never be able to walk again without pain.

■ ■ ■

On December 10 Gayer left a message on my answering machine to call him back as soon as I could. His line was busy for quite a while, but I finally got through.

"Dick Gayer," he answered.

"I hope this is good news, Dick."

"Extremely good," he said excitedly. "Judge Lynch has ruled in our favor! He is allowing us to take depositions from Teigen, Kuker, Stoops, and Rubino. He's ordered the government to turn over *all* its files on you, including your personnel file. The government also has to furnish us with all the documents Stoops and Rubino reviewed in making their decision."

Gayer was talking rapidly, and I took notes as quickly as I could. He said Judge Lynch had ordered the government to give us any FBI documents created by the bureau since 1985 relating to the employment of gay persons in the FBI.

I pounded the desk with my fist, but Gayer still wasn't finished. "The judge also ordered the government to provide us with any FBI documents created by the bureau since 1985 relating to the hiring, firing, and disciplinary practices of all FBI agents!"

"This is extraordinary, Dick!" I shouted. "I've never heard of the FBI being ordered to reveal this kind of internal personnel information. It will be the first time anyone has ever examined its treatment of gay employees."

"And also compare it with its treatment of other employees," Gayer interjected. "Let's hope that such records exist and that they give them all to us."

"Can they appeal the ruling?"

"Yes," Gayer answered. "But I doubt they will. They'll probably try, instead, to keep as much of the information as possible away from us by a motion for a protective order."

I think we both were too excited to talk any further and decided to begin planning our strategy the following day. I was anxious to call my family and friends with the news but found myself reviewing my notes. We desperately needed the bureau's disciplinary files and files on its treatment of gay employees and applicants. Without these it would be nearly impossible to support our claim that I had been denied equal protection under the law because I'm gay. It was a major victory for us. As I started dialing my parents' number, I felt for the first time we were going to win.

In the days that followed, Gayer and I had several discussions with Gary Hall about how best to proceed. We decided to gamble and go ahead with Teigen's and Kuker's depositions instead of waiting for the release of files. The files would have helped us prepare better, but there was no way of knowing how soon we would probably receive them. In all likelihood Judge Lynch would not allow us to depose these same people again. We would have to rely on our knowledge of the case and our combined professional skills.

Gayer and I spent the remainder of December and early January 1991 preparing for the depositions. I remembered Bob Woodward of the Washington *Post* once remarked, in regard to Watergate, that "God is in the details" of an investigation.

Gayer and I were looking for God.

■ ■ ■

My contact with gay publications around the country started to pay off. A woman who had been an FBI agent for two years got in touch with Gayer. She had been an outstanding employee, but in 1987 the FBI learned of her "lesbian activities." She had acknowledged her sexual orientation to OPR investigators, and the bureau threatened to reinterview her neighbors and friends if she refused to resign. She had also been told the bureau would make her a test case. She had resigned "for personal reasons." To assist us, the woman filed a "Jane Doe" affidavit.

She didn't want her real name used because she was seeking new employment.

The "Jane Doe" affidavit was an important first step in expanding my case to a class-action suit. Perhaps others would also come forward. Maybe the government's delays were starting to work against it.

33.

The nation's capital was in the midst of its most severe snowstorm of the winter when I arrived on the night of January 8, 1991. The road from Dulles Airport to the city was extremely icy, and several cars had spun out of control and been left abandoned.

The following morning I introduced myself to the owner and employees of the Olender Reporting Company in downtown Washington, D.C. They were friendly and even brought a pot of coffee to the conference room where the two depositions were to take place. I heard the outside door of the office open. "Good luck, Richard," I said, and he nodded, without looking up from his notes.

Tracy Merritt, the Department of Justice attorney, entered. With her was Toni Tell, an FBI supervisory agent who was on the legal staff at headquarters. Behind them was Bill Teigen.

I hadn't seen Teigen in nearly two years, and when I looked at him, some very strong emotions rose inside me. He offered his hand and asked how I was in a very friendly manner.

"Just wonderful," I answered.

I sat next to Gayer, wondering why I had shaken hands with Teigen. He had tried to destroy me and now acted as though we were old friends. Yet I needed to maintain control of my emotions if I was to be of any help to Gayer.

The irony of having two female attorneys along wasn't lost on me. In his nearly forty-eight-year reign as director Hoover had successfully prevented women from becoming agents. An assistant director of the FBI told us once that the possibility of having female agents was the "greatest threat facing the FBI in the future!"

Moreover, when OPR questioned me, I hadn't been allowed to have any attorney present, and I'd been threatened with being fired if I didn't answer all its questions. Teigen had two attorneys who could object to any question and instruct him not to answer. I couldn't question him or even talk during the course of the deposition. All I could do was pass notes to Gayer.

"What is your understanding of the FBI's policy on the employment of homosexuals?" Gayer asked, as an opening question.

Tracy Merritt immediately objected. Teigen wasn't the one to make policy, she said.

Gayer pressed anyway.

Teigen finally said, "My understanding is we don't have a stated policy. I don't know of a stated policy. . . ."

Gayer focused on Teigen's interrogation of me. He asked why Teigen had spent so much time probing the evolution of my sexuality if the bureau wasn't interested. He also rather abruptly asked Teigen: "Have you ever had sex with another man?"

This question apparently caught Teigen by surprise. His face reddened, and he glared at Gayer. Despite Merritt's objection, Teigen answered no.

"Is there anything in your sex life you don't want other people to know about?" Gayer went on.

"Mr. Gayer," Teigen answered coldly, "I think that question is out of line. My answer is no, but I think it is grossly out of line."

Gayer moved along without comment. He asked Teigen questions about his own sexual experiences, the ones he had told me about during the polygraph.

Merritt again objected. She said these questions were an invasion of his privacy. We hoped she would object. We would later argue to the judge that my privacy had been invaded, too; that a heterosexual's right to privacy should not be any more inviolate than a homosexual's rights.

Gayer asked Teigen if he had ever discussed homosexuality with other FBI employees, and Teigen answered that he had.

"Do you talk about homosexuals as faggots or queers?" Gayer asked.

"Do I?"

"Yes."

"Ever?"

Gayer was becoming impatient. "In the past ten years?"

Teigen hesitated once again. "In the past ten years, probably, yes."

"Have you ever heard such words used by other FBI employees?" Gayer then asked.

"Yes."

Teigen also admitted, under intensive questioning, that he believed homosexuals were more likely to succumb to blackmail than heterosexuals were. He told us, again after a barrage of questions, that no heterosexual he had ever polygraphed was asked explicit questions about his or her sexual life.

Gayer and I had done extensive research on the polygraph itself. Gayer now asked Teigen about its use and results. Teigen and Morgovnik had used the word "deceptive" to describe some of my responses on the polygraph, and the bureau had used this to fire me. It was also the basis for its constant refrain, in the media, that I repeatedly lied.

But when Gayer asked if it was not true that the polygraph machine really measured reaction to questions rather than truth or deception, Teigen answered, "Yes."

Gayer also got Teigen to admit that test results could be interpreted differently by different examiners.

Morgovnik and Teigen had been holding all the cards when I sat through hours of interrogation and testing trying to save my career. Now the bureau had to answer for its conduct. It felt good to be on the offensive.

Gayer looked at Teigen for a moment, then asked, "Do you find homosexuality to be offensive?"

"No," Teigen responded, and Gayer went in for the kill.

"Why did you tell Mr. Buttino that you found homosexuality to be offensive?"

"I didn't."

"Correct me if I'm wrong . . ." Gayer said. He glanced at me, and I nodded to go ahead. "It's your testimony under oath that at no time have you ever told Mr. Buttino that you found homosexuality to be offensive?"

Teigen apparently was knocked on his heels. "Is that my testimony, is that your question?" Teigen responded. He seemed confused. "Yes, that is my testimony," he finally answered.

I was looking directly at Teigen, but he avoided me. The bureau was saying I was a liar, and here was one of its own supervisors apparently caught in a lie. Gayer dropped the matter, but I knew we would get back to it later.

Gayer asked Teigen about his comment about other agents killing me in 1974 if they had known I was homosexual.

Teigen backpedaled. "Why did I tell him that?" he said, then argued that it was simply a topic under discussion.

"And if you had been one of these other agents, you would have killed Mr. Buttino?"

Merritt objected, but Teigen answered anyway, saying that killing was just a figure of speech.

"They might assault him in some way? Was that the meaning of your term 'killing'?" Gayer continued.

Teigen wouldn't answer the question directly, and Gayer eventually stopped this line of questioning. Teigen had already said enough to help our case.

We broke for lunch, and Teigen and Tell immediately left the room. Teigen ignored me completely as he passed by. I confronted Merritt before she left the room.

"I want you to know that Teigen committed perjury this morning when Gayer asked him if he told me he found homosexuality offensive," I said angrily. "You and everyone else in the room are witnesses to it."

Merritt stared at me but did not respond. A full-page article about my case had just come out in *Newsweek,* along with my photo, and I used it as a trump card. "You know that I'm not afraid to talk to the media. If Teigen doesn't tell the truth this afternoon about that statement, I'm going to the media when the deposition is over. I'm going to tell them that an FBI polygraph examiner lied under oath and in your presence."

Merritt still didn't respond. She left, and I closed the door behind her.

"I was just about to intervene," Gayer said.

"I did it on purpose," I said with a wink. "I have a feeling Teigen is going to change his testimony this afternoon."

"I hope so," Gayer replied. "It's something we need to have on the record."

When Teigen, Merritt, and Tell returned after lunch, they were decidedly more subdued than when they first arrived. Teigen seemed more irritable and hostile as the questioning progressed. Merritt continued objecting to Gayer's questions, and there were many heated exchanges.

As planned, Gayer asked about the capability of the polygraph room's being monitored, and Teigen said the room we used had a one-way mirror that wasn't working at the time.

I wondered how a one-way mirror could not be working. I felt as though he were distracting us for some reason. One of the forms I had signed said the room had the capability of being monitored.

Gayer moved to our next question. "Now, to the best of your knowledge, was any videotape recording made of anything you said or Mr. Buttino said?''

Teigen hesitated. I looked over at him. ''Yes,'' he answered.

The court reporter finished typing, and the room fell silent. Teigen and I both knew what had happened that afternoon, though words always failed me in trying to explain it to others. Until now my only evidence was my own recollection.

Gayer knew he was on to something and began slamming Teigen with question after question, making them up as he went along. Teigen slowly turned away from us, as though he were trying to get out of the line of fire. Merritt's and Tell's faces were stone cold, but I suspected they already knew about the existence of a tape.

Teigen explained that after my polygraph another FBI employee had asked him a question that made him wonder if a videotape had actually been made of the session. He went into the adjoining room and found a tape had in fact been made. Teigen said that it had been done without his knowledge and that it contained only a portion of the pre-polygraph interview.

Gayer bore in again, and Teigen kept stammering out his responses. Merritt objected whenever possible, but there was no denying what this meant. There was a ''smoking gun.'' We would have indisputable proof of how the FBI treated one of its own agents behind closed doors—a veteran agent who happened to be gay. The long lie of the FBI was about to come to an end.

Teigen had tried to find out who had made the tape, but failing that, he then told his supervisor about it. And still later he turned it over to his unit chief. Teigen admitted finding the tape on May 23, 1989, but not giving it to the unit chief until late 1990. He had kept the tape for more than a year and a half.

It seemed to me that Teigen had probably held on to the tape all that time thinking I would either resign or be fired. If that had happened, the tape would never become an issue. But he couldn't destroy it *unless* I resigned or was fired because others at FBI headquarters knew of its existence.

Teigen said he did not tell Stoops or Rubino, the two people responsible for firing me, about the tape. Teigen did say he discussed the tape with ''counsel.'' Teigen wasn't sure where the tape was at the moment but believed the FBI had given it to Tracy Merritt.

Gayer and I looked at her, and she nodded. She said she would turn it over to us.

In that afternoon session Gayer also got Teigen to admit he had in fact said he found me "offensive." I looked over at Merritt, but she continued to stare straight ahead.

Teigen said he used the word "offensive" referring to the first time we met, in San Diego. Another agent and I were in our office's polygraph room. Teigen said I was "inappropriately aggressive" when talking to him.

Gayer pressed him to explain, and Teigen said Buttino was "literally at my knees, knee to knee, and right in my face."

After more questioning, Teigen admitted that the room was small, that it contained a polygraph machine and a table—and that there were four agents present.

I passed Gayer a note. I could see Teigen look at me out of the corner of his eye. Gayer asked my question: "How close were you to Mr. Buttino before *he* was strapped to the [polygraph] machine?"

"Well, it varied."

"Were you ever essentially knee to knee?" Gayer cut in.

Teigen looked to Merritt for help, but she didn't offer any.

"Probably. Yes," Teigen answered.

Gayer smiled for the first time that day. He followed with several more questions. Teigen said his comment about finding me offensive might be on the videotape.

The questioning continued until 4:30 P.M. Before it ended, Gayer asked about Teigen's comment about my feeling "degraded" by the polygraph session. Gayer asked if Teigen normally made that comment to examinees. Teigen said he did not.

Why had he made it then, Gayer pursued.

"Because of the topic of conversation that we had been involved in all day and the impact of that topic in his personal and professional life."

"The topic being homosexuality?"

"Yes. And his honesty."

"No further questions," Gayer said, and Teigen, Tell, and Merritt left the room without comment or delay. Teigen neither looked at me nor offered his hand on the way out.

This was the first time I had seen Gayer conduct a deposition. The depth of his preparation and the acuity of his skills were impressive. His questioning reminded me of those bantamweight boxers who keep throwing punches and never seem to tire. I only wished I could have done some of the questioning.

"Great job," I said.

"Teigen's admission that he found you personally offensive is almost as good an admission as his saying he found homosexuality offensive," Gayer responded, with a shake of his head.

"He admitted it only because it's probably on the tape," I added.

■ ■ ■

The deposition of San Diego's ASAC, Tom Kuker, began the following morning. Our hunch was that Kuker had been in charge of San Diego's investigation. If that was true, deposing Kuker would provide valuable information and be crucial to undermining the government's case against me.

Kuker had told me that neither of the men interviewed knew me, nor I them, yet the FBI had claimed otherwise. The bureau said I was deceptive in my responses about having met W. J. and used it as further proof that I was lying.

We did not expect Kuker to be a hostile witness, so Gayer and I planned our strategy and style accordingly. When Kuker arrived the following morning, he had a bad cold, and we offered to postpone the deposition. He said he wanted to go on with it anyway and was sworn in.

I hadn't seen Kuker in almost a year. Dressed in a dark suit and tie, standing at about six feet two inches, Kuker looked like an agent who actually made arrests. Though Kuker seemed dispassionate, my work with him in the command post had shown me a different side of him.

Kuker told us at the outset of the deposition that he had in fact been in charge of the OPR investigation in San Diego. I was relieved. Most of our preparations were predicated on this.

He said that his primary concern after the San Diego office had received the note from W. J. "was that maybe an agent's life was in danger, somebody out there might be doing something, planning something, and we don't know about it. And that concerns me, no matter what the allegation was."

Kuker continued: "FBIHQ Office of Professional Responsibility was notified concerning the receipt of the letter and its enclosures and they are the ones that determined that Frank needed to be interviewed and they told me how to conduct that interview.'' Kuker emphasized that the sole purpose of his investigation was to determine the identity and motivation of W. J. and not to investigate me.

"Is it correct to say that you did not interview anybody relating to Mr. Buttino's character?'' Gayer asked.

"I knew what his reputation and character were, and subsequently the bureau found out based on the communication they read from me, so there was no need for me ever to interview anybody concerning his character.''

Just as I had suspected, the bureau had not conducted an updated background investigation of me as I had suggested, probably because it did not want the public to know it had a gay FBI agent.

In response to questioning, Kuker described me as a "superior agent'' and said I performed at that level until I was suspended from my job. He said that he and the SAC, Tom Hughes, had considered the fact that I was gay and under investigation at the time of the Rogers van bombing, but that this had not been not a deterrent in assigning me to a leadership role in the case. Kuker said his investigation had not uncovered any information that would cause the bureau to remove me from the Rogers case.

Gayer asked Kuker, as he had Teigen, if he knew "anything about the FBI's policy on the employment of homosexuals.''

"I don't know what it is in regard to employees,'' he answered.

No one we asked in the bureau seemed to know what the actual policy was. The official policy statements on the subject were, in addition, both confusing and ambiguous. They seemed purposely designed to disguise the bureau's true antigay nature.

Gayer asked about the nude photograph Rubino claimed I had lied about, and Kuker said that he had never seen such a photograph and that there was no evidence such a photograph ever existed. Kuker seemed to be hitting every ball out of the park for us. His statements undermined the bureau's own case against me. And he went on in this manner throughout the day.

According to Kuker, the bureau had not conducted handwriting analyses of the two people interviewed to see if one of them had written the W. J. note. The bureau had, however, analyzed my handwriting to see if I had written the note myself! For Gayer and me, this demonstrated that the bureau had never been truly interested in determining the truth. Its primary concern was to get rid of me.

Kuker restated what he had told me before, that he did not believe I had met the letter writer (even though the bureau claimed otherwise and used it as a reason to fire me). What was important about Kuker's statement now, however, was that it became part of the official record.

Kuker explained that OPR halted the investigation in May 1989, before he had determined who wrote the W. J. letter. OPR advised SAC Hughes to "package everything and discontinue the investigation." Kuker said he was frustrated by the decision because "at that time we were still trying to determine the identity of W. J. and would have continued to do so."

Gayer asked if "any evidence or anything at all" was uncovered in the investigation to suggest that an attempt to coerce me had occurred.

"No," Kuker replied without hesitation.

Gayer asked if I had been cooperative during the investigation and Kuker answered with an unequivocal "yes." He also testified he would have no problem working with me if I were reinstated.

I looked over at Merritt and Tell. Contrary to the day before, Merritt had been fairly quiet. These two days were not good ones for the government.

When Gayer asked if any FBI surveillance of me had been conducted, Merritt objected on the ground of law enforcement investigatory privilege. She instructed Kuker not to answer. Their silence on this issue made me wonder about the break-ins and damage to my house.

When the daylong deposition was over, I walked Kuker to the reception area. The attorneys remained behind. I thanked him for his honesty and apologized for having to put him through the deposition. He said he knew he would have to testify at some point.

"I hope people in the bureau don't misunderstand what I'm doing. I'm not looking to make disparaging remarks about the bureau or its employees. I just want my job back."

Merritt and Tell appeared at that point, and he wished me luck. We shook hands before he left.

34.

Gayer began receiving some of the court-ordered FBI files at the end of January 1991. My personnel file showed nothing negative except in reference to the recent investigation of my homosexuality. Each performance rating was either "excellent" or "superior."

In the file I came across a memorandum J. Edgar Hoover sent to Clyde Tolson on February 7, 1972. It was the day I met Hoover. "Today I saw Special Agent Francis C. Buttino, a Relief Supervisor in the Detroit Office, who is attending the Security-General In-Service Class. Mr. Buttino makes an excellent, above-average, mature, and substantial personal appearance and I would rate him above average. I think this Agent has the potential for advancement in the service."

The files detailing the bureau's efforts to identify W. J. were profoundly troubling. No wonder headquarters didn't want me to see this information. The investigation was shoddy and incomplete. Logical leads and follow-up investigations were not pursued, and the investigation itself was terminated without determining the truth. It reinforced my belief that the investigation was "result-oriented"—unlike anything I had ever seen in the FBI. The bureau intended to fire me from the start and used the polygraph results to justify it. It probably never expected to have to answer for its actions.

The incident files also started to trickle in now. They dealt with homosexual FBI applicants and the treatment of FBI employees suspected of being homosexual. Although names and other identifying data were "blacked out," the files gave us our first glimpse into the bureau's own homophobic closet.

The pattern regarding applicants quickly became apparent. Highly qualified and recommended applicants were rejected on the mere suspicion of their being gay or lesbian. In one file a supervisor commented that a special agent applicant "came across in mannerisms as being gay."

He added that this was "strictly an impression and not based on fact." The bureau viewed this impression as "derogatory information," and the applicant was reinterviewed regarding his "alleged homosexuality." He categorically denied being gay, and the interviewing agents asked for and received the names of women he had dated. The women were interviewed, and though they spoke positively about the applicant, he was not hired or told the reason why.

An applicant for an FBI clerical position was suspected of being gay by some of his neighbors because he had a male roommate. The bureau's background investigation had determined he was an outstanding applicant, but this "derogatory information" caused him to be rejected. This was not shared with the applicant, nor was he told why the bureau didn't hire him.

Slowly we also began receiving the FBI's files on employees suspected of being gay or lesbian. The mere suspicion of homosexuality was enough to initiate an investigation. Employees were subjected to surveillances, polygraphs, and interrogations regarding the most intimate details of their sex lives. The files showed that most resigned "for personal reasons."

■   ■   ■

The government had informed us that because there were no files labeled "homosexuality" per se, it would have to conduct a random search of all OPR files. Locating, reviewing, and then furnishing other such files to us, contended the government, could take quite some time. For this reason, Judge Lynch extended the government's deadline for turning them over. It was frustrating, but he also postponed indefinitely the government's motion to have the case dismissed.

■   ■   ■

John Graham and I, and other members of our newly founded support group SOLO (Society Of Law Officers), sat together at the Nicky Awards ceremony in February 1991. This annual event honors individuals for outstanding contributions to San Diego's gay and lesbian community.

Bob Burgreen, San Diego's police chief, received the Mayor George Moscone Award. He got a standing ovation as he walked to the stage. Burgreen told the gathering that his belief in tolerance for gays and lesbians was tested when John Graham came into his office to tell him he was gay. "I've known a lot of brave officers in my time, but none braver than John." With that, Burgreen held up the award. Looking in our direction, he exclaimed, "John, this one's for you!"

Later John Graham and I were honored as the first recipients of the Neil Good Award. Good had been a longtime gay activist in San Diego who had died a few years before. The emcee spoke of John's courage in coming out as an openly gay police officer and also said I was fighting for the rights of all gays and lesbians with my lawsuit against the FBI. We were cheered as we walked to the stage, and both of us spoke. When it was my turn, I said that Neil Good's courage, and that of so many others in the gay and lesbian community, had given me the courage to take my stand against the FBI.

A few days later I received a congratulatory letter from San Diego Mayor Maureen O'Connor. "I'm sure that your struggle is often lonely, frustrating and intimidating," the mayor wrote. "By your strength and perseverance you will empower many others who would otherwise be trampled by prejudice and injustice."

■ ■ ■

The Teigen tape arrived.

Gayer and I had decided that a transcript of the hour-and-forty-five-minute tape might assist us, and I agreed to do it. From the wiretap cases I had worked, I knew transcribing the tape would take at least a full week. I watched the tape for the first time and began to relive that day. I called Everett.

We met in the canyon near my house.

"I watched the Teigen tape today, Everett. I seriously wonder if I can go through all this again."

"I think it's ironic," Everett observed, seemingly on a different track, "that the bureau trained you to become one of their best investigators and now you're using your skills against them."

"I'm not really against them—" I said.

"I know you want your job back," Everett cut in. "And that's a noble thing. But think about it—the hunted has become the hunter."

We returned to our trucks.

"Frank, I'm proud of how far you have come since we first talked in Washington."

I reminded him that over two years had passed.

"This is another hurdle for you to overcome," he said. "You know what you must do, and you can do it."

■ ■ ■

Gayer called a few days later and said he had received more files from the FBI. "They're the most damaging yet to the government's case," he said. There was an uncharacteristic tone to his voice, and I decided to fly to San Francisco immediately. I picked up the files from Gayer and drove to Roger and Phil's house. No one was home, and I sat down and began to read the files.

They contained still more examples of the bureau's treatment of employees suspected of being gay. There was a pattern here, too. OPR would call the employees back to headquarters and confront them with the information. The employees were advised that the bureau would need to know the full details of their homosexual conduct, beginning with their first experiences. Employees were told that failure to answer any questions put to them during the inquiry could result in their being fired for failure to cooperate.

Additionally, OPR advised each employee that even after all this information had been provided in a signed statement, the bureau would need to conduct an updated background investigation of the individual. The investigation was necessary to determine suitability for continued employment and would include interviews with the employees' parents, family, friends, neighbors, and co-workers. The interview would focus on the employee's homosexual conduct.

Those bastards! I thought. *No wonder the government fought to keep these files from us! The FBI is the blackmailer!* It was the bureau that threatened to expose its employees' homosexuality if they wouldn't resign. Yet historically the bureau had used the blackmail argument as justification for excluding gays and lesbians from employment.

What I had done, though, was to sabotage this usual pattern of behavior. I had encouraged an updated background investigation. I had given the bureau permission to tell anyone it wanted I was gay. It couldn't blackmail me into resigning! And I had told the bureau I wouldn't resign. I had left it little recourse other than to fire me.

I opened another file. A veteran special agent was suspected of being gay. He was married with children and had an outstanding record. He was called back to Washington on what seemed to be a pretext because as soon as he stepped off the plane, the bureau began following him.

After several days of questioning on another issue, OPR confronted the agent with the allegation that he was homosexual. He categorically denied it and was asked to detail his conduct in Washington. Though he had been in public areas sometimes frequented by gay men, the agent had not been observed doing anything suspicious. Nevertheless, OPR continued to grill him. At the end of the second day he furnished a signed statement denying the allegation.

As I neared the end of the thick file, a sense of foreboding came over me. There were only a few pages left to read, and it seemed there was little left to explain how all this was resolved.

At the very end I read that the agent had returned to his field office and "committed suicide by shooting himself."

My God, I thought, *The bureau caused one of its own to kill himself.* I put my head back against the chair. My disbelief gave way to sadness and anger.

Roger came into the room a short time later, and I was still sitting in the chair with my eyes closed. He asked if I was all right, but I couldn't get the words out. He came over and put his arm on my shoulder.

Later I told Roger and Phil about the agent's suicide, and Roger exploded in anger. "I wonder how many other gay people's lives were ruined by the FBI! Look what they tried to do to you. The judge needs to know how they treat us!"

But Phil, as usual, was more subdued. "Remember him when you're sad and discouraged and wonder why you're going through all this," he said.

My efforts to sleep that night were disturbed by thoughts of the agent shooting himself. I thought about the extreme pressure he must have felt and my own experience with Teigen and the polygraph.

I turned on the light and opened the file. Most of the identifying information was blacked out, but I reread every page carefully. A suicide within the bureau was unusual. The agent had the same length of service as I. Suddenly I realized I had known him and had worked with him.

I thought about the phone call from the headquarters supervisor after the Teigen polygraph and his concern for my welfare. Later he had mentioned an agent's committing suicide under similar circumstances. The agent's suicide may even have caused someone at headquarters to turn on the videotape recorder during my session with Teigen.

I closed the file and turned off the light. I sat alone in the darkness. As the tears came down my face, for the first time in my life I felt old.

35.

In March I attended an open house at a building that would eventually serve as the new San Diego Lesbian and Gay Men's Center. While John Graham and I talked to visitors about SOLO, I saw Tom Homann enter the building. He looked extremely frail, and I went over to greet him. We spoke for a few moments, and then he said he had to sit. "I don't have much energy anymore," he said.

I sat beside him, and others came over to say hello. Tom still had that twinkle in his eyes, especially when I mentioned some of the positive developments in my case. "Oh, I think you're going to win," he reassured me.

"I couldn't have done it without you," I answered, getting up. We shook hands, and I said good-bye. A short time later I saw him leaving the building alone, and I had the feeling I would not see him again.

■ ■ ■

A week later I was asked to speak before the California legislature in Sacramento on behalf of Assembly Bill (AB) 101, which would prevent discrimination against gays and lesbians in employment and housing. I had previously spoken about my experience and the necessity for such legislation at public hearings held in Los Angeles.

Several of us, including Mitch Grobeson—the former Los Angeles police officer—told personal experiences of antigay discrimination. But the hearing room was packed with opponents of the bill, many of them religious fundamentalists. They quoted passages from the Bible to condemn us and warned of homosexual teachers' promoting their views and corrupting children. AB101, they said, would lead to legislation endorsing bestiality and incest.

It was my first real encounter with people whose hatred of homosexuals was so extreme and vociferous. Fortunately a number of state law enforcement officers were on hand to keep the situation under control. Later I told friends I felt like a lion being thrown to the Christians.

■ ■ ■

As we had hoped, Gayer began receiving phone calls from gay and lesbian applicants who had read about my case. A man in the Midwest had applied to be a special agent. He had a graduate degree, appeared to be well qualified, and had a honorable discharge from the military. When asked why he left the military, he said it was because he was gay. A female agent had responded: ''The FBI does not hire second-class citizens.'' The former applicant later furnished an affidavit to Judge Lynch of his experience and qualifications. He had an honorable discharge from the military and a graduate degree.

I traveled to San Francisco each time files from the FBI arrived. We finally received records detailing administrative action taken against all FBI agents over the two-year period of my battle. Our argument to the court was that my constitutional guarantee of equal protection under the law, a component of the Fifth Amendment, had been violated by the FBI. To prove this, we needed evidence that the punishment I had received exceeded the punishment administered to other agents for comparable offenses.

Despite the image Hoover and his successors carefully tried to maintain of incorruptible agents, my personal experience, and now the files, factually demonstrated otherwise. More than *one thousand* administrative inquires involving agents were contained in the files over the two-year period. The FBI was secretive even to its own rank and file, and it was a strange experience learning about many of these things for the first time.

One of them described an agent who had been involved in an automobile accident while driving a bureau car. He had consumed alcohol before the accident and was found to be ''less than forthright'' during the administrative inquiry. Other files disclosed instances of agents making unauthorized disclosure of FBI information and some even falsifying government documents. One agent ''falsified background investigation on a former Special Agent applicant'' while another ''submitted a fraudulent voucher for reimbursement of expenses not incurred.'' An agent falsified his attendance record. Files described agents lying in court proceedings or putting pressure on witnesses to lie.

The maximum punishment for these types of offenses ranged from censure to suspension without pay. But no top secret security clearances were revoked, nor were any of these employees fired.

In one instance an FBI supervisory special agent, married with two children, was arrested for felonious sexual conduct that took place in a public bookstore, and the agent lied during the FBI inquiry. The bureau gave him a letter of censure and fourteen days' suspension without pay. No probation was imposed on the agent because according to the file, "probation is inappropriate and unnecessary as this incident does not relate to the agent's work performance."

The number and nature of such instances by FBI agents were surprising to me. Because they remained secret, even to those of us in the bureau, the public was hard pressed to believe anything negative about the FBI when it came out. The bureau and agents were above reproach. When others heard my story, for example, the response more often than not was "Can't be—not the FBI."

Another group of files included gay-related correspondence between the FBI and colleges and universities, as well as individual citizens. In these the bureau was asked whether it discriminated on the basis of sexual orientation. Its response was that it had "an absolute policy" of not discriminating on the basis of sexual orientation itself, but "where homosexual conduct is indicated, it is considered a significant factor in FBI decision-making, with respect to both hiring and retention of employees."

The FBI's own files were clearly showing that applicants were summarily rejected and employees forced out when the mere suspicion of homosexuality was raised. The bureau was simply not telling the truth.

It appeared that the bureau hoped to confuse the public by arguing its unique distinction between sexual orientation and sexual conduct. To the FBI, *any* homosexual conduct was egregious. "It's like the bureau saying it doesn't discriminate against Catholics," I told Gayer, "as long as they don't go to mass!"

In March the government petitioned the court to protect portions of Teigen's deposition and remarks he had made on the videotape that dealt with his "personal sexual experiences." Attorney Tracy Merritt contended that "the personal privacy of William Teigen" ought to be protected.

We told the court that we agreed and that the FBI's questioning about my personal sexual experiences was likewise an invasion of privacy.

We planned to use the government's desire to protect Teigen's privacy in still another way. The government had claimed I was susceptible to blackmail because my homosexuality was a secret. We would argue that Teigen, too, was susceptible to blackmail because he had sexual secrets he did not want revealed.

Another major factor in the government's case against me was its reliance on the polygraphs. It relied on them even when some of Kuker's investigation contradicted the results. Teigen had admitted to us under oath that the polygraph was a reactive tool which could not actually determine if a person was lying or telling the truth, that the test itself could be affected by the examiner, and that the results could be interpreted differently by different examiners. However, Judge Lynch had not yet made a decision about the admissibility of polygraph results as evidence.

Then, in late March, Judge Lynch ruled that he "did not intend to take such evidence into account...." He expressed doubt, as well, whether the polygraph evidence would be admissible if my case went to trial.

■ ■ ■

I had never met Gary Stoops, the FBI's security programs manager, before our May 1, 1991, deposition of him in Washington. Stoops was responsible for the revocation of my top secret security clearance, which led to my firing. Now, roughly a year and a half later, he would have to defend his decision.

Stoops looked to be in his late forties, wore glasses, and had graying hair. He had joined the FBI the same year I did, 1969, but had spent most of his career behind a desk.

Dr. Franklin Kameny joined us that morning. Kameny was representing the gay FBI clerk whose security clearance had been revoked by Stoops. (After the filing of my lawsuit the Department of Justice overruled Stoops and allowed the clerk to return to work!)

Kameny was a pioneer in the gay rights movement, and I told him it was an honor to meet him. He was in his late sixties—short, stocky, and bald.

He responded loudly, "And it is indeed a pleasure to meet you."

I suspected that Dr. Kameny was hard-of-hearing.

Tracy Merritt and Tony Tell sat on each side of Stoops, and the questioning began. Gayer wanted to draw parallels between my case and that of the gay FBI clerk. He introduced Kameny as the clerk's "counsel of record" and asked Stoops to defend his reasoning in the case.

"We waive privacy with respect to Mr. [the gay clerk] and this proceeding," Kameny boomed.

Tracy Merritt objected quickly and angrily. "One, Mr. Kameny is not a lawyer," she said. "Two, Mr. [the gay clerk] is not here to give his personal waiver, and I am not going to allow Mr. Stoops to answer that question or any other question that identifies a third party by name."

Gayer ignored her objections and asked Stoops to defend his reasoning. Merritt interrupted. "I am going to object here. You're getting into attorney-client privileged information, and the witness is not going to answer. I instruct you not to answer," she told Stoops.

The deposition came to a halt, and a heated exchange took place off the record. When we resumed, on the record, Kameny pointed his finger at Merritt. His face reddened, and he exclaimed loudly, "I object to your interceding in the relationship between me and my client. Lawyers are not royalty in this country, and therefore, I have as many rights as you, even though I am not an attorney! I am on a par with you as far as that case is concerned. And I simply object to your rather arrogant attitude on this matter!"

"I am not going to sit here and listen to this!" Merritt told him. "You will leave the room, and we'll terminate this deposition if you are going to speak further. That is our position!"

Gayer wouldn't back down. "And we will come back here again."

Kameny did not leave the room, nor did Merritt, Tell, or Stoops. The deposition resumed, and as it progressed, Stoops's lack of preparation became evident. He said he could not remember basic details of the case. Like Teigen, he seemed to become more defensive and hostile as the day wore on.

The depositions had reinforced my belief that FBI headquarters had never anticipated having to defend its actions. Part of me felt vindicated because of the depositions, but the part of me that was still an FBI agent was embarrassed by the lack of professionalism exhibited by the two bureau representatives.

Gayer tried several times to get Stoops to clarify what he meant by "alleged homosexual activities." It was the reason why the FBI had even initiated its investigation of me. To Gayer and me the phrase sounded too much like "alleged Communist activities"—a repeated charge made by Senator Joseph McCarthy in the early 1950s. Stoops eventually got around to saying, in a somewhat twisted bit of logic, that homosexuality is not a concern if the FBI is *unaware* of it. He added, however, that when the FBI does become aware of it, it becomes a national security concern!

Gayer stared at Stoops. A small smile crossed Gayer's lips, and there was a slight shake of his head before he resumed his questioning.

We were able to get into the record that day how Stoops had relied mainly on the polygraphs in his decision to fire me. Stoops testified he had never talked with ASAC Kuker about Kuker's investigation to identify W. J. Stoops said the polygraph results took precedence over the FBI's own investigation anyway! Stoops stated that he had talked to Teigen about the polygraph results but that Teigen had never told him about the nature of my session with him or the fact that it had been videotaped.

Stoops couldn't remember who told him I was "uncooperative," even though he used this as a reason to revoke my security clearance. Gayer was furious. He wanted to know who, specifically, in the San Diego office gave Stoops this information.

"I don't know," Stoops answered. "I can't recall."

"Was it Mr. Kuker?"

"I don't know."

Stoops claimed he couldn't remember if the information was given to him orally or in writing. He thought it might have been in the form of a telephone call.

Gayer pressed.

"I don't recall," Stoops responded, "but my best recollection was that it came in written form."

Merritt was objecting that the "question had been asked and answered," but Gayer, looking directly at Stoops, said, "Isn't it true that you're lying?"

Merritt asserted that Gayer was badgering the witness.

"Do you know the meaning of the oath you took this morning, Mr. Stoops?" Gayer continued.

Stoops mumbled a "yes."

Later Stoops said that a supervisory special agent working under him had actually written my letter of suspension and that he, Stoops, had "furnished input and we made some changes and so forth." I made a note to myself: We would have to depose Brad Benson.

According to Stoops, he had revoked my security clearance because I refused to disclose the names of my homosexual associates.

"Are you aware that Mr. Buttino offered in writing to you, before you made your final decision, to name at least some of his gay associates?" Gayer asked.

"I don't recall that."

Gayer handed Stoops a copy of a letter I had written to him after my suspension. In it I had offered to disclose names after obtaining permission. We waited while Stoops and Merritt read the letter. Stoops looked up and said he didn't remember seeing the letter.

Unbelievable, I thought. Stoops had decided the fate of my career, and he didn't know all the facts! But what bothered me most was that he didn't even seem to care.

During the course of the day Gayer had become increasingly frustrated with Stoops. Gayer would say, bitingly, "I can't hear you with your hand in front of your mouth," or, "We are a master of evasive answers, I must say." Finally Gayer put it to Stoops directly: "You realize I am going to characterize your answer to the court as nonsense? With that in mind, do you wish to amplify your answer?"

Merritt kept objecting. We wanted her to. We would argue before the court that Stoops's decision was not credible because he was ignorant of my case.

One of the more frustrating moments came late in the afternoon. Gayer tried to get Stoops to answer yes or no whether I had harmed national security. Stoops finally answered, no.

"Thank you," Gayer said with sarcasm.

Still later Gayer told Stoops that Supervisory Special Agent William Teigen had sought a protective order to prevent details of his private sexual life from becoming known. Gayer asked Stoops if this meant Teigen had the potential of being coerced.

Stoops said he'd have to know more of the facts.

"Have you ever engaged in oral sex?" Gayer asked abruptly.

Tracy Merritt objected, instructing Stoops not to answer. I glanced at Kameny, and he winked back.

"I gave him the power to refuse to answer based on his privacy concern without any interference from counsel," Gayer said.

"I am not interfering," Merritt answered. "I'm posing the objection, and I will instruct the witness not to answer."

Gayer looked at Stoops. "Do you feel that question is an invasion of your privacy as a human being?"

Stoops smiled. "I look at it as I am not the one whose conduct is being reviewed here."

"Are you sure of that?" Gayer asked, returning the smile.

■ ■ ■

As the Department of Justice's chief security officer D. Jerry Rubino had the power to overturn Stoops's decisions. Rubino had in fact done so in the matter of the gay FBI clerk. The following morning we deposed Rubino.

Rubino appeared to be about fifty, was five feet eight or nine, and heavyset. Like Stoops, he seemed ill prepared. Questioning proved even more frustrating than questioning Stoops. Rubino also seemed more vague and evasive in his answers. For example, an early exchange between Gayer and Rubino went:

GAYER: *Does the name Thomas Kuker mean anything to you?*

RUBINO: *Would you repeat that?*

GAYER: *Thomas Kuker. Have you ever heard of that name in connection with Mr. Buttino?*

RUBINO: *I believe I have.*

GAYER: *Is it not true that Mr. Kuker was in charge of an investigation of Frank Buttino that was done in the San Diego area?*

RUBINO: *I believe that that is the agent involved in the investigation.*

Rubino testified that he had never talked with Kuker about my case. But Rubino stated that I had met and been coerced by W. J.

Gayer eventually got him to admit that Kuker had found no evidence to support his claims. Rubino also said he knew nothing of Teigen's treatment of me or the existence of a videotape.

Rubino had officially written, in upholding Stoops's decision, that my refusal to provide names of gay associates to the FBI was evidence of my failure to cooperate. Gayer showed him my letter to Stoops offering to do so. In one of his first direct responses of the day, Rubino said it was the first time he had seen the letter.

Gayer asked if the letter would have made a difference in his decision, and Rubino answered, "I am unable to answer that."

Gayer questioned Rubino about the FBI's investigation of W. J., pointing out some of its limitations, such as failure to fingerprint suspects, etc. "That is up to the FBI," Rubino said with a shrug. "I am not questioning the FBI's conduct of their investigation. I am not involved in that."

Gayer asked Rubino if he knew what FBI policy was regarding security clearances for employees who engage in homosexual conduct, but Merritt objected. "I can't answer that," Rubino responded. "I am not an FBI official. I don't know exactly. No, I don't."

Rubino said "I don't know," "I can't answer that," or "I'm not sure" so many times that Gayer's frustration eventually reached the boiling point. Ignoring Tracy Merritt's objections, Gayer said to Rubino, coldly, "Let me say this. In my opposition to the government's motion for summary judgment I will try to show that you're incompetent. Now, you have an opportunity in answering these questions to show that you know what you are doing and that as an adjudicator you know how to apply your standards which we discussed earlier to specific instances, to hypothetical cases. If you're unable to do that, I will argue that your opinion is worthless."

Rubino didn't respond.

Gayer shook his head and asked if there were personal things in Rubino's life that might cause him embarrassment if exposed.

Rubino cautiously responded, "Possibly."

Gayer closed in, "And you see no obligation on your part to reveal these things to anybody in the Department of Justice, do you?"

"No."

"It seems that you're applying a different standard to Mr. Buttino. Do I misunderstand you?"

"I object," said Merritt. "Mr. Rubino's conduct is not at issue here."

Rubino added, "I am not the subject of an official FBI investigation."

Gayer just nodded, going back to his questions.

When the deposition ended, I waited as Gayer collected his papers. For the past two days I had listened to total strangers responsible for judging me. Stoops had accepted the results of OPR's incomplete investigation, relying on unreliable polygraph results, and Rubino had not questioned any of it.

Gayer looked tired.

"Another fine job, Counselor," I said. "Too bad the public and the people in the bureau couldn't see what we've seen these past two days. It would help them understand how unfair and ridiculous all this is."

Gayer nodded. "Let's hope we have an opportunity to put both of them on the witness stand."

■ ■ ■

When I returned to San Diego, I learned that Tom Homann had died. Hundreds attended a memorial service for him. I asked to speak and related how Tom was my first attorney in my lawsuit against the FBI and that he had ably represented me. I said he was a legal professional with a keen sense of justice.

"He always told me what an interesting case mine was . . . and I would tell him it would be more interesting for me if it was happening to somebody else!" I said that Tom and I were contemporaries and went to high school at the same time. I said I believed Robert Kennedy's words, spoken at that time, aptly described Tom's legacy: "Each time a man stands up for an ideal, or acts to improve the lot of others, or strikes out against injustice, he sends forth a tiny ripple of hope, and crossing each other from a million different centers of energy and daring, those ripples build a current that can sweep down the mightiest walls of oppression and resistance."

36.

A few days after Homann's service my friend Ann Davis called. She wanted to meet me for dinner.

I could tell something was wrong upon seeing her face. "I'm concerned about what is going to happen to me at work when the bureau finds out about Jerry," she said. Her son Jerry was suffering from infections caused by AIDS.

"I know their attitude about gay people, and I'm concerned about my job." She paused for a moment before adding, "Frank, I can't afford to lose this job."

Ann had told me before how difficult it had become caring for Jerry in her home. Like K. D., Jerry did not want to die in a hospital. "His condition is getting worse, and he hardly eats anything at all." She struggled to hold back her tears. "It hurts so much to watch one of your own children die."

Ann and I had talked before about telling the bureau why she might need time off. "I think you should tell the SAC," I said. "Joe Johnson seems to be a kind and considerate type of person. He's a parent and should understand what you're going through."

"Frank," she said, "I continue to hear remarks and jokes about gay people and AIDS in the office. If they only knew how much it hurts."

It angered me. I leaned closer to her and lowered my voice. "The bureau has a lot of control over the lives of its employees, and after a while we all start to think alike. For an organization that is so involved with the public, the bureau really lives in an artificial world. It's about time it grew up and learned what the real world is like!"

I leaned still closer. "It needs to realize there are a lot of gay people in this society, and some are even their own employees or relatives of their employees. And some of these people have AIDS."

It was getting late, and the restaurant was emptying. Before we left, I assured her I would help in any way I could.

■ ■ ■

The third week in July was Gay Pride Week in San Diego. Kicking off the celebration were the annual Stonewall Awards, recognizing outstanding achievement and contributions to the gay and lesbian community. I received one of the awards and was selected, as well, to be one of the co-grand marshals of our parade. My counterpart was Karen Marshall, administrative director of the Lesbian and Gay Men's Community Center. Gay parades adopt a nationwide theme each year. In 1991 it was "Together in Pride."

Leading the parade that sunny afternoon was San Diego Mayor Maureen O'Connor, accompanied by her openly gay chief of staff, Ben Dillingham. Directly behind came the Gay Freedom Band, and I spotted Herb King playing the drums, marching proudly. Karen Marshall and I, in a horse-drawn carriage, were next—followed by hundreds of marchers, bands, and floats.

Some of the banners and signs in the parade and along the way said PRIDE, UNITY, JESUS LOVES US, and WE ARE HERE. Everywhere, in the parade and among those watching, were reminders of people living with AIDS and those who had died from the disease. The American flag and the pink triangle, symbol of the Nazi oppression of gays, hung next to each other on flagpoles or were draped over balconies.

Thousands had lined the streets, sitting on curbs or in lawn chairs. People watched, waved, and cheered, from porches, windows, and rooftops. I had never been in a parade before, and it was an extraordinary feeling. I saw Drew Mattison and other friends, and they waved and clapped as we passed by. Karen and I looked at each other, shaking our heads at the same time.

Along the parade route I spotted an FBI agent and his girlfriend, who also worked for the bureau. I waved hello, and the woman smiled and returned my wave. But the agent just stared, unsmiling.

A group of religious fundamentalists stood along the parade route. They held up a sign that said, JESUS SAVES SOULS FROM HOMOSEXUALITY, but we ignored them.

When I reached the end of the parade route, I stood alone and watched. City council members and other government officials marched, followed by three openly gay members of SOLO. A contingent of gay and lesbian veterans was greeted with loud cheering and clapping. But perhaps the most thunderous response of all was given to a group of older people, who walked behind a blue and white banner that said "P-FLAG—Parents and Friends of Lesbians and Gays."

I made my way to the pavilion in Balboa Park for the postparade rally. Karen and I, and a few other speakers, sat on the stage, watching as people began to approach the rally site. They came in the thousands, walking alone or with others, hand in hand, arms draped over one another—men with men, women with women, men with women. On foot, on bicycles, in wheelchairs, they approached in what was the largest such rally in San Diego history.

It was my turn to speak. Larry Baza, a parade organizer, said other gays and lesbians had been fired from the FBI and walked away—"but not Frank Buttino!" People began to cheer. I had never spoken before so many people, and the feeling was electrifying.

I extended my admiration to parade organizers, volunteers, marchers, and spectators alike. "Many of you have been coming to this parade for years, but this is the first Gay Pride Parade I've ever attended!"

This must have surprised many, for a great silence fell upon the crowd. I used the moment to proclaim, fist clenched, "I want to publicly thank the Federal Bureau of Investigation for tearing down the walls of my closet!"

The crowd roared.

"I am proud of who I am! And seeing all of you today, I can honestly say I have never been more proud of being gay!"

When the cheering diminished, I told them that as a fifteen-year-old boy I had taken up John Kennedy's challenge to do something for America. "Thirty years later our presence here today—and our continuing struggle for equality—are what we can do for our country!"

I spoke of my love for my job as an FBI agent and added, "How I conducted myself at work had nothing to do with whom I went home to at night. My lawsuit demands that people be judged by the quality of their character—and their ability to do the job!

"In the past," I said, "when I was sad and discouraged by the government's disgraceful treatment of me, I thought about so many of you who have fought so tirelessly and for so long on behalf of all of us.

"And when I was strapped to the polygraph machine and interrogated as to whether I was a spy, I thought about the millions of gays and lesbians who love their country and have served in our nation's military."

The crowd was cheering more frequently, and I had to pause for longer and longer moments. It was then I saw Everett and Richard, sitting next to each other, toward the front. They were smiling at me and I smiled back. I thought about K. D. and Tom Homann. I wondered if Brian was somewhere out there in the sea of faces.

"We have been rejected, mocked, scorned, humiliated, and condemned from the pulpit and by politicians—and still we're here!" I shouted.

"We have been denied jobs, harassed at our jobs, fired from our jobs—and still we're here!

"We have been told that whom we love, and what we love, and how we love is sick and warrants shame—and still we're here!

"We'll be here! We've always been here!

"We have contributed to the world's music, its arts, its armies, and the legion of ever-faithful, down through the centuries, who have stubbornly insisted that human beings can be more than they are! That they can be more caring and loving and compassionate!

"And we are here today . . . together in pride!"

part six
but a tiny ripple
ripple

37.

"I hope this isn't another postponement," I said, returning Gayer's message.

"Worse than that," he answered. "Judge Lynch transferred your case to a new judge. He knows it's a hot potato. The new judge is Saundra Brown Armstrong, a Bush appointee."

Here we go again, I thought. "How long will this delay things?"

"Several months," Gayer answered.

■ ■ ■

A year had now passed since I filed my lawsuit, and there was no resolution in sight. My legal expenses continue to mount. Each trip to Washington, D.C., for depositions cost an average of five thousand dollars. Gayer was sacrificing monetarily as well, still charging far less than the normal fee for this kind of litigation.

It would have been extremely difficult to hold another job while pursuing my lawsuit. Early on I had decided to devote all the time and energy I needed to the litigation. Under the circumstances who would hire me knowing I had been fired by the FBI and was intent on getting my job back?

With my brother Lou's help I began devoting more time to writing a book about my experiences. If the case was dismissed, the book might be the only way of revealing the FBI's treatment of gays and lesbians. Also providing me with a glimmer of hope was the fact that Judge Armstrong was both a woman and an African-American.

■ ■ ■

In August I became a volunteer at Mama's Kitchen, which delivered free meals to people with AIDS. Some AIDS patients were being assisted by family and friends, but others lived alone and were too weak, or too poor, to shop or cook for themselves.

As I began to deliver meals, the devastating effect the epidemic had on individual lives was sometimes overwhelming. But the beautiful and uplifting part of this experience with the plague was how heterosexuals and homosexuals alike had come together to help total strangers.

■ ■ ■

Ann Davis called to tell me that she talked to SAC Johnson about her son Jerry's condition. Johnson had, without hesitation, granted her a leave of absence as Jerry's condition worsened. He now wanted only his immediate family and a close personal friend with him. I could hear the pain and sadness in Ann's voice as we talked almost daily. One evening Ann said Jerry had asked, ''When I die, will the angels spit on me because I'm gay?''

■ ■ ■

Writing about my experiences caused me to think a lot about Brian again. ''We shared so much for so many years that I guess I always thought that we would be friends,'' I told Drew. ''His birthday is coming up, and I've thought about calling him. He's leaving for graduate school the first week in September.''

''Maybe time and writing the book have caused you to want to resolve some of the negative feelings you've had about Brian,'' Drew said. ''Maybe Brian wants that, too.''

I called Brian on his birthday but got his answering machine. Later that evening he returned my call, and I wished him a happy birthday. It was strange to hear his voice again, and he told me he had been planning to call me. He said he was leaving San Diego in two days and, when he was packing, found some things I might want. He asked to bring them over the next morning.

I was at my desk writing when I heard Brian's car pull into the driveway. I went outside to greet him. He was carrying a large box, so we couldn't shake hands.

''How have you been?'' I asked.

''Busy,'' he answered as he set the box down in the living room. ''I hate moving.''

I smiled. ''Especially without me there to help you.'' I had always complained in the past when I helped him move.

"Sure," he said, smiling back.

I told him a little about the case and the bureau files that proved the FBI discriminated against gay people.

"Just like we suspected," he said, nodding.

"I'm writing a book with Lou about my experiences during all this. You're in it, but we're protecting your identity. Your name is Brian in the book."

"I was a part of it," he commented without much emotion.

I told him I'd like to write to him, and he gave me his new address. We stood facing each other.

"How about a kiss?" I said, half-kiddingly.

He smiled. We put our arms around each other and kissed. We stood hugging a few moments longer.

"I love you," I said.

"I love you, too," he replied.

After he left, I looked inside the box and found an envelope with pictures of us together at one of Brian's annual "surprise" birthday parties.

Other than my family, my relationship with Brian had been the most important of my life. Brian had now given me the last tangible symbol of our lives together and perhaps by doing so had intended to end any kind of relationship. As I began writing again, I wondered if Brian felt the same void I now felt in my life.

■ ■ ■

In September I read Curt Gentry's controversial *J. Edgar Hoover: The Man and the Secrets*. It was the most thoroughly researched book about the bureau I had ever seen. Gentry made several references to the possibility that Hoover and Tolson were gay lovers. The book also mentioned my lawsuit. "Practicing homosexuals are still banned from Bureau employment," Gentry wrote, then predicted that if my lawsuit was successful, "others are expected to follow." This was also the month Ann's son Jerry succumbed to AIDS.

Gays and lesbians throughout California reacted bitterly as Governor Pete Wilson vetoed AB101, the bill banning discrimination based upon sexual orientation in employment. Wilson had voiced support for gay and lesbian rights in his campaign for governor, and our community had responded with its votes. The feeling of betrayal led to loud and sometimes violent protests across the state.

Several of us organized a protest march and rally in front of the California State Building in downtown San Diego. John Graham and I helped lead the march of nearly seven hundred protesters, and I was one of the speakers. As I walked beside Everett, I mentioned that my first and last protest march had been in Washington, D.C., in 1969. "It was an anti-Vietnam War march led let by Coretta Scott King. I was in new agents training and afraid the bureau would find out. My career would have ended before it began."

Everett grinned. "I was in that march, too."

■ ■ ■

In late summer a group of people calling themselves Concerned Citizens of America had marched in front of the San Diego Police Department headquarters. Fliers called for Chief Burgreen's resignation for promoting the "unnatural, anti-family, anti-American, anti-God crime of homosexuality." The group also called for the "immediate dismissal of the two criminals." They were referring to the two openly gay police officers John Graham and Rick Edgil. Concerned Citizens of America urged passage of a law requiring the death penalty "for those convicted of the crime of homosexuality." The group's leader told a nearby police officer that all gay people should be "lined up and shot."

■ ■ ■

Other members of the Society Of Law Officers (SOLO) came out on October 11, the annual National Coming Out Day. Natalie Stone became the first openly lesbian officer of the San Diego Police Department; her lifetime partner, Tricia Stone, the first open lesbian firefighter in the San Diego Fire Department.

The seven openly gay members of SOLO participated that evening in a march and rally in front of police headquarters to support Chief Burgreen's employment policies toward gays and lesbians. We spoke to the marchers, and as I rejoined the audience, a woman stepped in front of me. Her face was flushed with anger as she pointed her finger at me. "I'll never forgive you for twenty-one years of writing reports for the FBI on gay people!" she shouted.

I responded with an anger equal to hers. "You don't know anything about my record in the FBI. I never discriminated against anybody in or out of the FBI!"

It was the kind of criticism gays and lesbians who worked in law enforcement or similar professions sometimes heard. How could we work for people who traditionally discriminated against us? Early in my career I had asked myself the same question. Though the bureau as an institution had a reputation for being antigay, until my lawsuit I had never personally witnessed that policy in practice. There had been occasional antigay comments, but I had never seen antigay bias affect any of our investigations.

When pressed on this issue by gay friends, I would ask whether they believed every gay person who worked for an employer that was antigay should quit his or her job—including all the gays and lesbians in the military? Wasn't it far better that we remained in these professions and perhaps at some point changed the organizations from within? Or, if necessary, changed these organizations from the outside? With excellent work records we could refute the argument that we were incapable of performing these jobs.

I later talked to Drew about the confrontation and criticism I had received for insisting on nonviolent dissent.

"It's better to respond briefly and disengage," Drew commented. "People who confront others by shouting aren't interested in discussing an issue. They're more interested in attracting attention."

■　■　■

Two years had passed since I first requested files through the Freedom of Information Act. The information finally arrived, and I carefully read through it, hoping to find something that might help us.

Most of the information had already been provided in my lawsuit, but one new fact disturbed me. In a letter to OPR, ASAC Kuker stated that when Special Agent Bohlenbach received the W. J. note, its envelope had already been opened. Though it had been addressed to Bohlenbach and marked "personal," at least one other person in the San Diego office had seen its contents. It meant that as early as August 1988 others in the FBI had known of the allegation about my homosexuality.

Those close to me believed the FBI was involved in the harassment of my home. They viewed it as an attempt to harass and intimidate me into resigning. As an investigator I had always been careful about drawing conclusions without supporting evidence. But I wondered now about the opened letter and whether individual bureau employees had taken action on their own. In the past I had discounted that possibility. Perhaps at some level I didn't want to believe that anyone in the bureau would do that to one of his or her own.

■ ■ ■

On November 7, 1991, I turned on the television before leaving for Mama's Kitchen. Earvin "Magic" Johnson, one of the most famous and gifted basketball players of all time, was holding a press conference. He said that he had tested positive for the HIV virus.

It was the main topic of conversation at Mama's Kitchen that afternoon as we prepared to deliver meals. One volunteer said that it was tragic but that "one hundred and twenty-six thousand gay people had already died from AIDS and many straight people didn't seem to care very much."

I followed the reactions in the media to Johnson's revelation. One of the most poignant came from Mike Lupica, a sports journalist who had grown up near my hometown. Writing for the New York *Daily News,* Lupica said that when Rock Hudson died of AIDS, nearly everyone had then known somebody stricken with AIDS. "And now everybody knows someone who had tested positive. And maybe that was the only positive yesterday. Maybe the fight against AIDS puts a champion, as much as there has ever been in American sport, at the point now."

■ ■ ■

Gayer and I pressed for more depositions, but the government opposed each request. Our frustration mounted. Judge Armstrong had numerous cases before her, and we would have to wait. It seemed that the delays, legal maneuvering, and repeated trips to San Francisco were interminable.

Then one afternoon Gayer called, and he was extremely upset. The government claimed that a large number of FBI documents released to us had been found scattered along the streets of San Francisco. Department of Justice attorney Kevin Simpson, who had replaced Tracy Merritt, accused Gayer of being negligent and in violation of the judge's order that these files be kept confidential.

"As the new government attorney maybe Simpson is trying to intimidate us," I responded. "You'd think by now they'd realize we're not afraid of them."

Gayer's anger subsided. "Maybe the government's trying to send a message to other gay FBI employees that we can't be trusted to keep their names confidential if they join you in a class-action suit."

Several times during my lawsuit I had heard from others who knew current gay and lesbian FBI employees. They were careful not to disclose their friends' names but emphasized that the employees were following my case very carefully. These employees were afraid to come forward and join me, even anonymously, for fear of being fired. The above incident would probably become known throughout the bureau and make our attempt to identify others for a class-action suit even more difficult.

We decided to fight fire with fire and immediately responded with an angry letter to Simpson. The letter accused him of trying to make Gayer look untrustworthy to the new judge and of trying to send a message to gay and lesbian FBI employees that we couldn't or wouldn't protect their identities if they came forward. We said the government ought to "look elsewhere for the guilty party and start with the FBI." We demanded an apology from Simpson, telling him if he did not desist in these charges, we wanted to inspect the documents ourselves.

■   ■   ■

Beginning in early summer 1991, dozens of people were being viciously attacked on the streets in the Hillcrest and North Park areas of San Diego, and a number of these people were gay. In December one of these attacks ended in the death of a local seventeen-year-old high school senior who was walking to a local coffee shop with other friends. One of the attackers had called the boy a "faggot" before stabbing him several times.

The following day an emergency community meeting was held in Hillcrest, and several people, including me, publicly expressed anger over the boy's death. Not a single arrest had been made in any of the assaults, and we demanded that something be done immediately. The meeting received extensive media coverage, and a special police task force was assigned to the area. San Diego City Council Member John Hartley, along with members of SOLO and others, formed the Citizens Patrol. We operated as a mobile neighborhood watch and became the "eyes and ears" for police. We patrolled streets at night in our cars, using cellular telephones. Incidents in the area decreased dramatically.

■   ■   ■

We met Kevin Simpson, the Justice Department attorney, outside Judge Armstrong's courtroom prior to our December 31 hearing. He seemed friendly. With reference to the documents he had accused Gayer of mishandling, I introduced Dick to him with the observation "And here's the man you were going to throw into prison!"

As we sat in the courtroom waiting for the judge, I wondered why the Department of Justice had assigned such a young, relatively inexperienced attorney to my case. He looked to be only in his late twenties or early thirties. This was a high profile case with serious consequences for the FBI if we should prevail. Perhaps the Department of Justice wanted to send a message to the bureau. It was going to defend the FBI, but maybe it wanted the FBI to know that Justice did not believe in the case.

We all stood as U.S. District Judge Saundra Brown Armstrong entered the courtroom. She appeared to be in her early forties and was attractive, even-tempered, and polite. At the beginning of the hearing Judge Armstrong advised that the polygraph results would not be admissible as evidence in the trial. She also postponed her ruling on our request to take additional depositions. She set February 4, 1992, as the date she would rule on the government's motion for summary judgment. In the hearing that afternoon Simpson never brought up the matter of FBI documents being found on San Francisco streets.

38.

The year 1992 began with a phone call from a producer of *The Oprah Winfrey Show*. He asked if I would be a panelist on an upcoming show dealing with discrimination against gays and lesbians in the workplace. He said an estimated fifteen million people watched the program daily. After talking it over with Gayer, I agreed and two days later flew to Chicago. A limousine awaited me at the airport and transported me to a beautiful hotel in downtown Chicago.

Some last-minute switches were made in the program's format, and I was asked to sit in the audience rather than be on the panel. Before the program's final segment, during a commercial break, Oprah came over and introduced herself to me. We shook hands, and she then surprised me by wrapping her arm around mine as the camera moved in.

The audience became quiet, and the program resumed. Oprah said it was often difficult to tell if someone was gay. She introduced me, saying that mothers watching the show might think I'd be a "nice man" for their daughters. Oprah disclosed that I was gay and a special agent who had been fired by the FBI. She asked me to explain.

I briefly explained my situation and concluded with the observation that there was no federal protection for gay people in the workplace. In fact, I said, we were discriminated against by our own government. The show broke for a commercial, and Oprah commended me for my words.

Almost immediately a young man sitting nearby called Oprah over to talk animatedly about how the Bible condemned homosexuality. He said that she had to make that point on the show. Oprah listened patiently and then said, with utmost politeness, that she believed all people were created equal and everyone should be treated the same way. When the program ended, she shook hands with everyone in the audience.

■ ■ ■

One evening in late January I received a phone call from a young-sounding man who said he was an FBI agent. I had been in touch with others who knew him and was expecting his call. His first concern was whether the bureau was monitoring my telephone. I told him I didn't think so, but to be careful in what he said. I, too, was careful about what I said, just in case this was a setup by the bureau.

The caller said he was gay and had experienced severe and humiliating harassment by the FBI since it first suspected he was gay. But neither his supervisors nor OPR had confronted him on the issue.

I told him that other gay employees in the FBI, no matter how exemplary their record, had been harassed by the bureau in the past. I cautioned him about taking a polygraph if he was confronted. I also said the bureau would ask him to divulge the names of gay friends or gay FBI employees.

As he described the harassment he had experienced, the pain in his voice was clear. I thought of the agent who had committed suicide and my own ordeal. When he finished, I suggested he obtain counseling to help cope with the stress. I also advised him to document everything happening to him.

Toward the end of our conversation he thanked me for my advice. I told him to call me if he needed my help.

"What do you think your chances of winning are?" he asked.

"I don't know," I answered. "But I'm afraid if I lose, the witch-hunt for gays and lesbians in the bureau will begin."

■ ■ ■

I flew to San Francisco on February 3, 1992, the day before Judge Armstrong was scheduled to make her decision on the government's motion to have my case dismissed. As usual I drove to Gayer's residence. He waited until I sat down at his dining-room table before giving me the bad news.

"I just received a call from Judge Armstrong's clerk. He said tomorrow's hearing has been canceled."

I shook my head. Another delay. When was this ever going to be resolved?

Gayer seemed as disappointed as I was. "The clerk said Judge Armstrong had made her decision, and that was the reason for canceling the hearing. She didn't need to hear any oral arguments." He anticipated my next question.

"The clerk gave no indication as to how she would rule. He said only that we would be notified by mail in a few weeks."

I returned to San Diego that same afternoon. Richard, K. D.'s life companion, was waiting for me at the airport. I had already phoned him with the disappointing news and was surprised to see a big smile on his face.

Richard handed me an envelope. "It's an early birthday present for you. I thought it might cheer you up."

I looked inside. There were two tickets to see Rosa Parks that evening.

■ ■ ■

The audience was packed with adults and children of all races, talking excitedly. There was singing, poetry reading, and stories depicting Rosa Parks's single act of courage and how it had turned this nation upside down.

Rosa Parks, in 1955, had refused to surrender her seat to a white man on a segregated bus in Montgomery, Alabama. This was in violation of city law, and her arrest sparked a massive boycott of the city bus system. It also marked the entrance of a little-known minister by the name of Martin Luther King, Jr., into the civil rights struggle. Historians were to view Rosa Parks's action as a turning point. Within a year of her arrest, the U.S. Supreme Court struck down segregation statutes as unconstitutional.

The lights from television cameras flicked on, and people applauded, cheered, and stomped their feet. Almost as a wave the entire audience stood up, Richard and I among them, as a small, slender woman with beautiful white hair walked onto the stage.

She looks like a saint, I thought. *So dignified and serene.*

Her words that night were simple and brief, and she received another standing ovation. All she had wanted, back in 1955, was "to be treated like a human being."

As she passed by us, Richard put his hand on my shoulder. I remembered telling Hughes and Kuker about her the afternoon they took my badge and credentials away.

■ ■ ■

I took my "little brother," Andy, to see a small part of the AIDS quilt. It was on display at the university where K. D. had taught. We passed by his house.

Hundreds of people were there to see the quilt, and many cried openly as they walked or stood beside the panels. At the closing ceremony new panels were accepted from families and friends who had recently lost loved ones to the disease.

Neither Andy nor I spoke for a long while after seeing the quilt. The last time the quilt was on display in San Diego, I was an FBI agent and hadn't gone to see it. I was afraid somebody might see me and wonder if I was gay.

■ ■ ■

A week had passed since Judge Armstrong canceled the hearing, and I was starting to get anxious. Then, on February 13, as I worked at Mama's Kitchen, I called my answering machine to check on messages. I immediately recognized Gayer's distinctive voice. Gayer said, "Please call me as soon as possible. Judge Armstrong has denied the government's motion for summary judgment."

Tears started in my eyes, and I let out a yell. I told my startled covolunteers the news, and they began to cheer. I called Gayer when I returned home. He was more excited than I had ever heard him. "The judge could have issued a one-page decision, but she didn't. Her ruling is twenty-three pages long and is devastating to the government's position!"

"Congratulations, Dick. You've done an extraordinary job."

I called my family and friends and began to receive phone calls from reporters who wanted my reaction to the news. Several local radio and television stations carried the story that evening, and late that night I received a fax of Judge Armstrong's decision.

Judge Armstrong rejected the government's argument that revocation of my security clearance "is not judicially reviewable." She said I had "submitted evidence—and indeed it is undisputed—that the FBI has had a history of anti-gay discrimination." Judge Armstrong pointed to the FBI's own files as proof that it had a "significant interest . . . in anything hinting of homosexuality in the lives of its employees" and castigated FBI policy which "punishes gay employees for being less than candid about their homosexuality when it is undisputed that at least until very recently, the FBI would clearly have purged any employee for being candid about one's homosexuality."

Judge Armstrong stated that she doubted an investigation into my fitness for a security clearance would have ever been initiated if it weren't for the fact that I am gay. She said she could not "help but wonder . . . whether there is anything to indicate that Buttino's lack of candor would have become an issue but for society's prejudice against gays and the FBI's history of anti-gay discrimination. . . ."

Unbelievable, I thought. What Judge Armstrong had written was even stronger than what Gayer had related.

Judge Armstrong continued that the FBI would be hard pressed to justify antigay bias by invoking "national security" because of the equal protection clause of the Constitution and because I had given the bureau unrestricted permission to tell anyone I am gay. She stated that "national security" had been used to justify the internment of Japanese-Americans during World War II and to justify the segregation of blacks and whites in the U.S. armed forces until 1948.

Finally, Judge Armstrong questioned why I was not reinstated when other agents who lied in the course of their jobs received far less punishment. She concluded by saying she had "serious questions as to the rational basis for a policy which does not permit the reinstatement of a gay Special Agent whose 20-year record is unblemished but for a short-lived deception regarding his homosexuality."

I was stunned by the clarity and power of what Judge Armstrong had written. She had seen through the FBI's double standards and its attempt to conceal the reason I was fired. By citing the military segregation of blacks and whites and the internment of Japanese-Americans, a federal judge had joined gays and lesbians to the American civil rights struggle.

The judge's ruling meant we would have a trial. Under the law there would not be a jury and Judge Armstrong would be deciding the case. Perhaps the FBI would see the handwriting on the wall and agree to a settlement. I started thinking about going back to work.

I reached Gary Hall by phone, and he congratulated me. "It's a major victory," he said, adding, "and don't forget it was an African-American woman who backed you. She knows about discrimination from the inside out." Gary is African-American too.

I told Gary I was more optimistic than ever about being reinstated.

"They're not going to give you your job back," Gary said flatly. "I know the bureau from its treatment of other agents. Accept a financial settlement, and get on with your life."

"But it's a matter of principle, not money, Gary."

"I hear you, Frank. But I think you really ought to consider it. And knowing how the government operates, they will probably make you a very generous offer.''

"It's not their money. It doesn't come out of their pockets," I responded. "If I don't go back to work, the bureau will go on discriminating against gays and lesbians, and nothing will have changed. People will say I was in it all along for the money, that everyone has a price."

Gayer and I quickly put together a settlement offer to the government. I agreed to drop my lawsuit if I received back pay and legal fees and had my pension restored. The FBI would also have to issue a formal, written statement that it will ''consider homosexual orientation and conduct in the same way it considers heterosexual orientation and conduct [and] will treat associations among homosexual persons in the same way it treats associations among heterosexual persons.'' We asked that the FBI end its harassment of all gay employees and that I be reinstated to my job.

Despite what Gary Hall had said, I remained optimistic. Judge Armstrong's ruling was a devastating indictment of FBI history and current policy. I also believed the bureau would want to avoid a trial and public exposure of its historic treatment of gay and lesbian applicants and employees as well as of the misconduct of heterosexual agents.

More former gay and lesbian FBI employees contacted Gayer with additional stories of being discriminated against by the bureau. If the bureau did not reinstate me, we planned on resubmitting a new request for certification as a class-action suit. Undoubtedly the bureau would want to avoid additional negative publicity. The class-action suit brought by Latino agents had been a public relations disaster for the FBI.

My optimism was short-lived. Within a few days we heard back from the government, and it rejected our settlement offer. As Gary Hall predicted, the FBI advised Kevin Simpson that my reinstatement was out of the question. It was the second time the bureau had rejected our settlement offer, and I was more disappointed than before.

A few days later I received a phone call from someone close to the top administrators at FBI headquarters. The caller went right to the point: "You know why they're not reinstating you. They're concerned about what the country will think of the bureau's having homosexual agents. The FBI is concerned with its image. Nothing else matters.''

Gayer and I went ahead with plans to take depositions from other FBI officials and agents. The government's request to the court to depose me was also approved. I would face Simpson on my next trip to Washington.

■ ■ ■

March 1992 was an extremely busy month. I worked on my book nearly every day while assisting Gayer for the upcoming depositions. I also spent considerable time preparing for my own deposition. I expected the government would be playing hardball with me in light of the positive developments in the case.

The annual Nicky Awards were also held in March, and I was voted "Man of the Year" by members of San Diego's gay and lesbian community. Mayor Maureen O'Connor sent another letter of congratulations afterward. It said, in part, "I hope the accolade someday has an honored position in your office at the Bureau, where upcoming agents can learn and profit from your ordeal and perseverance. You are a true hero and I am most proud of your accomplishments." I framed the letter and put it next to the Nicky Award on my wall. Someday both would be on my desk in the bureau.

A few days before I left for Washington for the depositions, a producer from *60 Minutes* called. We had spoken before about a program on gays and lesbians in law enforcement. He informed me that the producers now wanted to include me in the program. We agreed on April 4th as the date Mike Wallace would interview me at my home. I was told an estimated fifty million people would be watching the show.

39.

Department of Justice attorney Kevin Simpson seemed to have a fairly good overall grasp of my case but was confused on a few of the details. Some of his deposition questions surprised me, as if he were in my corner, not the bureau's. At one point, for example, he asked if I would have conducted the investigation of W. J. differently from the way the bureau had done it. I jumped at the chance to demonstrate how shoddy and inept the bureau's investigation had been.

I would have assigned a team of agents to work full-time on the investigation, I said, and they should have been asking me questions, too. "I have done investigations that took two, sometimes three years to complete. Six months, and this one was over."

The bureau did not show me photographs of the individuals it interviewed, I said, and neither had it checked for fingerprints on one of the men. It also had not conducted a handwriting analysis to determine if either man had written the letters. I explained that a number of leads and other logical investigative possibilities had not been pursued. I analyzed some of the conclusions the bureau reached, trying to show how they were not supported by the facts.

"[I]f a person really wanted to find out the truth," I concluded, "they could have done it. But they weren't interested in that," I said. "They were just trying to get rid of another homosexual FBI agent."

None of Simpson's questions really challenged me, but as the day wore on, I found myself increasingly weary of it all. I was tired of going over the same information again and having to explain everything I had done. I had been doing this for nearly four years. Yet at the end of my deposition I again wondered whether the Department of Justice was simply going through the motions of defending the FBI.

■ ■ ■

We deposed Ray Arras the following day. He was the OPR investigator who had been involved in all of OPR's interviews of me. He was prepared and did not seem hostile in answering Gayer's questions. Like Kuker, Arras would help undermine statements made by Stoops and Rubino.

For example, Arras testified there was no evidence I had ever been threatened or coerced by anyone, that there was no evidence to suggest I had ever met a W. J. or either of the two individuals interviewed by the FBI. Gayer got a small yet significant point into the record. Arras said I was "asked" to name gay associates, not "compelled" to do so. Not naming gay associates was one of the reasons the bureau gave for firing me.

Arras said that I had been "very cooperative, very articulate" during his interview of me and that in his judgment, I had never lied to OPR. In response to questioning, Arras said he had been involved in five or ten cases concerning homosexuals in his tenure at OPR and had investigated two cases involving homosexuals since my case began. In response to Gayer's last question, Arras said it was possible that W. J. was in fact somebody in the FBI.

■ ■ ■

The following morning Ralph Regalbuto, the unit chief of OPR, was deposed. Regalbuto said he had become head of OPR in 1989 and was not familiar with details of my case. He stated that since June 1989 he was aware of at least ten to twenty OPR investigations involving homosexual activity on the part of FBI employees. Like Arras, Regalbuto also admitted that after being assigned to OPR, he had overseen the investigation of several cases involving homosexual FBI employees. Gayer asked if he was aware of any gay people employed as special agents for the FBI. Regalbuto answered, "Not to my knowledge."

Regalbuto testified that OPR would look into an allegation of homosexual conduct because "the issue is one of security of information . . . to see whether information from FBI files has been disclosed as part of the overall allegation."

When prodded by Gayer, Regalbuto stated that it could become "germane" for OPR to determine whether the homosexual conduct engaged in included oral and anal sex. "We want to amplify and clarify the record" was his explanation.

Gayer pressed Regalbuto on how OPR classified investigations involving homosexuals in the FBI. Categorization would undermine bureau claims it did not discriminate against a class of people. Regalbuto said that OPR did not classify cases according to the subtopic "homosexual conduct."

■ ■ ■

Supervisory Special Agent Bradley Benson had participated in the last OPR interview of me. We were deposing him because Stoops had told us that an underling had actually written most of the letter proposing revocation of my security clearance. My hunch was that it had to be Benson.

Benson said at the outset that I had been cooperative, had never been coerced, and probably never knew W. J.

Gayer, as usual, sought to establish the unequal treatment of gay FBI employees vis-à-vis heterosexual employees and asked if Benson ever engaged in potentially embarrassing conduct. Benson answered yes.

"Does that make you a security risk?" asked Gayer.

"No," he answered.

Benson testified that there was no requirement for gay FBI employees to declare their sexual orientation to the FBI or to their parents. Benson had asked about this during his interview of me.

Benson acknowledged having played a major role in Stoops's decision to revoke my top secret security clearance. Like Kuker, he expressed frustration that so many issues had not been resolved in the bureau's investigation of W. J. But unlike Kuker, he seemed to hold *me* responsible for the FBI's inability to determine the truth. To Gayer's astonishment and mine, Benson offered several possible scenarios to explain the W. J. letters.

According to one script, someone had revealed my homosexuality so I could become a standard-bearer for gay rights. Although I may have been reluctant at first, Benson thought that at some point during OPR's investigation of me I might have decided to become a gay rights cause.

Another scenario involved a "Fatal Attraction" possibility. According to Benson, I might have been the victim of a love affair that had gone "sour" and W. J. had written the letters as revenge.

Perhaps the strangest explanation of all was that I had experienced a "mid-life crisis" and had written the letters to both the FBI and my parents as a way of disclosing my homosexuality.

I stopped taking notes. This was ridiculous. The FBI hadn't determined the truth, and one of the people most responsible for my firing actually thought I was W. J.!

Gayer pressed for other possibilities, and Benson shocked us further by saying he thought the letters might have been the work of a hostile intelligence service trying to compromise me. Gayer asked why such a service would alert the FBI I was gay if it was trying to use that information against me, but Benson didn't have an answer. He said that the letters may have been a "possible incremental step to Mr. Buttino's involuntary coercion."

He added, "I tried to relate a little earlier that in my experience with national security investigations and efforts of hostile intelligence operatives toward an individual, that it is not one, big compromise that characterizes the operation but a series of little exercises before the hook is set, so to speak, and before the individual is fully compromised into becoming a spy."

Gayer had been growing increasingly angry during the course of the scenarios. He said now, "So when you talk about the possibility of coercion, you are talking about the possibility that Mr. Buttino might succumb to an attempt to coerce him, is that true?"

Benson said it was.

"I find that highly offensive and insulting," Gayer responded angrily.

■ ■ ■

In her deposition Supervisory Special Agent Sandra Fowler denied telling me that OPR investigated at least one case a week involving a homosexual FBI employee. I had written that down in my notes at the time. I didn't think she was lying; she probably had simply forgotten.

Gayer asked why she had questioned me about intimate details of sex with men but didn't ask for details about my sexual relationship with a female FBI agent.

"Because in our view," she answered, "there was less of a potential for a security problem in a heterosexual relationship."

"Have you ever been asked in a formal setting by an FBI employee about the details of your sexual conduct?" asked Gayer.

"I have not," Fowler answered.

Like Kuker and Arras, Fowler said I had been cooperative and had not lied.

■ ■ ■

Early Saturday morning, April 4, 1992, a *60 Minutes* crew arrived at my house. Everett was already there, and Richard was planning to come over a little later. The crew immediately transformed the living room into a makeshift television studio and hung black curtains over all the windows.

As I was fixing my tie, I told Everett that I was not going to be intimidated by Mike Wallace. "If it looks like I'm scared," I said, "it might reinforce some people's views that gay people are weak and easily intimidated."

Everett smiled, helping me with my tie. "You'll do fine. You've come too far for that to happen."

I asked him how I looked.

"Handsome as ever," he said, and moved to hug me.

"Don't!" I said in mock protest. "You'll wrinkle my shirt!"

I put my hand on Everett's shoulder as we walked into the living room. "I'm glad you're here," I said.

Mike Wallace arrived, and we were introduced. The final camera and sound adjustments were being made, and Wallace and I took our seats, directly opposite each other, virtually toe to toe. I felt a little nervous, but I hoped the interview would contribute to more tolerance and understanding of gay people.

Wallace asked his first question, and I listened carefully, pausing a moment before answering. A few questions later he asked if I thought J. Edgar Hoover was gay.

"Mike," I said, "I believe a person's sexual orientation or their sexual activity is a matter of personal privacy. And that should extend to an individual whether he's living or deceased."

Wallace's questions were tough but fair. He asked me to characterize Director Sessions's involvement in my case, and I said Sessions was aware of my situation but had "washed his hands" of any personal involvement.

I acknowledged that I had not told the truth about the W. J. letter, and Wallace asked why the FBI should continue to trust me. I said that after this initial denial I had told the FBI the truth. I also mentioned examples from FBI files in which heterosexual agents had lied about far more serious matters and received far lesser punishments. Wallace followed up with questions about the blackmail issue and national security. "There has never been a case in American history of a gay person being blackmailed to betray the country," I responded.

Several times during the interview I spoke of my respect for the FBI and said how much I enjoyed being a special agent. I did this because it was the truth. I did not want to be viewed as a bitter ex-employee and tried to be calm and careful in my responses.

The interview lasted for about forty-five minutes. When it ended, Wallace asked me to sit without speaking while they continued taping cutaway shots. The room was quiet except for the sound of Wallace's voice, which was not being recorded. He told me that the past few days interviewing gay and lesbian law enforcement officers had been particularly moving for him and his crew. He said he never met more articulate, sensitive, and competent people. "Every once in a while we do a program that's a public service," he commented. "I think this program is going to change the way America thinks about gay people."

■ ■ ■

Near the end of April it was reported that the FBI had settled discrimination claims made by a group representing more than three hundred African-American FBI agents, who had threatened to file a class-action suit if such an agreement wasn't forthcoming. Although the FBI wouldn't publicly admit to discrimination, a spokesperson acknowledged that there had been statistical "disparities" between black and white agents in several categories—most notably in promotions and assignments. A female agent and leader of the group reacted to this, saying that the FBI's reasoning appeared to be a "face-saving explanation, as opposed to reality."

The reality was that among the bureau's ten thousand agents, only 5 percent were African-American, 5 percent Latino, and 10 percent women. This was, of course, far less than the proportionate size of these groups in the general population. Still, I couldn't help viewing the settlement as a positive sign as far as my lawsuit was concerned. Maybe it would discourage the FBI from continuing its fight against another minority within the bureau.

■ ■ ■

Mike Fitzgerald, an attorney with the prestigious San Francisco law firm of Heller, Ehrman, White & McAuliffe, had contacted me in early April. Mike was in his early thirties, a Harvard graduate with a law degree from the University of California at Berkeley Law School, and a former assistant U.S. attorney. He said he had read about my case and believed the government was being terribly unjust to me.

I later met Mike in person at his Los Angeles office, and his law firm offered to assist me on a pro bono basis. Mike had an excellent reputation as a trial attorney, and he was a welcome addition in my legal battle. The costs of my court fight were continuing to mount, so I had to change my mind about accepting pro bono work. I was still paying Gayer, however.

A few weeks later I introduced Mike Fitzgerald to Gayer and Gary Hall as we waited outside Judge Armstrong's courtroom. Kevin Simpson, the government's attorney, approached and shook hands with all of us. "We're going to kick your ass!" Gary told him.

Judge Armstrong set December 14 as the beginning date for my trial. We estimated it would take approximately five days. She denied the government's request to reconsider her summary judgment decision. Judge Armstrong stated that despite her previous ruling, the FBI continued to make an "artificial" distinction between security clearances and employment and was confusing matters even further by trying to draw a distinction between sexual orientation and sexual conduct.

Several days later I received a copy of a letter Kevin Simpson sent to Gayer. Gayer called my attention to one paragraph in particular. OPR Unit Chief Ralph Regalbuto had been asked in our deposition of him if the FBI categorized cases involving homosexuals and had answered no. But now, in the letter, Regalbuto said "that although he never used a code for homosexual conduct to classify or describe an OPR investigation, such a code was created for use by the OPR in approximately 1987." The code for homosexual conduct, the letter continued, was "09(d)," a subset of the "unprofessional conduct category."

This was still another smoking gun. Despite bureau denial and the sworn testimony of FBI agents and Justice Department officials, the FBI had in fact classified a group of people according to their sexual orientation. Placing this group in the subset "unprofessional conduct" demonstrated there was no distinction between sexual orientation and sexual conduct. If you were gay, you were gone.

■   ■   ■

In August we returned to Washington for still more depositions. Mike Fitzgerald had now become a major asset in my lawsuit and helped with these depositions. Since his offer of assistance, Mike and his firm had already devoted a considerable amount of time, energy, and resources to my case.

A retired former personnel officer for the bureau testified that a lie under oath by an FBI employee would be treated seriously. It would ordinarily not result in termination, he said, but the employee might receive a harsh letter of censure and possible suspension. He said an initial lie, later corrected, would definitely not result in termination. He also advised us that private heterosexual conduct between consenting adults was not investigated by OPR. The current personnel officer we deposed testified that the bureau viewed homosexual conduct as a negative factor and that the bureau's policy had not changed in the past ten or fifteen years.

We also deposed the former head of the bureau's applicant unit. He testified that homosexual conduct by an applicant was a "significant factor" to be looked at from a security perspective. He estimated that during his seven years as head of the applicant unit possibly fifteen applicants were suspected or known to be gay. To the best of his knowledge, he said, none of these people had been hired.

During the week the former head of OPR, who had supervised the investigation of me, testified. He said that any allegation of homosexual conduct, even between consenting adults in private, would be regarded by OPR as potentially "serious misconduct." Allegations of similar heterosexual conduct, however, would *not* be investigated as serious misconduct. He said that the FBI would view a gay employee writing to meet another gay person or meeting another gay person in a gay bar as exhibiting "notoriously disgraceful conduct," a disciplinary offense which could result in the gay employee's being fired.

This former head of OPR also volunteered that he had suspected other FBI employees of being gay. I knew Gayer would pursue it. "What had made you suspect that generally?" Gayer asked in a low-key manner.

"Mannerisms," he responded, "the way they spoke, the way they dressed, other characteristics of how some homosexual people conduct themselves in meeting and greeting people."

I was surprised that someone at that level in the FBI would think in these stereotypes, and astonished that he would actually volunteer them under oath.

Gayer asked if he thought these people might be of some danger to the FBI because they were gay.

"Yes," was his answer. He voiced his concern about "whether or not these people were security risks, whose interest they really have at heart." When pressed, he stated that he had not communicated his security concerns about these employees to anyone.

One after the other, the FBI's own people were admitting to discrimination based upon sexual orientation. It seemed as though they either didn't realize what they were admitting to or felt there was nothing wrong about such discrimination. The bureau's carefully crafted, ambiguous public policy statements were being shredded, first from the FBI's own files, now by the words of its own administrators.

■ ■ ■

We also included the words of others in our court fight. For example, we planned to have Dr. Gregory R. Herek testify as an expert witness. Dr. Herek was a research psychologist at the University of California at Davis and the author of numerous articles on homophobia, perceptions of homosexuals by heterosexuals, and similar topics.

Dr. Herek was to testify that there is no psychological research to support stereotypes that gays and lesbians are mentally unbalanced, subject to blackmail, or more likely to break the law than heterosexuals. He was also to argue that gays and lesbians as a group share no distinctive psychological traits other than their sexual behavior.

Dr. Lawrence J. Korb was assistant secretary of defense in the Reagan administration and a senior fellow at the Brookings Institution. He was to testify as an expert on the Pentagon and its policies.

Dr. Korb was to explain to the court that the Department of Defense itself had abandoned ''security'' as a justification for its own antigay policy. The official justification is the need of soldiers or sailors to live together with no privacy and similar concerns peculiar to the military. Dr. Korb would testify that this justification is in fact not the motivation behind antigay discrimination. The real motivation is the military's prejudice against anyone ''different.'' This arises, Korb would argue, because of the military's hierarchical, closed structure.

Korb's testimony would be relevant because the military rejection of security justifications cast doubt on whether the FBI could still rely on such justifications to exclude gays and lesbians from employment.

■ ■ ■

As we prepared for the trial, we determined that since I had filed my lawsuit, at least four other gay FBI employees, including a special agent, had been allowed to continue working for the bureau. We suspected that the FBI had not fired them because it feared firing them might cause them to join my lawsuit. We were pleased that perhaps my lawsuit had saved these careers, and maybe we had already begun to change the bureau's antigay policies. But we still wondered what would happen to these employees if my suit failed.

Other former gay FBI employees continued to contact us, as did an applicant for the special agent position. Dana Tillson was a highly qualified candidate who the bureau suspected, during its background investigation, might be lesbian. She was asked intimate details about her sex life, including whether she engaged in oral sex. Tillson's application was subsequently rejected. Now she joined our efforts to expand my lawsuit into a class-action suit.

■ ■ ■

"Pride Equals Power" was 1992's nationwide gay pride celebration theme, and once again Mayor O'Connor led the San Diego parade.

I marched with eight other openly gay members of SOLO, most of whom were in uniform. When we reached the corner of Sixth and Robinson in Hillcrest, the crowd spotted us for the first time. The sound of their applause and cheering was deafening, and we locked hands and raised them in salute to the crowd. I thought about what I had been through the past four years and how brave the young officers were beside me. I felt tears come down my face, but I was no longer ashamed of them.

San Diego Police Chief Burgreen, honored by the gay and lesbian community as "Friend of the Year," rode behind us in an open convertible. He was the first San Diego police chief ever to participate in a Gay Pride Parade. At the end of the parade route Chief Burgreen invited me to ride with him.

"Chief, did you ever think you'd see gay police officers walking down the street holding hands," I asked.

"Times have definitely changed," he said with a grin.

■ ■ ■

The *60 Minutes* program aired on September 13, 1992. It was the opening segment on the season première, and it also was the twenty-fifth-anniversary season. Many of my gay friends came to my house to watch it with me.

Mike Wallace opened the segment by referring to the upcoming 1992 presidential election. "There is no issue, none, on which George Bush and Bill Clinton differ more sharply than on homosexuality."

During the campaign Governor Clinton said he supported equal rights for gays and lesbians. If elected, he said, he would sign an executive order banning discrimination against gays and lesbians in the military.

Most of the *60 Minutes* program focused on gay and lesbian police officers, but several minutes were devoted to the FBI and my case. As I watched, I hoped it would help change people's attitudes toward us.

■ ■ ■

Three weeks had passed since Judge Armstrong heard oral arguments on our motion to certify my lawsuit as a class-action suit. On the afternoon of September 29, 1992, Gayer called.

"I know this is good news, Dick," I said before he even had a chance to begin. "I know it because it's exactly three years to the day that I was suspended from the FBI."

"It *is* good news!" Gayer responded. "Judge Armstrong has certified the class action! Let me read you her order: 'It is hereby ordered that plaintiff's motion for class certification is granted for a class comprised of all past and present employees and all applicants of the FBI, who are gay, or who engage in homosexual conduct with consenting adults in private.' "

Judge Armstrong's decision changed the significance of my challenge to the FBI. My lawsuit became more than an individual employee suing for reinstatement. I now represented an unknown number of past and present employees and applicants who had been victims of the bureau's anti-gay policies. If the lawsuit was successful, it would profoundly change the FBI.

■ ■ ■

Gayer, Fitzgerald, and I spent the next few months preparing for the trial, which was set to begin on December 14.

I was elated when Governor Clinton was elected President in November. The media immediately focused on his campaign promise to end the ban on gays and lesbians in the military. Then a Los Angeles federal judge's ruling catapulted the issue to center stage. The judge ordered the Navy to reinstate Petty Officer Keith Meinhold, who had been discharged during the summer for being gay.

On November 13 the mandatory pretrial settlement conference was held in San Francisco. In view of Governor Clinton's election promises and the ruling in the Meinhold case, I was more optimistic than ever about my being reinstated. But once again the FBI refused to allow me to return to work or to promise to end its discrimination against gay and lesbian applicants or employees.

Although disappointed by the government's intransigence, Gayer, Fitzgerald, and I resumed our preparations for the trial. A few days later, Judge Armstrong's clerk advised us that because of scheduling conflicts, the trial had been postponed until June 1993.

epilogue

As a young man I had learned that my secret thoughts and desires were considered taboo and that if I acted on them, I would be a social outcast. These beliefs had come from the most unlikely sources: the very people and institutions I had been taught to trust and respect. Early in life I built my own private closet to protect me from others—and from myself.

Living a "double life" meant expending enormous amounts of time and energy *being careful*. I kept my work and usually even my identity as an FBI agent secret from people. My closet kept my homosexuality hidden from most of the others. As I approached middle age, secrecy had become the operative principle in my life. But I also began to see the enormous price I had paid for my secret life. By keeping my distance and avoiding intimacy, I had isolated myself from others—even my family and closest friends.

I could never have imagined that being fired from the FBI would become the best thing that ever happened to me. On the day I decided to stand up to the bureau and file my lawsuit, my closet door swung open, and I took my first steps toward a new life. Being open about my sexual orientation enabled me to be more honest about myself to others. For the first time I felt connected to other people, and in return they were connecting to me.

The media attention resulting from my lawsuit also swept me involuntarily into the ongoing struggle for gay and lesbian civil rights. Suddenly I had become part of something far greater than myself. Seeing Rosa Parks and remembering her singular act of courage rekindled the idealism that had originally motivated me to join the FBI. It reminded me again that the movement for civil rights in our society has been comprised of ordinary people whose courage changes history.

The postponement of my trial, this time for six more months, could have been a major disappointment to me, but there was something different in the air that November. Candidate Bill Clinton had promised to overturn the Pentagon's ban on gays and lesbians in the armed forces, and now he was going to be President.

I knew the obstacles we faced as a minority were still enormous. I knew that an end to ridicule and hatred would not disappear in my lifetime—or perhaps in several lifetimes. But there was also no mistaking that we had become part of the nation's agenda.

So instead of feeling disappointed, I began to see myself as but a tiny ripple, joining others in creating a mighty wave. And that wave would one day sweep down, as Robert Kennedy had predicted, "the mightiest walls of oppression and resistance."

Our time had come. All we ever wanted was to be treated like human beings.

glossary

This is a list of terms, phrases, abbreviations, organizations, and bureau euphemisms that appear in this book.

ASAC—pronounced *ay-sack,* assistant special agent in charge. FBI administrator who is second-in-command of an FBI field office. In large offices, one of several second-ranking administrators.

bureau—within the FBI refers to FBI headquarters in Washington, D.C.

case agent—the FBI agent in charge of an investigation.

cash incentive award—a monetary award from FBI headquarters in recognition of outstanding work by bureau employees.

censured—disciplinary action taken against an FBI employee by FBI headquarters. Can range from a letter of censure to suspension.

contact agent—FBI agent assigned to meet periodically with an undercover FBI agent to handle administrative and personal issues.

CPUSA—Communist Party USA.

DEA—Drug Enforcement Administration, a federal agency whose jurisdiction involves enforcement of federal drug laws.

FBI Academy—the physical complex of buildings on the U.S. Marine Corps base in Quantico, Virginia. It is used for training FBI agents and other local, state, and federal law enforcement personnel. The Forensic

Science Research and Training Center, operated by the FBI laboratory, is also a part of the FBI Academy.

FBIHQ—FBI headquarters, the J. Edgar Hoover Building, located between Ninth and Tenth streets on Pennsylvania Avenue N.W., Washington, D.C.

FCI—foreign counterintelligence.

FD-302—the standard form which the FBI uses to report information that may be used as evidence in court.

field office—one of fifty-six regional units of the FBI offices located in most major cities throughout the United States and including San Juan, Puerto Rico.

field supervisor—a supervisory special agent (SSA) who manages the work of a squad of agents within a field office.

high-profile—highly publicized.

HIS—hostile intelligence services.

HQ—FBI Headquarters.

LCN—La Costa Nostra.

light cover—a limited undercover assignment which doesn't require an extensive false identity.

OC—organized crime.

Operation Airlift—Code name for the undercover operation of the Miami FBI at Fort Lauderdale Executive Airport in 1982 and 1983.

out in the cold—term used to describe an agent working on his own in an undercover assignment.

relief supervisor—an FBI agent who assists a field supervisor manage the agents and cases on a squad.

SAC—pronounced by enunciating the three letters, never ''sack.'' Stands for special agent in charge, an agent in command of one of the bureau's field offices or, in the largest offices, one of several top-ranking FBI administrators.

special—an investigation important enough that FBI headquarters assigns a number of agents to it; receives special attention and commitment of bureau resources.

special agent—any FBI agent.

SSA—an FBI supervisory special agent.

supervisor—a supervisory special agent working in a field office or FBI Headquarters.

United States attorneys—principal federal prosecutors in a federal judicial district.

Weathermen—the militant, terrorist faction that split off from Students for a Democratic Society and claimed responsibility for bombings in the late 1960s and early 1970s.

appendix

ORIGINAL
FILED
FEB 12 1992
RICHARD W. WIEKING
CLERK, U.S. DISTRICT COURT
NORTHERN DISTRICT OF CALIFORNIA

IN THE UNITED STATES DISTRICT COURT
FOR THE NORTHERN DISTRICT OF CALIFORNIA

FRANK BUTTINO,)) Plaintiff.)) vs.)) FEDERAL BUREAU OF INVESTIGATION,) et al.,)))) Defendants.))	No. C–90–1639–5BA ORDER GRANTING IN PART AND DENYING IN PART DEFENDANTS' MOTION FOR SUMMARY JUDGMENT

OVERVIEW

Plaintiff Frank Buttino brought this lawsuit to challenge the revocation of his security clearance and the termination of his employment as a Special Agent with the Federal Bureau of Investigation (the "FBI"). Plaintiff claims that he was deprived of his right to due process under the Fifth Amendment of the United States Constitution, his rights to freedom of speech and freedom of association under the First Amendment, and his right to equal protection under the Fifth Amendment. He also brings a <u>Bivens</u> claim against FBI Director William Sessions.

COPIES MAILED TO
PARTIES OF RECORD

The matter is currently before the court on defendants' motion for summary judgment.[1] Having carefully considered all of the papers submitted by the parties, the court HEREBY GRANTS summary judgment as to plaintiff's due process and First Amendment claims and DENIES summary judgment as to plaintiff's equal protection claim.[2]

BACKGROUND

Frank Buttino joined the FBI as a Special Agent in 1969. During his twenty-year tenure with the agency, his assignments included undercover work and criminal and foreign intelligence. He performed investigations involving espionage, Chinese affairs, and terrorism. He received four special commendations as well as numerous cash awards for his service as a Special Agent, and the FBI has stated that it has no information to indicate that plaintiff ever failed to safeguard either the classified information or the money with which plaintiff was entrusted during his tenure with the agency. Mr. Buttino is gay.

In August, 1988, the FBI received an undated, handwritten letter stating that Buttino engaged in homosexual activity and enclosing a second handwritten letter to "James" signed "Frank," describing certain homosexual activities. The FBI then initiated an administrative inquiry regarding Mr.

---

[1]Plaintiff has also amended his complaint to expand this case into a class action. The class has yet to be certified and this summary judgment motion is directed only at plaintiff's individual claims.

[2]Plaintiff's equal protection claim is the primary focus of this lawsuit. The due process claim is precluded under <u>Dorfmont v. Brown</u>, 913 F.2d 1399 (9th Cir. 1990), <u>cert. denied</u>, 111 S.Ct.1104 (1991), <u>see</u> Discussion, Section I, <u>infra</u>, and plaintiff has offered no response specific to defendants' arguments for dismissal of the First Amendment claims. The <u>Bivens</u> claim is not addressed by either party. The Discussion, <u>infra</u>, focuses on the equal protection claim.

Buttino which resulted in the FBI's revocation of Buttino's Top Secret security clearance and, in turn, the termination of his employment.[3]

The parties agree to little else about the facts. Defendants describe plaintiff as being "repeatedly deceptive" during their investigation while Buttino denies all deception other than initially lying when he denied writing the note to "James." Buttino states that he understood that he would have been fired if he had admitted the truth about the note, and that he corrected the lie when he was called back to FBI Headquarters on the matter five weeks later.

The defendants say that plaintiff's security clearance was revoked because he was deceptive, because he disclosed information he was not supposed to, and because he was uncooperative in their investigation. Plaintiff claims his security clearance was revoked because he is gay, consistent with the FBI's traditional anti-gay policy. He says the FBI's contention that he was fired because of his "lack of candor" is a mere pretext for the agency's anti-gay discrimination and that non-gay employees "guilty" of similar degrees of lack of candor or improper disclosure of information do not suffer punishment anywhere near that which he suffered.

Buttino seeks reinstatement. He has given the FBI "unrestricted permission" to tell anyone they desire about his sexual orientation and conduct.

DISCUSSION

I. The Reviewability of Plaintiff's Equal Protection
   Challenge to the Revocation of his Security Clearance.

Defendants first argue that the revocation of plaintiff's security clearance is "not judicially reviewable" because such determinations are highly discretionary and are constitutionally committed to the Executive Branch. They cite Department of the Navy v. Egan, 484 U.S. 518 (1988) and Dorfmont v. Brown, 913 F.2d 1399 (9th Cir. 1990), cert. denied, 111 S.Ct. 1104 (1991), in support of this argument. It is clear under Egan and Dorfmont that courts should be highly deferential in reviewing the denial or granting of security

---

[3]On September 25, 1989, the FBI's Security Programs Manager, Mr. Gary L. Stoops, proposed revoking plaintiff's security clearance, and plaintiff was then placed on administrative leave. Mr. Stoops informed plaintiff of the FBI's final decision to revoke his security clearance on January 31, 1990. Plaintiff appealed the revocation of the security clearance to the Department of Justice, and by letter dated May 29, 1990, Department of Justice Security Officer, D. Jerry Rubino, notified plaintiff that the revocation of his security clearance was affirmed. Because every FBI employee must have a Top Secret security clearance, plaintiff's employment with the FBI was terminated by letter dated June 20, 1990.

clearances for the reasons defendants indicate. Dorfmont, in fact, specifically held that a person cannot raise due process challenges to the revocation of a security clearance.

Defendants overstate the scope of Dorfmont, however. Dorfmont specifically refrained from ruling that all constituional attacks on security clearances cannot be heard, and acknowledged that Webster v. Doe, 486 U.S. 592 (1988), Dubbs v. CIA, 866 F.2d 1114 (9th Cir. 1989) ("Dubbs I"), and High Tech Gays v. Defense Indus. Sec. Clearance Office, 895 F.2d 563 (9th Cir. 1990), "stand for the proposition that federal courts may entertain colorable constitutional challenges to security clearance decisions." Dorfmont, 913 F.2d at 1404. Significantly, Dubbs I and High Tech Gays both involved equal protection challenges to security clearance determinations.

Not only did Dorfmont stop short of holding that equal protection challenges to security clearance decisions are nonreviewable, but Dorfmont certainly did not speak to the situation in which there is an allegation of the government's pretextual revocation of a security clearance, which is really the essence of plaintiff's complaint. Indeed, only a strained reading of Dorfmont (when considered in tandem with High Tech Gays and Dubbs I) would support the shielding of the government's revoking a security clearance where such revocation is a mere pretext for the implementation of a discriminatory policy. To construe Dorfmont in that way would be to invite those government officials, who have both the authority to make security clearance determin-ations and the desire to discriminate against a certain class of persons, to effect such discrimination through their security clearance decision-making authority with the comfort of knowing that the nonreviewability of the "merits" of security clearance determinations would serve to immunize the discrimination from judicial review. Defendants have not persuaded the court that either Dorfmont or any accepted constitutional principles compel such a result.

In fact, Judge Eugene Lynch of this District expressly rejected rendering equal protection challenges to security clearance determinations nonreviewable per se in Dubbs v. CIA, 769 F. Supp. 1113 (N.D. Cal. 1990) ("Dubbs II"). In so doing, Judge Lynch stated:

> The court accepts, as a general matter, the language in Egan which indicates that courts ought to be extremely deferential in reviewing issues such as the denial or granting of security clearances that are constitutionally committed to the Executive Branch and involve highly discretionary decisions requiring specialized expertise. See Egan, 484 U.S. at 527–530, 108 S.Ct. at 824–826. However, such deference to

Executive Branch decisions does not require the Judiciary to abdicate its authority under Article III to decide whether or not an individual's right to equal protection under the Federal Constitution has been violated.

Dubbs II, 769 F. Supp. at 1116 n.3. Judge Lynch continued:

> More importantly, defendants' argument requires this Court to presume that they have acted rationally in the present case and would be acting rationally in any case where they deny an individual a security clearance because of her homosexual orientation and conduct. This standard, while not wholly unprecedented in constitutional jurisprudence, would effectively eviscerate the Dubbs [9th Circuit] panel's decision that plaintiff's equal protection claims are colorable [citation omitted], something which this Court is not at liberty to do in the absence of a contrary decision from the Ninth Circuit or a higher court.

Id. at 1116–1117.[4]

Judge Lynch's refusal to condone the abdication of an Article III Judge's authority to adjudicate constitutional equal protection claims notwithstanding the need for deference to Executive Branch decisions rests on more, of course, than mere separation-of-powers technicalities. The implication of the judiciary's divesting itself entirely of its role in reviewing colorable constitutional claims is, to put it mildly, unsound as a matter of policy because the result of adopting such a rule would be to effect the wholesale shielding of any actual deprivations of equal protection occurring in the course of the Executive Branch's allocation of security clearances.

To be comfortable with such a rule is to be blind to the historical reality that "national security" has frequently been asserted as the ostensible justification for sweeping deprivations of equal protection which, with hindsight, are nearly universally condemned and readily regarded as, at best, grossly disproportionate to the national security concerns at one time asserted as justifications.[5]

---

[4]Judge Lynch's reasoning is not undermined by the subsequent Dorfmont decision, because, as indicated, Dorfmont was specifically limited to due process challenges and acknowledged that other Ninth Circuit cases condoned equal protection review of security clearance determinations. Likewise, defendants' suggestion, in their reply brief at 11 n.9, that High Tech Gays may undermine the reviewability of gay equal protection claims (since High Tech Gays established that gay equal protection claims are (only) subject to rational basis review) is unsupportable. Judge Lynch explicitly addressed that point in Dubbs II, see 769 F. Supp. at 1117, and pointed out that the very fact that High Tech Gays engaged in a rational basis review of the gay plaintiffs' equal protection claim is squarely inconsistent with defendants' notion that such claims are nonreviewable.

[5]The internment of Japanese Americans during World War II (in order to safeguard against "sabotage and espionage," see Hirabayashi v. United States, 320 U.S. 81 (1943), and Korematsu

Accordingly, neither the governing authority nor considerations of policy justify adopting a rule of law by which courts would be barred from engaging in any equal protection review of security clearance decisions.[6] Buttino's equal protection challenge to the FBI's revocation of his security clearance is not, therefore, inherently nonreviewable. As such, the court must proceed to considering whether a reasonable jury could find that plaintiff was discriminated against because of his homosexuality in the revocation of his security clearance, and, if so, whether there was a rational basis for such discrimination.

II. Is there a Triable Issue of Fact as to Whether Plaintiff's Security Clearance Would Have been Revoked and His Employment Terminated But For the Fact that He is Gay?

Federal Rule of Civil Procedure 56(c) provides for summary judgment "if the pleadings, depositions, answers to interrogatories, and admissions on file, together with the affidavits, if any, show that there is no genuine issue as to any material fact and that the moving party is entitled to a judgment as a matter of law." Summary judgment should be granted "unless there is sufficient evidence favoring the nonmoving party for a jury to return a verdict for that party." Anderson v. Liberty Lobby, Inc., 477 U.S. 242, 249 (1986). If the only conclusion a reasonable jury could reach is that Mr. Buttino's security clearance would have been revoked even if he were heterosexual, then as a matter of law plaintiff could not succeed on his equal protection claim and summary judgment would be appropriate.

Defendants argue that summary judgment must be granted because plaintiff "completely fails to present any colorable evidence" that his security clearance was revoked because he is gay. Defendants' argument fails for two reasons.

A. Defendants Have Not Satisfied their INITIAL BURDEN on a Motion for Summary Judgment

First, defendants are wrong in their threshold assumption that they have

---

v. United States, 323 U.S. 214 (1944)) and the strict segregation of Blacks and Whites in the United States armed forces (in order to preserve "morale" necessary to effectively defend the national security), terminated in 1948 by Exec. Order No. 9981, 3 C.F.R. 722 (1941–1948), are but two examples. (The fact that, as Hirabayashi and Korematsu illustrate, even the judiciary has, at times, failed to curb unconstitutional abuses of security-related discretion hardly supports the further shielding of such discretion from judicial review as defendants would have this court do.)

[6]The Supreme Court has also made clear that even the "extensive rummaging around in" a national security agency's affairs that would likely occur in the course of judicial review of an agency's termination of a gay employee does not justify preclusion of such review. See Webster, 486 U.S. at 604.

met their initial burden on a motion for summary judgment[7] by submitting the declaration of D. Jerry Rubino, the Department of Justice Security Officer who affirmed the FBI's revocation of plaintiff's security clearance on appeal. Even taken at face value, Mr. Rubino's declaration does not demonstrate the absence of a genuine issue of fact as to whether plaintiff's security clearance would have been revoked but for plaintiff's homosexuality. Although Mr. Rubino apparently had the authority to set aside the FBI's decision to revoke plaintiff's security clearance,[8] his statement that his affirmance of the FBI's revocation of the security clearance was made on the basis of reasons other than plaintiff's homosexuality[9] does not go to the principal allegations of discrimination in plaintiff's lawsuit: namely, that the FBI's own investigation and determination of plaintiff's fitness for continued service were attained by (and predetermined by) anti-gay bias within the FBI. Indeed, Mr. Rubino presumably did not even become involved in the matter until after the FBI had completed its investigation and had revoked plaintiff's security clearance which plaintiff then appealed to the Justice Department. Defendants have not, accordingly, met their initial burden on the motion for summary judgment of demonstrating the absence of a genuine issue of fact on the strength of Mr. Rubino's declaration.[10]

B. Plaintiff, In Any Event, Has Presented Evidence from Which a Reasonable Jury Could Infer Discrimination

Second, even if defendants had satisfied their initial burden by virtue of

[7]The moving party bears the initial burden of demonstrating the absence of genuine issues of material fact. Celotex Corp. v. Catrett, 477 U.S. 317, 327 (1986).

[8]Plaintiff disputes this authority "in part." Pl.'s Response to Defs.' Statement of Undisputed Material Facts at 2:20–3:3. But plaintiff's "dispute" of that authority appears to be more of a restatement of his argument that the FBI has an anti-gay policy rather than a presentation of any evidence refuting Mr. Rubino's authority to set aside the FBI decision.

[9]Mr. Rubino states that his decision was based upon his belief that Mr. Buttino placed himself in a position that may have subjected him to coercion or pressure to act contrary to the best interests of the national security, was not truthful in answering questions posed during the FBI's inquiry [the court ruled on December 31, 1991 that inferences of untruthfulness on plaintiff's part will not be drawn to the extent that they depend exclusively on the results of polygraph examinations], and failed to cooperate fully during the administrative investigation. Declaration of D. Jerry Rubino, ¶6.

[10]Defendants' suggestion that plaintiff can only withstand summary judgment by directly attacking Rubino's credibility is therefore inapposite, since even if wholly credible, Rubino's declaration does not put to rest the question of whether the FBI used plaintiff's homosexuality against him. Frederick S. Wyle Prof. Corp. v. Texaco, Inc., 764 F.2d 604, 608 (9th Cir. 1985), cited by defendants, is distinguishable in that the court there found that there was not a genuine issue of material fact in the absence of any reason to suspect the affiants' credibility. In any event, a plaintiff can show pretext, as Buttino alleges here, even without directly impeaching the credibility of the employer's proffered explanation, if the plaintiff otherwise directly persuades the court that a discriminatory reason "more likely motivated the employer." Cotton v. City of Alameda, 812 F.2d 1245, 1248 (9th Cir. 1987) (quoting Texas Dep't of Community Affairs v. Burdine, 450 U.S. 248, 256 (1981)).

Mr. Rubino's declaration, the court finds that plaintiff, in his opposition, has presented ample evidence from which a reasonable jury could infer, notwithstanding Mr. Rubino's declaration, (1) the existence of anti-gay bias within the FBI generally and (2) the specific effect of such bias on the investigation into, and the decision regarding, plaintiff's continued fitness for a security clearance.

The evidence presented by plaintiff from which a jury could infer such discrimination includes, inter alia:

1. The Disparity in Plaintiff's Treatment after the FBI Learned He was Gay and the FBI's Interest in the Names of OTHER Homosexuals in the FBI

Plaintiff has attested to the vast disparity between the FBI's interest in his personal life when the agency assumed plaintiff was heterosexual and when they learned he was gay, as well as to the FBI's attempts to get him to divulge the names of other gay people in the agency:

> For 19 years of my employment with the FBI they assumed I was heterosexual and did not ask me about personal details of my heterosexual conduct or the names of my heterosexual friends. When I disclosed that I engaged in heterosexual sex with a female FBI agent they did not ask for any details about this conduct or this person's name. However, they wanted to know every detail about my homosexual conduct, including exactly what kinds of sex acts I engage in with other men. They also wanted the names of other homosexuals in the FBI and the names of my homosexual, but not heterosexual friends.

Declaration of Frank Buttino at 4:4–11.

2. The Fact that the FBI Investigated Plaintiff upon being Advised that Plaintiff Engaged in Homosexual Activities

Defendants themselves describe the investigation into whether plaintiff was a security risk as being in response to the FBI's being advised ''that plaintiff engaged in homosexual activity.'' One reasonable inference is that the FBI would not have considered information that a highly commended twenty-year Special Agent ''engaged in heterosexual activity'' grounds to undertake an investigation into his continued fitness for a security clearance, and that the very investigation resulting in plaintiff's termination would therefore not have been undertaken if plaintiff were not gay.

3. Evidence that the FBI's Punishment for Plaintiff's ''Lack of

Candor'' was More Severe than the Agency's Punishment for Lack
of Candor Generally

Plaintiff has submitted evidence from the FBI's own documents which
indicates that the measures taken against Mr. Buttino (revocation of his
security clearance and dismissal) were more severe than the FBI otherwise
takes in cases of similar—or more serious—findings of ''lack of candor'' and
improper disclosure of information. See Exs. 11, 12 to Declaration of Richard
Gayer; Pl.'s Opp'n at 9–11. Those documents suggest that the typical
punishment for indiscretions of roughly similar seriousness appears to be
censure, probation of six months to one year, and suspension without pay for 7
to 60 days.

4. The Evidence of the FBI's Undisputed History of Anti-Gay Discrimination

Plaintiff has submitted evidence—and indeed it is undisputed—that
the FBI has had a history of anti-gay discrimination. In 1979, the FBI
formally represented to the United States Court of Appeals for the District of
Columbia:

> The Federal Bureau of Investigation has always had an absolute
> policy of dismissing proven or admitted homosexuals from its employ.

Ashton v. Civiletti, 613 F.2d 923, 926 (D.C. Cir. 1979). As recently as four
years ago, the D.C. Circuit explicitly found that the FBI still had a policy of
discrimination against gays. Citing various statements and letters by the FBI,
the court concluded that ''we still can find no indication that the FBI
renounced homosexuality as a basis for reaching employment decisions. . . .
Arguably, the FBI has committed itself not to consider the sexual orientation of
an applicant who can show he does not engage in sex, but it clearly has done
no more.'' Padula v. Webster, 822 F.2d 97, 101 (D.C. Cir. 1979). And in a
June 5, 1989, letter from Milt Ahlerich, Assistant Director, FBI Office of
Public Affairs, the FBI specifically referred to the Padula case in which the
D.C. Circuit found the FBI still had a policy of discrimination and stated:
''[T]here are no plans underway to change the FBI's policy regarding
homosexuals.''[11]

---

[11]Defendants contend that the ''past'' policies of the FBI, and in particular the findings of
the Ashton case, are irrelevant here because those policies have undergone ''some modifications'' since Ashton was decided. Defs.' Reply at 17 n.16. Defendants cite Cotton v. City of
Alameda, 812 F.2d 1245, 128 (9th Cir. 1987) to support their position. Cotton, however, only
questioned the relevance of past policies that were ''terminated'' and said nothing about discriminatory policies that were merely ''modified,'' the former, of course, being precisely the

5. The Declaration of Other Gay or Lesbian Employees and Applicants

Plaintiff has submitted declaration of five individuals—three former FBI employees, a current employee, and a rejected applicant—all of whom attest to anti-gay bias within the FBI. A reasonable jury could certainly construe these declarations as corroborating plaintiff's characterization of the FBI's treatment of employees it learns are gay. The declarations evidence the FBI's extensive inquiries into its gay employees' private sexual activities— including detailed inquiries into specific private sexual acts and the exploration of childhood sexuality. The declarations describe the FBI investigators' attempts to obtain the names of other gay employees in the FBI. The declarations describe the FBI's threats that gay employees "resign quietly" or risk being fired. And, significantly, at least one of the declarations asserts that the FBI investigators made allegations of "lack of candor" by "twisting" the gay employee's words "at every turn."[12]

The court is bound, on a motion for summary judgment, to draw all

issue here. The distinction is significant because the similarities of the current policies to the past policies could conceivably be more telling as to the true character of the current policies than are the "modifications" that may have occurred over time. There are, for example, strong inferences that a reasonable jury could draw regarding the credibility of the current explanations for the FBI's policies toward gays (which goes to those policies' "rationality" under the Constitution—see Section III, infra), were the FBI's current (public) pronouncements of its policies somehow reach the identical conclusions that the past ones did (i.e., that the employment of gay persons creates significant security risks) notwithstanding the disappearance, at least in public pronouncements, of the patently unsupportable reasons which were offered in the past to justify the same conclusions now reached. See Senate Committee on Expenditures, Employment of Homosexuals and Other Sex Perverts in Government, Interim Report, S. Doc. No. 241, 81st Con., 2d Sess. (1950) (Senate Committee report indicating that the FBI was integral to a crusade in the 1950's to eliminate all "homosexuals and other sex perverts" from not only its own employ but from all federal government agencies because they constituted security risks.

[12]The court believes that items 1 through 5, supra, (and probably #1 alone) are sufficient to establish a triable issue of fact as to whether or not plaintiff's homosexuality was the real (or principal) reason for the revocation of his security clearance. The court notes, however, that plaintiff has submitted even further evidence which simply reinforces the court's finding that there is, at least, a triable issue of fact on the question of whether Mr. Buttino would not have been fired but for his homosexuality. Such further evidence includes, inter alia:

a. Internal FBI files which indicate significant interest on the part of the FBI in anything hinting of homosexuality in the lives of its employees; and

b. Director William Sessions' statement in his September 6, 1990 letter to Congressman Don Edwards that the Director was unaware of "any" openly gay Agents in the FBI, rendering questionable the effective validity of defendants' purported policy of tolerating "open" gays. See Defs.' Statement of Material Facts Not in Dispute, ¶13. (The parties note that two (of the FBI's 20,000) employees have retained their employment notwithstanding the recent discovery that they are gay. Plaintiff points out that such discovery appears to have occurred since the filing of this lawsuit. Pl.'s Opp'n at 19 n.21.)

justifiable inferences in the non-moving party's favor. Anderson v. Liberty Lobby, Inc., 477 U.S. 242, 255 (1986). In view of the foregoing evidence submitted by plaintiff, the court believes that a reasonable jury could conclude that plaintiff's security clearance would not have been revoked and his FBI employment would not have been terminated if plaintiff were not gay.

III. If There Is a Triable Issue of Fact as to whether Plaintiff Was Discriminated Against Because He is Gay, Is it Nevertheless Clear that there was a Rational Basis for so Discriminating Against Him?

Notwithstanding the triable issue of fact as to whether plaintiff was discriminated against because he is gay, summary judgment would be appropriate if such discrimination is nevertheless rationally related to a legitimate governmental interest. High Tech Gays, 895 F.2d at 571.[13] The legitimacy of the government's interest in safeguarding classified information is incontrovertible. Id. at 574. The only question is whether the FBI's discrimination against gays, if proven, is rationally related to that legitimate governmental interest.

A. The Applicability of High Tech Gays

Defendants do not mount a significant argument to support a finding, at this juncture, that the FBI's alleged discrimination is rational as a matter of law. They cite High Tech Gays as ostensible authority for the proposition that even if the facts plaintiff alleges are true, the FBI would have had a rational basis for revoking plaintiff's security clearance. For at least three reasons, however, High Tech Gays does not compel a finding (on this motion for summary judgment) that the FBI's discrimination against gays, as alleged by Mr. Buttino, is rational as a matter of law.[14]

---

[13]The court notes that the requirement that anti-gay discrimination be subjected only to "rational basis" review, rather than to either "heightened" or "strict" scrutiny, is the object of considerable distinguished criticism. See, e.g., the opinion of the Chief Judge of this Court, The Honorable Thelton E. Henderson, in High Tech Gays v. Defense Indus. Sec. Clearance Office, 668 F. Supp. 1361, 1368 (N.D. Cal. 1987), rev'd, 895 F.2d 563 (9th Cir. 1990); the concurring opinion of the Honorable William A. Norris of the Ninth Circuit in Watkins v. United States Army, 875 F.2d 699, 711–731 (9th Cir. 1989), cert. denied, 111 S.Ct. 384 (1990); the concurring opinion in the same case of The Honorable William C. Canby, Jr. of the Ninth Circuit, 875 F.2d at 731; L. Tribe, American Constitutional Law §16–33 at 1616 (2d ed. 1988); J. Ely, Democracy and Discontent at 162–164 (1980); the editors of the Harvard Law Review, Sexual Orientation and the Law 54–61 (1989); Note, An Argument for the Application of Equal Protection Heightened Scrutiny to Classifications Based on Homosexuality, 57 S. Cal. L. Rev. 797, 816–27 (1984).

[14]Defendants make a "see also" reference to Padula v. Webster, 822 F.2d 97 (D.C. Cir. 1987) in which the D.C. Circuit found there was a rational basis for the FBI's discriminating against a lesbian applicant. Defendants do not make too much of the case, however, presumably because the court explicitly found that the FBI actively discriminates against gays, see Section II. B. 4., supra, which is exactly what defendants are denying in this case. Moreover, the D.C.

First, the existence of the anti-gay policy in High Tech Gays was not disputed. There, the Department of Defense expressly conceded its policy of conducting expanded investigations into the backgrounds of all gay and lesbian applicants for security clearances, such that the court, unlike here, was able to assess the rationality of a known quantity. The current status of this case is much more analogous to Dubbs II, 769 F. Supp. at 1118, decided after High Tech Gays, in which the court identified the need, as a trier of fact, to "first make findings regarding the factual issues of what the CIA's policy toward homosexuals and/or persons who engage in homosexual conduct actually is" before it could determine whether there was a rational basis for that policy. As in Dubbs II, it would be anomalous indeed for this court to sanction, as conclusively rational, discrimination whose very existence is denied by its alleged perpetrator.[15]

Second, High Tech Gays found the Department of Defense's policy to be rational only after an evidentiary inquiry specific to the question of the rationality of the relationship of the policy to the government interest the policy was purported to serve. Finding specific evidence that hostile Soviet intelligence elements targeted American homosexuals for blackmail, and after weighing evidence submitted by the plaintiffs offered to refute the rationality of discrimination in that context, the court concluded that the expanded inquiry into gay persons' security clearance applications was rationally related to the government's interest of safeguarding national security. High Tech Gays, 895 F.2d at 574–578. Here, the FBI has not purported to submit evidence by which this court could make an assessment of the rationality of its alleged discriminatory policy.[16]

Circuit's reasoning in Padula, which cited in support of its finding that the discrimination was rational the fact that homosexual conduct "generate[s] dislike and disapproval among many . . . who find it morally offensive" is arguably of questionable soundness in the Ninth Circuit after Pruitt v. Cheney, 943 F.2d 989 (9th Cir. 1991), which held that discriminatory policies which simply give effect to society's prejudices do not suffice under the rational basis test. See discussion, infra.

[15]This is not to say that a court, on a motion for summary judgment, could never find a rational basis for discriminatory conduct where a defendant denies the existence of such discrimination. On the contrary, a blanket rule to that effect would put a defendant in the untenable posture of having to forfeit his opportunity to pursue summary dismissal if he chooses to deny the allegations of unconstitutional discrimination. The key inquiry would appear to be whether the evidence the parties set forth in connection with a motion for summary judgment leaves the court, as it does here, with genuine issues of fact both as to the existence of discrimination and as to the character of such discrimination which so obscure the nature of the discrimination as to deprive the court of a firm sense of the actual discrimination whose rationality the court must ultimately assess.

[16]Again, Dubbs II is germane:

After determining the policy and the government interests served by it, this Court

Third, the court in any event has serious reservations about somehow treating as binding on this action the Ninth Circuit's ruling in High Tech Gays that the Defense Department's discriminatory policy against gays was rational, where the current validity of the very basis for that ruling (evidentiary findings that the K.G.B. specifically targeted American homosexuals) would appear to be in question in light of the post-High Tech Gays demise of the Soviet Union and the uncertain future, if any, of the Soviet Secret Police. David Wise, "Closing Down the K.G.B.", N.Y. Times, November 24, 1991, § 6, at 30.[17] High Tech Gays binds this court to apply only a rational basis review to cases of actual anti-gay discrimination, but nothing in that case, or in any other Ninth Circuit case for that matter, directs this court either to ignore its obligation to assess the rationality of a discriminatory policy or to embrace obsolete justifications therefor, and this court declines to do so.[18]

B. Serious Questions as to Rationality

Moreover, in the Ninth Circuit's most recent pronouncement regarding the

then must determine what are the reasons for this policy which indicate, or fail to indicate, that this policy is rationally related to these interests.

This Court believes that this also is a factual issue. . . .

Assuming that the factual issues [regarding the existence and nature of, and the reaons for, the policy] are settled, this Court will then decide, as a matter of law, whether the identified policy is or is not rational.

Dubbs II, 769 F. Supp. at 1118.

[17]It is noteworthy, too, that subsequent to the date on which the arguments in High Tech Gays were submitted, an internal Defense Department study, addressing the issue of "the suitability of homosexuals for positions that require national security clearance," was made public. The study's conclusion: "the preponderance of the evidence presented in this study indicates that homosexuals show preservice suitability adjustment that is as good or better than the average heterosexual." Michael A. McDaniel, Defense Personnel Security Research and Education Center, "Preservice Adjustment of Homosexual and Heterosexual Military Accessions: Implications for Security Clearance Suitability," Defense Personnel Security Research and Education Center (January 1989).

[18]Defendants' implicit attempt to rely on Mr. Rubino's testimony to satisfy the rational basis standard, Defs.' Mem. at 11–12 n.6, simply represents a misapplication of that standard. On an equal protection claim, the rational basis standard is not applied—as both parties' papers loosely suggest at times—by posing a general inquiry into the inherent rationality of a certain government action (i.e., the revocation of a security clearance); the inquiry, rather, is whether there is a rational basis for the government discriminating on a certain basis in taking such action. High Tech Gays, 895 F.2d at 571. Therefore, the fact that there may have been a rational basis for Rubino's affirmance of the FBI's decision, which Rubino denies incorporated anti-gay discrimination, accomplishes little, if anything, here. For if plaintiff does not prove that the FBI revoked his security clearance because he is gay, then plaintiff could not succeed on his equal protection claim and there is no discrimination whose rationality needs to be assessed. See Dubbs II, 769 F. Supp. at 1118. If, on the other hand, plaintiff establishes that he was discriminated against because he is gay in the decision to revoke his security clearance, then the court would have to inquire into the rationality of the FBI's discrimination against gays in its security clearance determinations. Id. Rubino's declaration (denying as it does that such discrimination was present) does not purport to offer reasons why such discrimination is rational.

review of equal protection challenges to anti-gay discrimination, the court embraced what it called "active" rational basis review even in cases where the defendant agency is, like here, one whose national security decisions are entitled to considerable judicial deference. Pruitt v. Cheny, 943 F.2d 989 (9th Cir. 1991). Pruitt cited with approval the line of Supreme Court cases which hold that the government's implementation of policies which simply give effect to society's prejudices do not suffice under rational basis review. The Ninth Circuit quoted Palmore v. Sidoti, 466 U.S. 429, 433 (1984) which stated:

> The Constitution cannot control such prejudices but neither can it tolerate them. Private biases may be outside the reach of the law, but the law cannot, directly or indirectly, give them effect.

Pruitt, 943 F.2d at 994.

Especially in light of Pruitt, the court is of the impression that even if it were to undertake, at this juncture, an inquiry into the question of the rationality of the FBI's alleged anti-gay discrimination, by considering among other things the extent to which defendants' statements in the record regarding the FBI's policy toward gays indicate the rationality of such a policy or the lack thereof, the court would be left, at best, with serious questions as to the policy's rationality.

Among the court's questions as to the rationality of the policy is how, for example, the FBI can rationally implement a policy which (as defendants themselves describe it) requires gay employees to be simultaneously "open" and "discreet" as to their homosexual conduct. Defs.' Statement of Material Facts Not in Dispute, ¶13.

The court also has questions as to the rationality of a policy which punishes gay employees for being less than candid about their homosexuality when it is undisputed that at least until very recently (and certainly for most of Mr. Buttino's tenure at the FBI) the FBI would clearly have purged any employee for being candid about one's homosexuality.

The court cannot help but wonder, moreover, whether there is anything to indicate that Buttino's lack of candor would ever have been an issue but for society's prejudice against gays and the FBI's history of anti-gay discrimination, and if not, whether a policy which dismisses someone for lack of candor under those circumstances has, especially under Pruitt, a rational basis under the equal protection clause of the Constitution.

Finally, the court has serious questions as to the rational basis for a policy which does not permit the reinstatement of a gay Special Agent (whose twenty-year record is unblemished but for a short-lived deception regarding his homosexual activities), where that employee has expressly given the FBI "unrestricted permission" to tell anybody it wants about his sexual orientation and sexual activities.

CONCLUSION

There exists a triable issue of fact as to whether Buttino's security clearance would have been revoked and his employment terminated if he were not gay. Because the court cannot conclude from the record that such discrimination, if it occurred, was in any event rational, the court cannot say that plaintiff's claim under the equal protection clause will necessarily fail. Defendants' motion for summary judgment as to the equal protection claim is therefore DENIED. Summary judgment is also DENIED as to plaintiff's Bivens claim, which was not addressed in defendants' papers. Summary judgment as to plaintiff's First Amendment and due process claims is HEREBY GRANTED.

IT IS SO ORDERED.

DATED: Feb 11, 1992   Saundra B. Armstrong
                                      SAUNDRA BROWN ARMSTRONG
                                      United States District Judge